INSIDE SCIENCE FICTION

Second Edition

JAMES GUNN

The Scarecrow Press, Inc.
Lanham, Maryland • Toronto • Oxford
2006

SCARECROW PRESS, INC.

Published in the United States of America
by Scarecrow Press, Inc.
A wholly owned subsidiary of
The Rowman & Littlefield Publishing Group, Inc.
4501 Forbes Boulevard, Suite 200, Lanham, Maryland 20706
www.scarecrowpress.com

PO Box 317
Oxford
OX2 9RU, UK

Copyright © 2006 by James E. Gunn

British Library Cataloguing in Publication Information Available

Library of Congress Cataloging-in-Publication Data

Gunn, James E., 1923–
   Inside science fiction / James Gunn.—2nd ed.
      p.   cm.
   Includes bibliographical references and index.
   ISBN-13: 978-0-8108-5714-8 (pbk. : alk. paper)
   ISBN-10: 0-8108-5714-6 (pbk. : alk. paper)
      1. Science fiction—Study and teaching.   2. Science fiction—History and
criticism.   I. Title.
   PN3433.7.G86   2006
   809.3'8762071—dc22   2005028528

∞ ™ The paper used in this publication meets the minimum requirements of
American National Standard for Information Sciences—Permanence of Paper
for Printed Library Materials, ANSI/NISO Z39.48-1992. Manufactured in the
United States of America.

*For teachers and
students everywhere*

CONTENTS

INTRODUCTION

In 1970 my personal situation changed. I had spent a great deal of my life in educational establishments of one kind or another. I had been writing a great many different things, including plays, verse, articles, and news stories for a variety of media, and had turned to writing science fiction in 1948. Ultimately, I spent nearly four years writing science fiction full time (and part time after that) before I was led into other activities at the University of Kansas, including teaching, editing alumni publications, and, for twelve years, directing public relations.

I left that position in 1970 and became a full-time English professor because I wanted to spend more time teaching and writing. One of the comments the chairman of the department passed along from the full-time faculty was that "some of the younger faculty hoped I would be willing to teach a course in science fiction."

As I record more fully in the articles that start this volume, the study of science fiction was just getting started, and its teaching was not much older. Every teacher had to create his or her own approach, reading list, and study plan, and there were very few books to consult. My response was to write a history of science fiction, which was published in 1975 as *Alternate Worlds: The Illustrated History of Science Fiction*, and I later put together the six-volume historical anthology that I called *The Road to Science Fiction*, as well as the study of Isaac Asimov's work that was published as *Isaac Asimov: The Foundations of Science Fiction*.

But others were responding to the same needs. Editors were putting together books about science fiction and soliciting chapters, science fiction magazines were accepting and even encouraging articles about science fiction, and even general interest magazines and newspapers were becoming interested in the genre. So I had a number of invitations to write chapters for books and articles for magazines and newspapers, many of which I accepted. Eventually,

I had enough of these contributions to fill a couple of volumes. The book you have in your hands is one of those volumes. The other is *The Science of Science-Fiction Writing* (Scarecrow Press, 2000).

I call this book *Inside Science Fiction* because it is a series of perspectives about science fiction from someone who grew up with the genre and has spent a good portion of his life reading it, writing it, editing it, writing about it, teaching it, and associating with a great many people who are involved with it in almost every capacity imaginable. As the only person who has been president of both the Science Fiction Writers of America (SFWA) and the Science Fiction Research Association (SFRA), I have had the opportunity to know not only both sides of the road but also the people who live and work there. Sometimes, as chapter 8, "Teaching Science Fiction Revisited," illustrates, I have even tried to mediate misunderstandings between them.

Within *Inside Science Fiction* you will find thoughts about a variety of aspects of this odd genre, as it has been called by others before me. Not as tightly organized as a book setting out to treat a single aspect of a subject, this collection of perspectives has the virtue of ranging broadly and exploring not only well-traveled roads but strange byways as well. Another advantage of this approach to a subject is that it can be diverted into a serious consideration of an aspect of science fiction that would seem inappropriate for a work organized around a single purpose.

This volume is both broader (all over) and deeper (in places) than my other books on the subject. You will find, for instance, autobiographical details; considerations of the academic situation of science fiction and how science fiction became separated from the mainstream to become a genre; a look at how the magazines created the genre and how the editors shaped it; accounts of how science fiction people resisted academic interest, how academics looked at the field, and the disagreements between critics and writers; an analysis of how science fiction (including my own stories) got mangled by film and television but were treated well by radio (with a few exceptions); and some speculations about how science fiction has influenced everyday life (and, in turn, been influenced by it).

The first edition of this book was published in 1992. This edition contains new chapters describing perspectives brought on by the intervening dozen or so years, and revision of the older chapters to bring them up to date. Science fiction is the literature of change, and the analysis of change must change as well. Whenever either reaches its goal, it no longer will be science fiction.

1

GETTING INSIDE SCIENCE FICTION

1

THE EDUCATION OF A SCIENCE FICTION TEACHER

When I began writing science fiction in 1948, I had the feeling that I was the inheritor of a tradition whose origins were lost in antiquity. The editor of *Astounding Science Fiction*, John W. Campbell Jr., seemed to me to have been in his position for almost as long as the genre had been in existence, and Isaac Asimov and Robert A. Heinlein, who filled the pages of *Astounding* with stories devastating in their originality and Olympian in their inevitability, had been shaping the genre for almost as long.

None of it quite that way. In one sense, the genre was only twenty-two years old. Campbell was only thirty-eight and had been editor of *Astounding* for only ten years; Asimov was twenty-eight, just three years older than I was, and Heinlein was only forty-one.

I did not become aware of these realities, either literally or psychologically, until some years later. How I learned about SF,[1] what I learned about it, and how it emerged from its pulp ghetto into academic acceptance is the story I want to tell in the next few pages.

Looking back upon that time long ago, I realize that I should have been more knowledgeable. Articles about the origin of SF must have appeared in various magazines that I read in my youth. A good, short history of science fiction was included in Groff Conklin's big 1946 anthology, *The Best of Science Fiction*, but that, too, made little impact at the time. What one discovers in one's early years, like one's parents, seems to have always existed.

"The Education of a Science Fiction Teacher" was first published in the *Kansas Quarterly* 10, no. 4, in Fall 1978.

Students often ask how I happened to become a writer, and particularly a science fiction writer. I tell them that it is a matter of imprinting, the way a chicken is imprinted by the first moving object it sees when it emerges from the shell. All the writers I know fell in love with reading at an early age and thought of it as a magical process in which they wanted to participate as soon as possible.

I was nine or ten when I began reading SF in magazines, although I was even younger when I discovered some Edgar Rice Burroughs Tarzan novels in the back closet of my grandmother's home in Girard, Kansas, where they had been put away a couple of decades earlier when my father or uncles had finished with them. That was in the 1930s.

At that time, dozens of pulp magazines rainbowed the magazine racks with their bright covers at newsstands and corner drugstores. The general adventure magazines, such as *Argosy* and *Bluebook*, were still being published, but the era of the category pulp magazine was at hand—detective magazines, westerns, sports magazines, love stories, and the hero pulps: *Doc Savage*, *The Shadow*, *Operator #5*, *The Spider*, *G-8 and His Battle Aces*, and dozens more.

I read them all. My father or my five uncles would bring them home. They only cost a dime each, and they would be read by a half-dozen of us, including my older brother, and then I would trade them, two for one, at the used magazine store called Andy's down on Twelfth Street. (If I had them now, all those ten-cent magazines that passed through my hands and mind, I would buy myself a house or several cars, because today they are selling for ten dollars or more per issue!)

Once in awhile, I would come across a unique kind of pulp magazine that pleased me in a special way; sure, it had adventure, but it also contained ideas, discoveries, inventions, future events, different kinds and ways of life, and ways of thinking about life stranger, certainly, than I had ever dreamed of. It was a science fiction magazine, and it was called *Amazing Stories* or *Astounding Stories of Super Science* or *Wonder Stories*.

There were never enough of them to satisfy my growing appetite, and I ransacked the shelves of the Kansas City library system, including the big, gray gothic building downtown, where I discovered Jules Verne and H. G. Wells, an occasional H. Rider Haggard or an M. P. Shiel (which weren't quite right, but they would ease withdrawal symptoms in an emergency), and sometimes a strange mixture, such as the musings of Olaf Stapledon. I learned to skip Verne's interminable lectures on natural history and to differentiate between Wells's scientific romances and his later propaganda novels (although at the time I had no idea why these otherwise exciting writers should lapse occasionally into what I considered banality).

Only much later did I begin to piece together a kind of definition of science fiction and a chronology of its development into a genre. Conklin helped, and in 1950, August Derleth—who founded Arkham House in 1939 to reprint the works of H. P. Lovecraft and went on to reprint other science fiction novels and collections—put together a historical anthology, *Beyond Time and Space*, that provided examples.

Between the two of them, they traced the origins of science fiction back to Jules Verne and his *voyages extraordinaires* beginning in 1863;[2] or to Richard Adams Locke's 1835 spoof for the *New York Sun*, later reprinted as *The Moon Hoax*; or to Edgar Allan Poe and his "Ms. Found in a Bottle" that won an 1833 contest run by the *Baltimore Saturday Visitor*;[3] or to Nathaniel Hawthorne's symbol-laden stories such as "The Birthmark," "The Artist of the Beautiful," or "Rappacini's Daughter," all published in the early 1840s; or even to Mary Shelley's *Frankenstein*, published in 1818.

They pointed out examples of fantastic writing with an air of credibility that had been created before the nineteenth century. In September 1978, I reprinted many of them in an anthology published by Mentor entitled *The Road to Science Fiction: From Gilgamesh to Wells*, and traced some common elements to the earliest epics, including *Gilgamesh* and *The Odyssey*, and to the first trip to the moon: Lucian of Samosata's second-century A.D. "A True Story." In that book I defined science fiction as:

> the branch of literature that deals with the effects of change on people in the real world as it can be projected into the past, the future, or to distant places. It often concerns itself with scientific or technological change, and it usually involves matters whose importance is greater than the individual or the community; often civilization or the race itself is in danger.

Since technological change became a part of human experience only after the Industrial Revolution, earlier fiction (or writing resembling fiction) did not deal with change and was not, strictly speaking, "science" fiction.

The aspect of change that was common to virtually all of the early examples was the journey. The journey was not only a conventional device for launching a series of adventures, but it also provided credibility to the strange lands and creatures and customs that the adventurers found along the way or at the end of their trips. Thus, Marco Polo's account of his thirteenth-century journey to China did not differ significantly in its appeal from the fourteenth-century fiction *The Travels of Sir John Mandeville*. Real or imaginary, the two journeys made believable the distant places of the world, and the fact that the places were distant made credible their strange inhabitants and ways of existence.

Even the Utopias that became popular after Thomas More's sixteenth-century prototype, including Campanella's *The City of the Sun* and Francis Bacon's *The New Republic* in the seventeenth century and Jonathan Swift's antiutopian *Gulliver's Travels* of the eighteenth century, began with journeys. Science fiction is not simply fantasy—a narrative of events that could not happen—but a narrative of events that have not happened yet or have not happened that we know of. The efforts of the author to present the events as believable leads the reader to consider under what circumstances the fantastic can be brought into the natural world. The utopianists had the same aim: to help their readers suspend their disbelief and transfer innovative political concepts from the imaginary society to the real one.

Journeys were used for other purposes than to provide credibility for an ideal society. Johannes Kepler whisked his protagonist off to the moon (in his seventeenth-century *Somnium; or, Lunar Astronomy*) by a demon summoned by his mother, a witch, but once there, the purpose was to allow the author, a contemporary of Galileo, to describe physical conditions on the moon. Cyrano de Bergerac, on the other hand, sent himself to the moon (in his seventeenth-century *A Voyage to the Moon*) in a variety of comic methods, none of them intended to be credible, in order to satirize his contemporaries.

Throughout the nineteenth century, authors were creating works in which the older traditions of journeys and adventures were intermixed with newer concerns about the ways in which life was being changed by science and technology. Edward Everett Hale wrote a novel entitled *The Brick Moon* that was serialized in *Atlantic Monthly*; Fitz-James O'Brien wrote a number of fantastic stories about strange events and mad scientists; Edward Bulwer-Lytton, Samuel Butler, W. H. Hudson, William Morris, and William Dean Howells wrote utopian novels; even Mark Twain wrote a time-travel novel, *A Connecticut Yankee in King Arthur's Court*, and a pre-vision of television in "From the 'London Times' of 1904." But modern science fiction began with H. G. Wells.

Wells had learned Darwinism in T. H. Huxley's classroom, and this concern for evolution imbued his scientific romances with an underlying unease about the future of the human species. His truly science fiction works were written before 1901, and his short stories and novels, from the 1895 *The Time Machine* to the 1901 *The First Men in the Moon*, established many of the concepts and methods upon which science fiction would build.

The larger story, about the scientific and social influences that shaped the developing genre, I have told elsewhere, including the story of the growth of a new reading audience and the pulp magazines (beginning in 1896 with *Argosy*) that evolved from the boys' magazines to satisfy the appetite of a new audience for adventure stories of all kinds, and the creation of the category pulp magazines as the tastes of the audience began to differentiate. *Amazing Stories*, and later *Wonder Stories* and *Astounding Stories*, were the category science fiction magazines of the late twenties and early thirties, and they encapsulated only one genre among many.

For the first time, however, science fiction had a recognizable home and a name. No longer were its stories and novels isolated examples of imagination at work on contemporary problems and future possibilities; no longer were they called, variously, extraordinary voyages or scientific romances. *Amazing Stories* publisher and founder Hugo Gernsback (an immigrant from Luxembourg who was fascinated by electricity and radio and published a variety of popular science magazines about them) called it "scientifiction" and added the word to the spine to explain what the magazine published. When he created *Wonder Stories*, Gernsback changed the name to "science fiction." He also identified the new genre with the pulp medium in which it would be published almost exclusively for the next twenty years. By 1926, Verne, like Swift's *Gulliver's Travels*, had become identified as children's literature; Wells, popular and respected in his early days, had been dismissed for his propagandizing. Gernsback reprinted them both, along with Edgar Allan Poe, and inspired new writers to produce stories for his magazines. Together, they created a pulp ghetto in which the genre was nurtured into maturity, but from which it would have difficulty escaping.

Teaching science fiction during that twenty-year period of isolation would have been unthinkable. But the postwar anthologies, and the reprinting of magazine serials in book form, began to rehabilitate the genre. Even as early as my first story, I was thinking of writing SF, and I signed my first ten published stories with a pseudonym to preserve my real name for scholarship. I stopped when I saw how unnecessary (and counterproductive) a pseudonym was.

Still, even by 1950, when I was ready to begin work on a master's thesis about SF, one of my professors commented that he considered science fiction as "at best subliterary." As if to confirm his opinion, some twenty thousand words of the thesis were serialized in a pulp science fiction magazine.

By then, other criticism had begun to appear—little of it in newspapers or journals, where SF was cavalierly dismissed without a reading until recently—in the SF fan magazines, which had been springing up since 1930 as an outgrowth of amateur journalism and enthusiasm for SF. The thought of teaching it, or studying it, no longer seemed so incredible. A fan named Sam Moskowitz negotiated the offering of an evening class at the City College of New York in 1953 and 1954 and Mark Hillegas taught a course at Colgate in 1962. Other courses sprang up here and there as readers, some of them fans such as Thomas D. Clareson at Wooster, or writers such as Jack Williamson at Eastern New Mexico University, came into academic positions and persuaded their departments to allow the teaching of literature that had recently edged over the border into respectability.

I taught my first course in 1969. It may be a commentary on how swiftly SF has been accepted that, within a few years, the University of Kansas would offer a summer workshop on the teaching of science fiction, an annual course at the junior/senior/graduate level, an occasional graduate course, half a dozen courses at the sophomore level, a graduate seminar, and an occasional course in other departments, such as anthropology.

Today, hundreds, perhaps thousands, of courses are taught in colleges and universities across the country; many more are taught in high schools and junior high schools and even primary schools (the back-to-basics movement reduced the opportunity for such courses, but they are making a comeback in the third millennium). Students came to my summer workshop from all levels of education, from Texas and Michigan, New York and Oregon, and even two teachers from Canada, one from Australia, one from New Zealand, two from Argentina, one from the Netherlands, one from Denmark, one from Japan, and three from the People's Republic of China.

Critical acceptance of the genre was given significant impetus by the Christian Gauss Seminar in Criticism offered by Kingsley Amis at Princeton in 1959, published the next year as *New Maps of Hell*. The first conference on science fiction under the Modern Language Association was held in 1958 and has been an occasional feature since. Scholarly studies by H. Bruce Franklin, Mark Hillegas, and I. F. Clarke began to appear in the mid-sixties (J. O. Bailey's pioneer survey, *Pilgrims through Space and Time*, was published in 1947), and more recent work came from such scholars as Leslie Fiedler and Robert Scholes.

Some of the more fascinating studies continue to be done by fans such as the late Sam Moskowitz. Fans have provided an unusual measure of support for the genre: from their ranks have come not only writers, editors, and publishers but also scholars, collectors, and bibliographers. They do more than publish fanzines and put on conventions.

The first academic journal in the field, *Extrapolation*, began publication in

1959; the second, *Science Fiction Studies*, in 1974. Fanzines of varying degrees of seriousness and scholarly detachment have existed almost from the beginnings of magazine SF, and some of the earliest criticism by critics such as Damon Knight and James Blish was published there. The Science Fiction Research Association (SFRA) was founded in 1970. The first full histories of the genre began to appear in 1973: first Brian Aldiss's *Billion Year Spree*, then my own *Alternate Worlds*;[4] after me, the deluge.

Science fiction has evolved in other ways as well. From its splendid isolation in the magazines, it has spread into hardcover and paperback books, general magazines, motion pictures, comics, television, records, popular songs, and everyday language. More than two thousand works of science fiction and fantasy are published annually; half of the best-grossing films of all time are science fiction or fantasy. The television series that developed the greatest following in syndication is science fiction, and successor and competing series are commonplace.

What happened to create this incredible blossoming? Many explanations can be offered. Technology—particularly the technology of atomic war, atomic energy, and space travel—has produced a world that is recognizably the world described in early science fiction stories; as Isaac Asimov has pointed out, "We live in a science fiction world." In the early days of the magazines, the average reader was a teenage male who was alienated from his contemporaries by appearance, circumstance, or intelligence and turned to the literature of ideas for acceptance. Today, alienation from society is more common, in the sense that the average young person is willing to accept deviation from a social norm and is less likely to believe that the answers society offers to life's problems are the only answers, or even the right ones.

The world has problems for which tradition provides no solutions, which may be unsolvable. Young people who have given up hope have taken up astrology, drugs, UFOs, mysticism, and fantasy; those who still have faith in the power of the human mind to find answers are reading science fiction. Their parents and grandparents rejected the notion that life could be different, in spite of the evidence around them. Their children know that life will be different.

What was an escape literature, a pulp genre beneath academic consideration, has become relevant and respectable. It is being taught not only in English classes but in classes on religion, philosophy, and the various behavioral sciences. All of this, even SF's new popularity, has not been greeted universally with enthusiasm by those within the science fiction ghetto. Science fiction has had so many booms and busts that success brings out the Jeremiahs, and respectability, its Doubting Thomases. At the organizing meeting of SFRA, one fan wrote on the blackboard, "Let's take science fiction out of the classroom and put it back in the gutter where it belongs." A former editor of *Analog* (*Astounding* renamed) attacked SF teachers for their inexcusable ignorance of the genre, and writers have raised the specter of the perversion of science fiction to satisfy its teachers and scholars.

It seems likely, however, that the teaching of science fiction is not a fad. In these days of growing apathy about learning, SF classes are large and enthusiastic, and enthusiasm can be used as the entering wedge for the love of learning. It offers the opportunity to stretch the imagination as well as exercise the mind; it can dramatize contemporary problems and consider other ways of existing, behaving, organizing, perceiving, thinking. It is a literature of ideas and a literature of change—it can be a literature of education.

Science fiction has come a long way since I sat down to write my first story. Today, I have been writing SF thirty-five years longer than science fiction magazines had been in existence when I began. Hugo Gernsback is dead and John W. Campbell Jr. is dead, Isaac Asimov, Robert Heinlein, Theodore Sturgeon, and A. E. van Vogt are dead, but the magazines that one created (although *Amazing Stories* goes in and out of existence) and the other edited are still being published while most of the other pulp magazines are long gone. Science fiction itself is still lively, still evolving, still young. There is so much about science fiction that still remains to be discovered.

NOTES

1. The preferred academic abbreviation for science fiction is SF, not "sci-fi." "Sci-fi" is a term coined by Forrest J Ackerman that is usually applied to films or to the entire field by "mundanes," but this distinction is fading and Ackerman's invention may yet prevail.

2. Verne's first *voyage* was *Five Weeks in a Balloon*, which was not SF. His second novel, *Journey to the Center of the Earth*, and his third, *From the Earth to the Moon*, in 1864 and 1865, respectively, were SF.

3. "Ms. Found in a Bottle" was more mystery than SF, but "Mellonta Tauta" (1849) was probably the first true story of the future.

4. *Alternate Worlds: The Illustrated History of Science Fiction* (New York: Prentice-Hall, 1975).

2

FROM THE PULPS TO THE CLASSROOM

The Strange Journey of Science Fiction

Science fiction has traveled a strange road from isolation, in part self-imposed, to critical and academic acceptance. From the marvelous adventures of Edgar Allan Poe, through the extraordinary voyages of Jules Verne, to the scientific romances of H. G. Wells, under whatever name science fiction has passed over the century and a half during which it has existed, it has always seemed like an unwelcome relative at the feast of literature.

Even its creators looked down on it. Poe preferred his mood stories and his tales of ratiocination to his more science fictionish pieces. Wells thought more highly of his contemporary novels of manners than the pessimistic scientific romances of his early days. Wells's admirers, Joseph Conrad and Henry James, much as they liked his scientific romances, kept after him to give up his journalistic ways with a story and devote himself to high art, but Wells "was disposed to regard a novel as about as much an art form as a marketplace or a boulevard." I have no evidence to support the notion, but I would not be surprised if Jules Verne liked *Mathias Sandorf* and *Michael Strogoff* better than *Journey to the Center of the Earth* and *From the Earth to the Moon.*

There may be an illuminating irony in the fact that in almost every case, the science fiction has endured and the rest has faded. At the time they were written, poor relation to literature or not, prototypical science fiction passed in the great society of books as fiction of only small difference from the rest, perhaps

"From the Pulps to the Classroom" was first published in *Algol* 14, no. 1, in Fall 1976–Winter 1977. It also appeared in *The Science Fiction Reference Book*, edited by Marshall B. Tymn (Mercer Island, Wash.: Starmont House, 1981).

more popular than some, perhaps less artistic than others, but part of the general spectrum of literature.

But the creation of the mass magazines in the latter part of the nineteenth century and the development of the all-fiction pulp magazines (beginning in 1896 with *Argosy*), and the creation of the category pulp magazines (starting with *Detective Story Magazine* in 1915), encouraged the separation of families into genera and genera into species, and in each closed environment the families of fiction began to evolve separately. In 1926, science fiction split off from the parent stock with the founding of *Amazing Stories* and began its evolutionary struggle toward some ideal form.

When science fiction enclosed itself in what would later be called a ghetto, it dropped out of critical view. As late as 1914, Sam Moskowitz pointed out, the *New York Times* was reviewing books such as Edgar Rice Burroughs's *Tarzan of the Apes*. By 1926, not only were such reviews unlikely but science fiction was scarcely being published in book form, and what was published—stories from the early pulp magazines and books by Burroughs and A. Merritt—were not available in many public libraries.

Many fantasy books were available during this period, and they were reviewed. Fantasy always has enjoyed better critical acceptance than science fiction, perhaps because it is less concerned with reality, and therefore less threatening—certainly because it was more traditional and thus responded to existing critical techniques—but most of all, because fantasy could not be subtracted from the history of literature without stripping literature of its origins and half its substance.

Science fiction, however, was ignored by publishers and critics. It was a latecomer, a product of the Industrial Revolution and the Age of Reason and the Scientific Enlightenment, and to overlook it was the act of a gentleman and a connoisseur. Science fiction was brash and crude, it smelled of oil and hot metal, and where science fiction was brashest and crudest and most typical, in the science fiction magazines, was where it was ignored by everyone except its fans, those strange new creatures that Hugo Gernsback discovered when he published *Amazing* and called by name in his third issue. Books to come out of this environment—real science fiction with the smell of the pulp magazines still on them—had to wait until the mid-forties, mostly until the two big 1946 postwar anthologies, Groff Conklin's *The Best of Science Fiction* and Raymond J. Healy and J. Francis McComas's *Adventures in Time and Space*, and the fan presses that began preserving for posterity fan favorites such as the works of H. P. Lovecraft and Edward Elmer "Doc" Smith.

Twenty years, almost to the day, science fiction spent in its pulp ghetto, and almost another twenty years elapsed before the critics noticed that something new had emerged from that period of isolation. It is that period and that process—those years between 1946 and the present—that I wish to describe here, because it has helped to shape the present situation of science fiction and we can move on more confidently in the academic consideration of science fiction if we know where we have been and where we are and how we got there.

By 1946, of course, Donald A. Wollheim had already edited a couple of science fiction books, one for Pocket Books and one for Viking; J. Berg Eisenwein and Phil Stong had edited even earlier anthologies; August Derleth had founded Arkham House and published Lovecraft's *"The Outsider" and Others*; and J. O. Bailey had completed his pioneer dissertation, *Pilgrims through Space and Time* (the preface to the 1947 Argus book was dated December 1945). A few critical studies had been published before Bailey's, such as Philip Babcock Gove's *The Imaginary Voyage in Prose Fiction*, which would be followed in 1948 by Marjorie Hope Nicholson's *Voyages to the Moon*. But Bailey's was the first critical study actually to concern itself with science fiction, even if he refers to it throughout his book as scientific fiction.

The most important books in the critical appreciation of science fiction, however, were the Conklin and Healy and McComas anthologies. I know what they represented to me—a World War II veteran returning after three years to finish his final year of college—they provided an overview and understanding of the recent accomplishments of science fiction that I could not have obtained by a perusal of all the science fiction magazines published between 1926 and 1946, even if they had been available anywhere west of Sam Moskowitz and east of Forrest J Ackerman. Groff Conklin's and John W. Campbell Jr.'s introductions to Conklin's anthologies were particularly helpful; I like to think of them as the opening wedge of critical understanding that later would allow science fiction to slip into the tunnel vision of the mainstream. Another pioneer book of criticism, the slim, red volume called *Of Worlds Beyond*, edited by Lloyd A. Eshbach and published by his Fantasy Press, came along in 1947 as another revelation.

Conklin followed his epic collection with other anthologies, which not only made stories from the magazines more broadly available but also continued his critical and taxonomical approach to the field. He was joined by others, particularly Derleth, whose anthologies for Pellegrini & Cudahy, beginning in 1948 and culminating for me in the 1950 collection *Beyond Time and Space*, were unusually helpful. A double handful of fan presses would follow Arkham House in keeping science fiction books in print until the commercial publishers caught on to the sudden new surge of interest, just as Advent Publishers was virtually alone in publishing science fiction criticism for more than a decade.

Other contributions to a critical consideration of science fiction would follow: My master's thesis was completed in 1951 and some twenty thousand words of it were published in *Dynamic Science Fiction* in 1952—probably the only thesis ever serialized in a pulp magazine—thanks to editor Robert Lowndes. Reginald Bretnor edited an exciting and important collection of essays about science fiction, *Modern Science Fiction*, for Coward-McCann in 1953. Rumors of other studies and dissertations floated around, and about this time, Jack Williamson was working on his study of Wells, which would eventually find its way into Leland Sapiro's *Riverside Quarterly*, about the only place to find serious literary criticism of science fiction, and then into a book, *Critic of Progress*, published by Mirage Press. Other consciousness-raising reviews and essays by Damon Knight and James Blish appeared in fan magazines and later were collected into *In Search of Wonder* and *The Issue at Hand* in 1956 and 1964, respectively. But all of these efforts were largely missionaries talking to the already converted.

The emergence of science fiction from its exile was represented in the fifties by the interest of the occasional literary figures such as Basil Davenport and Clifton Fadiman. Both were associated with the Book of the Month Club. Davenport wrote an introduction or two, edited anthologies, and wrote *An Inquiry into Science Fiction* in 1955; Fadiman edited *Fantasia Mathematica*. Both allowed themselves to appear on the back cover of the *Magazine of Fantasy and Science Fiction* saying something in praise of science fiction and the magazine. Unlike other magazines, *Fantasy and Science Fiction* tried to broaden its base of readership, extending pseudopods into the mainstream by reducing reliance upon conventions, insisting on skillful writing and a greater concern for the complexities of character and of language, associating science fiction with more literary works in the fantasy tradition, reprinting stories from the experimental mainstream, and by including critical or biographical headnotes. And their back-cover ads consciously tried to attract non–science fiction readers.

Then the critical situation for science fiction began heating up. In the publishing field, conditions were not promising: the big magazine boom of the early fifties had collapsed, dragging some old standards down with it; the surge of new science fiction writers which always seems to accompany magazine booms had slowed as well; Anthony Boucher had retired as editor of the *Magazine of Fantasy and Science Fiction* and Horace Gold was in his last couple of years as editor of *Galaxy*; the early enthusiasm created by the founding of Ballantine Books had dwindled; and such path-pointing books as Vonnegut's *The Sirens of Titan* and Walter Miller's *A Canticle for Leibowitz* had not yet been published. In fact, conditions were pretty much as usual for science fiction—lousy. But I did get a letter from my agent, Harry Altshuler, that Bantam Books was looking for some new writers, and shortly after that Bantam's SF editor, Dick Roberts, accepted *Station in Space*. Some vibrations were making themselves felt perhaps, but little was happening, except that some college professors, led by the late Professor Scott Osborn of Mississippi State University, organized the first Conference on Science Fiction under the auspices of the Modern Language Association. That was 1958. A year later, the first academic journal in the field, *Extrapolation*, was founded.

Meanwhile, something extraordinary was happening at Princeton. Kingsley Amis, a recognized English poet and author, presented a series of lectures for the Christian Gauss Seminar in Criticism in the spring of 1959 in which he proclaimed his long-time admiration for science fiction. A year later the lectures appeared in book form as *New Maps of Hell*, and various surprised popular media, reviewing the book, began to reconsider their own policy of consistently ignoring or denigrating the science fiction that had somehow reached their desks. *Time* magazine, which previously had mentioned science fiction only to ridicule, started publishing an occasional favorable review and included one retrospective look at Richard Matheson's *I Am Legend*, which had been published only in paperback. And other magazines and newspapers began to include articles about science fiction authors and individual works, including the *New York Times*, the *New Yorker*, the *Christian Science Monitor*, the *Wall Street Journal*, *Publishers Weekly*, and many others, although some of them would not discover science fiction until much later.

One small event in the real world might have been a precipitating factor: in 1957, the U.S.S.R. launched its first satellite, *Sputnik*. With that event, space travel became plausible, and with it the fiction that had dealt so consistently with space flight. Just as the atomic bomb had confirmed science fiction's worst nightmares, the space accomplishments confirmed its fondest dreams.

Other major critics were making themselves heard: H. Bruce Franklin's study of nineteenth-century American science fiction, *Future Perfect*, was published by Oxford University Press in 1967, and I. F. Clarke's *Voices Prophesying War* in 1966. C. S. Lewis's essay "On Science Fiction" was presented as a talk to the Oxford University English Club in 1955, and his "Unreal Estates" was recorded as a discussion in 1962, but they did not get into print apparently until the latter was published in Lewis's *SF Horizons* in 1964, and both were published in *Of Other Worlds* in 1966.

Other distinguished voices raised on behalf of science fiction have been those of Leslie Fiedler and Robert Scholes, professors of English at the State University of New York at Buffalo and at Brown University, respectively. Oddly enough, their views have been expressed in essays with similar titles: Fiedler's "Cross the Border, Close the Gap," and Scholes's "As the Wall Crumbles," in *Nebula Award Stories #10*. Both have other critical works about science fiction, in particular, Fiedler's historical-critical anthology *In Dreams Awake* and Scholes's *Structural Fabulation*.

I met Fiedler first. At the Science Fiction Research Association (SFRA) meeting in Toronto in 1971, he seemed a novice at science fiction, as eager to learn as he was to teach, but a quick study, and by the Nebula Award Day in New York the following spring, where I invited him to speak, he had much to say. For too long, he said there, critics had been trying to tell readers why they should like what they don't like. What they ought to be doing, he said, is trying to find out *why* people like what they like. Why, for instance, has H. Rider Haggard's *She*, in spite of its artistic deficiencies, never been out of print since its publication in 1886?

Fiedler seemed to like science fiction, not because it was good but because it was vulgar—no, that's not quite right, because vulgar, or pop, literature is good. In "Cross the Border," he wrote, "We have . . . entered quite another time—apocalyptic, anti-rational, blatantly romantic and sentimental; an age dedicated to joyous misology and prophetic irresponsibility; one distrustful of self-protective irony and too-great self-awareness." The answer, he wrote, is to turn frankly to pop forms, such as the western, science fiction, and pornography. In New York, he asked for a cross-fertilization of science fiction and pornography such as he saw in some of the work of Philip José Farmer. One wonders where Fiedler's desire to break new critical trails, and his attempts to shock his readers into new awarenesses, leaves off.

In his anthology *In Dreams Awake*, Fiedler wrote that science fiction writers, often accused of "slapdash writing, sloppiness, and vulgarity," cannot learn from

> the floggers of a dead avant-gardism, capable of creating neither myth nor wonder, only parody and allusion. No, it is precisely out of "slapdash writing," "sloppiness," and especially "vulgarity," as exemplified in, say, Shakespeare, Cooper, Dickens, and Twain, that myth is endlessly reborn, the dreams we dream awake.

Being loved by Leslie Fiedler was a bit like being loved by a lion: we weren't sure we were being appreciated for the right reasons.

On the other hand, we felt more comfortable with Robert Scholes—at least I did—because he related us to the rest of literature rather than setting us off because we were different. Scholes is a leading critic of contemporary literature, particularly that branch of contemporary fiction for which he supplied a name in his book *The Fabulators*.

I met Scholes at a science fiction gathering, too—the World Science Fiction Convention in Washington, D.C., in 1974—and later asked him to contribute an essay to the volume of *Nebula Award Stories* that I edited. In "As the Wall Crumbles," he put the literary position of science fiction this way: "Pleasure in fiction is rooted in our response to narrative movement—to story itself. This is a fundamental kind of pleasure, almost physical, and closely connected to physical sensations like those of motion and sex."

Much "mainstream" fiction, he went on, is so overburdened with a weight of analysis and subtle refinement of consciousness that we do not get from it the pure fiction pleasure that lies at the heart of our need for narration.

> One result of this situation is that many people may resort, more or less guiltily, to "lesser" forms of fiction—outside the mainstream of serious literature—for a narrative "fix," a shot of joyful storytelling. . . . What most people need in fiction is something that satisfies their legitimate desire for the pleasures of story-telling, without making them feel ashamed of having some childish and anti-social impulse. We need recreational texts, good stories that leave us refreshed without any feeling of guilt. We need stories that are genuinely adult in their concerns and ideas while satisfying our elemental need for wonder and delight. Science fiction at its best answers this need better than any other form of contemporary fiction. And it does more.

Now, as a science fiction writer and reader, I say, "That's more like it!"

Scholes also speaks the more esoteric language of academia. That is a valuable asset, because it allows him to attack the stronghold of scorn and indifference with its own weapons. In *Structural Fabulation*, which is not only the name of his book but the name he gives science fiction, Scholes traces science fiction to the romance (in the traditional division of fiction between realism and romance); he divides the romance into the pure romance (sublimation with minimal cognition, sometimes called "escapism") and the didactic romance (or fabulation, as in allegory, satire, fable, and parable); the didactic romance he divides, in turn, into speculative fabulation (or romances of science, such as More's *Utopia*) and dogmatic fabulation (romances of religion, such as Dante's *Divine Comedy*); and speculative fabulation he divides, at last, into pseudo-scientific sublimation (space opera, and so forth) and structural fabulation.

Structural fabulation, or science fiction, is "the tradition of More, Bacon and Swift, as modified by new input from the physical and human sciences." And Scholes restates the message of "As the Wall Crumbles" in more academic language:

> We require a fiction which satisfies our cognitive and sublimative needs together. . . . We need suspense with intellectual consequences, in which questions are raised as well as solved, and in which our minds are expanded even while focused on the complications of a fictional plot.

And he goes on,

> In works of structural fabulation the tradition of speculative fiction is modified by an awareness of the nature of the universe as a system of systems, a structure of structures, and the insights of the past century of science are accepted as fictional points of departure.

Scholes has other pleasant things to say about science fiction: the Hugo Award is at least as reliable an indicator of quality as, say, the Pulitzer Prize for fiction, and the most appropriate kind of fiction that can be written in the present and the immediate future is fiction that takes place in future time. But most of all he urges his "fellow teachers and makers of curricula to open their courses to the literature of structural fabulation and allow it to contribute to that critical revaluation of our literary past which functions so powerfully to keep that past alive."

Other critics have worked within the field itself, struggling with definitions and classification, strengthening our internal structures. I could mention names like Thomas Clareson and Darko Suvin, Dale Mullen and Robert Philmus, as well as Joanna Russ and Samuel Delany, who are critics as well as writers of fiction, but I am primarily concerned here with the ways in which the outside world—the *mundane* world, the science fiction fan language would call it—has become reconciled to science fiction.

The process of reconciliation, of acceptance, of discovery, continues. And that continuing process of opening the science fiction treasure-house to an unsuspecting and up-to-now largely unappreciative non–science fiction reading public is the condition of science fiction criticism today.

Meanwhile the concept that science fiction was a branch of literature that could be taught to the better understanding and appreciation of students began occurring to a few teachers here and there. Sam Moskowitz conducted an unrelenting quest for encyclopedic knowledge of science fiction and preeminence in the science fiction fan world, a quest recorded in his history of fandom, *The Immortal Storm*, whose fruits are the biographies of science fiction authors and editors published first in Ziff-Davis magazines in the late fifties and early sixties and then in the books *Seekers of Tomorrow* and *Explorers of the Infinite*. He told about organizing an evening course in science fiction for City College of New York in 1953 and 1954. But the first course taught within the official curriculum of a college is believed to be Mark Hillegas's course at Colgate in 1962. Jack Williamson began teaching a course at Eastern New Mexico University in 1964, and Tom Clareson was not far behind at Wooster.

My own science fiction teaching began in 1969. About the same time, Robin Scott Wilson began his Science Fiction Writers Workshops at Clarion and Stanford launched a summer Science Fiction Institute. Courses have blossomed since then. Jack Williamson's last survey in 1972 counted some 240 college courses. Judging by a little experience and a lot of intuition, I would say that there is scarcely a college in the nation that does not have at least one science fiction course a year, and if a college doesn't have a course, it is because the faculty can't find anyone to teach it rather than that they believe it is beneath them.

At the University of Kansas, the single annual course that I began teaching in 1971 to as many as 165 students expanded to include courses offered at the sophomore level in science fiction and fantasy; graduate-level courses, including a couple of seminars; a course in the writing of science fiction; and a summer program for teachers. There are special reasons for such growth at Kansas, of course, but I suspect that similar developments were occurring at other places around the nation: junior colleges, four-year colleges, universities—at last count, the nation had some two thousand colleges and universities, and it may be a reasonable estimate that they are teaching some two thousand science fiction courses, but a thorough survey still remains to be done.

What began as an attempt by a few pioneers to teach students what the teachers themselves found uniquely fascinating, and what they were uniquely equipped to teach, changed into a kind of self-preservation in the late sixties when student power became an issue and relevance became a byword, and in the seventies when vocationalism began diverting students away from the humanities toward business, journalism, engineering, social work, and the social and behavioral sciences. The question of jobs became the issue, not just for the students but for the faculty as well; the end of automatic enrollment increases and the beginning of enrollment drops made the attractiveness of course offerings a subject for concern in English departments everywhere.

I do not like to think, nor would I suggest, that colleges have taken up science fiction only in response to the need for inducing students to take some kind of English course, but it may not be unfair to propose that the pioneers were not so much trailbreakers for the wagon trains of settlers that would follow as the first scouts for a pack of migrating lemmings.

The question of qualified teachers was raised early. I began to think about it in 1969, when a combination of circumstances that I have related elsewhere led me to consider the development of a series of lecture films featuring science fiction writers and editors talking about those aspects of science fiction that they knew best. Basically, I hoped to provide help for teachers who felt unprepared, unqualified, and unable to cope with their new assignment. There were many of them in the early seventies. When I was president of the Science Fiction Writers of America in 1971–1972, I received one or two plaintive letters a week from teachers saying that they had been assigned a science fiction class, they had never read science fiction before, and could I send them a list of what to teach and suggestions about how to teach it.

It was enough to make a professor go write a book. I didn't—not about the teaching of science fiction—but others wrote or compiled such books. I'll get to them a little later, and to the book I did write.

That science fiction lecture series developed more slowly than I ever could have imagined. It was an education for all of us in the difficulties and costs of making films. But we eventually completed eleven films, in color, ranging in length from twenty to forty minutes. They have been seen all over the world, and it is a source of considerable satisfaction to me that students, wherever they are, have had the opportunity to hear the history of science fiction from the lips of Damon Knight and Isaac Asimov, its ideas from Frederik Pohl, its techniques from Poul Anderson, its themes from Gordon Dickson, its film history from Forrest Ackerman, its relation to the mainstream from John Brunner, and its new directions from Harlan Ellison, as well as Jack Williamson describing the early days of the magazines, Clifford Simak reminiscing about his career, and Harry Harrison and Gordon Dickson discussing with the late John W. Campbell Jr. a story idea that later developed into an *Analog* serial. Those films are more historical today, but they have been made available on DVD, and they provide a unique glimpse into the science fiction of the 1960s.

During the period that science fiction was spreading like a plague from space through colleges and universities, it also was beginning to swim upstream—to mix a metaphor—into high schools and junior high schools and even primary schools. The primary schools had different motivations from the colleges. Some of them wanted to provide incentives for poor readers and discovered that some students could graduate from television cartoons to comic magazines to science fiction stories; anything was legitimate that got students interested in reading. At the other end of the academic spectrum, gifted students often were bored with the pace of primary education, and science fiction, with its concern for ideas and themes, kept their attention and their involvement. More recently the Harry Potter books have provided striking evidence that young readers will still respond to engaging characters involved in difficult and fantastic situations.

In addition, the loosening of academic disciplines in primary schools—perhaps part of the same movement toward relevance that may be responsible for the increasing difficulties with the written language that students are bringing into college—provided a place in the secondary curriculum for a spreading system of elective mini-courses. Among the mini-courses, almost always, was a science fiction option; administrators soon found that science fiction courses were always overenrolled. Meanwhile, teachers in disciplines other than English discovered that through science fiction they could get students to consider the human aspects of science, sociology, politics, philosophy, religion, and other intellectual areas to which they might come unwittingly, or without understanding, in the abstract.

Whatever the reasons—I do not pretend that my list is comprehensive—science fiction courses proliferated in high schools until they may have rivaled woodworking or home economics.

All of this movement of science fiction into the academic curriculum had its inevitable reactions: delight, sometimes mixed with disappointment, on the part of students; consternation and bewilderment and sometimes a sigh of relief on the part of teachers; and disapproval, in general, on the part of the science fiction community. Writers and editors and readers saw science fiction threatened by the same hand that had, they thought, throttled the life out of Shakespeare and beat the dickens out of Dickens, and by the same desiccating mouth that had turned history into dust. Moreover, they thought, the hand and the mouth weren't even prepared; they had no idea what science fiction even felt like, much less what it was really about.

People such as Lester del Rey and Ben Bova and Harlan Ellison saw, in the new academic interest, disaster for science fiction. Teachers were using science fiction merely as a stepping-stone for their ambition; they were riding the winds of popularity. They were liking science fiction—if they did—for the wrong reasons, and they would turn students off to science fiction faster than the authors and the magazines were turning them on.

Much of this resentment of the science fiction community against academia seemed to come to a focus at a two-day meeting at Kean College of New Jersey in the spring of 1974. There I heard writers complaining bitterly about what was being taught and who was teaching the courses. Harlan Ellison had horror stories about his campus visits and what teachers were doing to science fiction there, and even the reasonable Fred Pohl viewed the situation with alarm.

Phil Klass, who wrote so many magnificent stories under the pen name of William Tenn, had described the situation even before that 1974 meeting. In a "Science Fiction and the University" issue of the *Magazine of Fantasy and Science Fiction* in May 1972, he wrote an article entitled "Jazz Then, Musicology Now" in which he worried about the impact on science fiction of academic interest. Then Ben Bova published an editorial in the June 1974 *Analog* raising serious questions about the preparation of teachers and the academic exploitation of science fiction. He asked why the SFRA was not setting and demanding professional qualifications among science fiction teachers, and he feared "a variation of Gresham's law in which the bad teaching and schlock movies and TV shows will drive out the good ones."

In rebuttal, in the November 1974 issue of *Analog*, for which Ben should be given credit—when I dropped into his office after the Kean College conference he asked me to write it; even better, he offered to pay me for it—I tried to respond to the fears that Ben's editorial had voiced. That article is called "Teaching Science Fiction Revisited" and can be found in this volume. (Ben also included my response in a slender volume of his editorials, published as *Viewpoint* by the New England Science Fiction Association [NESFA] Press in honor of Ben's guest of honor appearance at the Boston Science Fiction Convention [Boskone]).

That editorial had an amusing sequel. Lester del Rey wrote a rebuttal to my remarks, and that of others, about science fiction as a ghetto. In the March 1975 issue of *Galaxy*, he began his article by saying it wasn't a ghetto at all, that he had always read and written extensively outside the field, and he ended his piece by saying, "Stay out of my ghetto."

So much for ghettos.

One of the problems I didn't mention in my guest editorial in *Analog* was the difficulty with teaching tools. I'm not talking about scholarship here, although scholarship clearly contributes to teaching through insights and through the education of teachers. I am talking about the books the students handle and, hopefully, read: the textbooks and the anthologies and the novels.

Although Bruce Franklin's *Future Perfect* was published in 1966, it was concerned with nineteenth-century science fiction, a topic more scholarly than teachable, particularly in the introductory classes most of us taught. The first teaching anthologies were Robert Silverberg's *Mirror of Infinity* and *The Science Fiction Hall of Fame*. The second of those, preferable because of the number of stories it offered and the selection process by the authors themselves, and Richard Ofshe's *Sociology of the Possible* were not published until 1970. The last never had a cheap edition, I think, and the first two were not available in paperback until a year or two later. Sam Moskowitz's books of biographical sketches, *Explorers of the Infinite* and *Seekers of Tomorrow*, were published before 1970 but, though useful, were more reference works than texts, and in any case were not available in paperback (or in any other form, for a while) until Hyperion Press reprinted them. The same is true of his fascinating studies of early science fiction, *Science Fiction by Gaslight* and *Under the Moons of Mars*.

Tom Clareson's *SF: The Other Side of Realism*, with its useful reprints of scholarly and popular articles, and Dick Allen's *Science Fiction: The Future* were published in 1971. Don Wollheim's personal history, *The Universe Makers*, was also published in 1971, and Clareson's academic anthology, *A Spectrum of Worlds*, in 1972; neither has appeared in paperback. It is instructive about the youth of our field that Harrison and Pugner's *A Science Fiction Reader* did not appear until 1973; the first thorough history of the field, Brian Aldiss's *Billion Year Spree*, appeared the same year, although Sam Lundwall's *Science Fiction: What It's All About* was published in 1971 (Aldiss's book has been revised as *Trillion Year Spree* [2001]). Two books for high school teachers, Calkins and McGhan's *Teaching Tomorrow* and Hollister and Thompson's *Grokking the Future*, came out in 1972 and 1973; Beverly Friend's *Classroom in Orbit*, in 1974. The discursive symposium, Reginald Bretnor's *Science Fiction, Today and Tomorrow*, appeared in 1974, in paperback in 1975.

My own illustrated history, *Alternate Worlds*, was originally scheduled for 1972 and could have been published in 1973, but various problems including complexity and a change in editors delayed it until fall 1975. This book is now out of print.

By the summer of 1975 I could prepare for the students in my institute a list of fifty-five books of academic interest or usefulness just from those I could see on my shelves.

I would like to return for a moment to the matter of price and format: these are serious matters, particularly at the college level where a semester's course may involve ten to fifteen novels or short story collections. With this many required texts, none of them can be expensive; they must be in paperback—and in print. Being published in paperback in our field means that the books go out of print as rapidly as they become available. A case in point is Jack C. Wolf and Gregory Fitz Gerald's useful anthology, *Past, Present, and Future Perfect*, which was published by Fawcett in 1973 and has been unavailable ever since. My own four-volume, historically organized anthology for Mentor Books, *The Road to Science Fiction*, was an attempt to remedy this situation; it once more is in print from Scarecrow Press, and volumes 5 and 6, with coverage of British and international science fiction, are available from White Wolf.

The problem of availability has been even a greater problem in the science fiction novels themselves. Paperback publishers traditionally have been geared to the rhythm of the newsstands. The publishers throw a big printing of books onto the stands for a period which may last from a month to three months; at that point the newsstand proprietors replace the old books, tear off their covers, and return the covers for credit. Not all your piety nor all your wit will get a reorder out of such a publisher; he doesn't have the warehouses or the mechanism. The books will be out of stock or out of print until the next printing, if any. I have often received notices from the university bookstore that one-third to one-half of my book orders were out of stock or out of print. Teachers of science fiction got used to scrambling for replacements, or, if we were more sophisticated, to ordering 50 percent more titles than we intended to use. The latter solution, though it had the psychological advantage of cynicism, often left us with two or more books serving the same purpose. The situation has been ameliorated in recent years by the trend toward publication in trade paperback and reprint programs by several academic publishers.

Even this situation has eased as paperback publishers have become educated to the fact that science fiction is not the same as mysteries, westerns, nurse novels, and gothics, which may well be interchangeable. The publishers are keeping science fiction books in print and in stock longer; special educational flyers from half a dozen paperback publishers list their science fiction for the classroom. If nothing else, teachers may have helped the science fiction community achieve a momentary victory in its long campaign to convince publishers that science fiction books sell year after year and should be kept in print.

Four publishers brought old "classics" back into print, beginning with Hyperion and followed by Arno, Gregg, and Garland; Hyperion and Gregg came out with a second series, and Gregg with a continuing series until it was suspended in the early 1980s. The price of the books, however, as well as their antiquity, made them additions to scholarly resources rather than to classroom teaching, although the Garland and the Gregg series did include a number of titles from the so-called Golden Era of Science Fiction. Students, at least, can find the books in the library.

Avon Books started a Rediscovery series that it said was "dedicated to making important and influential works of science fiction available once more—and on a continuing basis—to discerning readers." That promising dedication would have been even more promising were it not for the suspicion that these "important and influential works" were also those books that happened to be available, either because the rights belonged to Avon already or because the rights had been reverted to the author by the original paperback publisher. Unfortunately even for this limited value, the series was soon cancelled, as was Crown's hardcover Classics of Modern Science Fiction series.

The situation of the classroom teacher has been complicated by several new factors. The first is the back-to-basics movement in high schools, which has limited, if not eliminated, the mini-course and placed greater emphasis on traditional areas of learning. At the college level, the original student enthusiasm that produced such remarkable enrollments seems to have diminished to more manageable levels, as the appeal of the new and exotic wore off and pent-up demand was satisfied. Enrollments have dwindled from the hundreds down to the fifties, forties, and even thirties—still adequate and perhaps even better for teaching purposes, but a sign that science fiction will have to find its place in the curriculum and its support from something more substantial than novelty. In some places, however, science fiction courses have been cancelled not because they were underenrolled, but because they were *too* popular.

The second factor is the spectacular success of science fiction films. *Star Wars* became, for a time, the biggest-grossing movie in the history of the film business (and its sequels have not been far behind), and it was succeeded at the top of the money list by another science fiction film, *E.T., the Extra-Terrestrial*. Other science fiction films, such as *Close Encounters of the Third Kind*, *Star Trek: The Motion Picture* and its sequels, *Superman* and its sequels, *Dune*, *Total Recall*, and a number of other films have not only cost previously unbelievable amounts of money to make (before *2001: A Space Odyssey*, at least) but some also have been big moneymakers (such as *Terminator 2: Judgment Day*, which cost a record $100 million, but earned over $200 million in the first year). As a consequence, teachers will have to cope with student interest stimulated first by film rather than by books, and it is a sad truth about the relationship between science fiction and film that the visual media have seldom done movies that are both good films and good science fiction (the only real exceptions I know are *2001* and the 1936 film *Things to Come*, but I have written about this subject extensively in an essay called "The Tinsel Screen," which is included in this volume). Even *Star Wars* is primarily a fairy tale, and *E.T.* is basically a lost animal film like, say, *Lassie, Come Home*. They are marvelous films, but not good examples of science fiction.

The third factor is the sudden popularity of fantasy, particularly heroic fantasy, perhaps inspired by the success of Tolkien's *The Lord of the Rings*, recently filmed to great acclaim. The distinction between fantasy and science fiction is not easy to make, and many experts claim that there is no difference, but to me it is critical to the successful teaching of science fiction. Fantasy can be just as effective as any other form of literature, but commercial success often means that the marketplace is flooded with publications that are produced to order according to formula, and bad fantasy finds its way into print more easily than bad (in the sense of "without originality" or "sloppily executed") science fiction. The demand upon teachers is not only to be more discriminating in the choice of texts but to be more certain of their own values as they teach.

The problems brought about by the increased publication of generic fantasy complicate the problems already produced by the vast increase in the publication of science fiction and fantasy. From 348 books a year in 1972, originals and reprints, hardcovers and paperbacks, publication totals increased steadily until they peaked in 1979 at 1,288—approximately a hundred a month—far more than any single person can survey, much less evaluate. That number dropped to 1,047 by 1982 but reached nearly 2,000 by 1989 and has been more than 2,000 almost every year since. Today, one of every four or five books of fiction is science fiction or fantasy. What this means in practice is the desirability of dependable methods of information, evaluation, and discrimination.

Extrapolation was joined in 1973 by a second journal, *Science Fiction Studies*, and they have since been joined by other media of information and analysis. These media include the British journal *Foundation*, the monthly news magazines *Locus* and *Science Fiction Chronicle*, and the *New York Review of Science Fiction*. Most of these are valuable, and perhaps essential, to the well-informed science fiction teacher and scholar.

The SFRA, which offers *Extrapolation, Science Fiction Studies*, a newsletter, and discounts on *Foundation* and other scholarly magazines as benefits of membership, has been joined by a second organization, the International Association for the Fantastic in the Arts (IAFA), which developed out of the International Conference for the Fantastic in the Arts.

Publication of scholarly books in the field has expanded almost as rapidly as the field itself. Oxford University Press's early interest culminated (and terminated) in a series of one-author studies under the general editorship of Robert Scholes, but it was succeeded by a variety of publishers, led by Bowling Green University Popular Press, Greenwood Press, the late Borgo Press, Southern Illinois University Press, and in 1984 UMI, all with ambitious publishing programs. Other presses remain open to books about science fiction and fantasy, such as Harper & Row (and its successors), which has published a variety of useful books in the past (such as the two collections of essays *Science Fiction, Today and Tomorrow* and *The Craft of Science Fiction*, edited by Reginald Bretnor) and has published two SFRA anthologies.

The many guides to the field should be noted as well, including Neil Barron's several editions of *Anatomy of Wonder* and companion books, Peter Nicholls and John Clute's *Encyclopedia of Science Fiction*, Donald Tuck's *Encyclopedia of Science Fiction and Fantasy*, Cowart and Wymer's *Twentieth-Century American Science Fiction Writers*, Curtis C. Smith's *Twentieth-Century Science Fiction Writers*. There are numerous bibliographies and guides to the literature, including the several indexes to the magazines, Hal Hall's *Book Review Indexes*, William Contento's *Index to Science Fiction Anthologies and Collections*, and the Locus annuals, as well as my own *The New Encyclopedia of Science Fiction*.

One fourth and final complication should be noted. After generations as a ghetto literature and a minority literature (Damon Knight has called it "a mass medium for the few"), science fiction has begun to make the best-seller lists routinely. At one time in 1982, seven books out of the top ten best-sellers on the *New York Times* list were science fiction or fantasy, including novels by Isaac Asimov, Arthur C. Clarke, and the late Robert A. Heinlein, the three best-known contemporary writers of science fiction. Whether this is a persistent phenomenon, and if so, what this will do to the public position, teaching, and study of science fiction, remains to be seen. One consequence may be that novels may be written to the requirements of the best-seller genre: that is, to appeal to broad interests rather than those that are deep but narrow, although it should be noted that the Asimov, Clarke, and Heinlein best-sellers succeeded in part because of audiences they had built for their work.

The magazines have not shared in the general increase in popularity. Their numbers and their circulations continue to decline, although innovative production and circulation methods have maintained a slender profitability. For a dozen years, *Omni* experimented with a slick magazine approach to science fiction and related content. Created in 1978, its circulation reached nearly a million a month, though largely as a magazine of colorful illustrations, graphics, and popular science leavened with a bit of fiction, until its publisher, Bob Guccione, gave it up. More teachers would do well to consider using magazines in their classrooms (a number of publishers have offered special classroom arrangements), and interested teachers, readers, and writers should subscribe to the big three (*Analog, Asimov's,* and *F&SF*) to preserve them, since if they go the field loses its center.

If there is uncertainty in the teaching of science fiction, that is nothing new. In the late 1960s, Arthur Clarke recommended a motto for the Science Fiction Writers of America: "The future isn't what it used to be." It has been a strange journey for science fiction, and it may never reach its final destination (considering the nature of the literature, it would be surprising if it did), but the trip has been exhilarating. Science fiction teachers may as well take a deep breath and hang on tight . . . the best may be yet to come!

3

SCIENCE FICTION AND THE MAINSTREAM

S cience fiction is a relatively recent invention.
So is the mainstream.

We can uncover predecessors and cite precedents but they only obscure the fact that the first successful science fiction writer—in the sense that science fiction made him immensely popular and a sizable fortune—was Jules Verne, whose first science fiction novel, *Journey to the Center of the Earth*, was published in 1864, a century and a half ago.

The word *mainstream*, on the other hand, is not listed in any metaphorical sense in that ultimate authority on word origins, *The Oxford English Dictionary*. *Merriam-Webster's International* did not list it until its 1961 edition, *Random House*, until 1968; and neither of them mention its literary meaning.

Clearly the use of the term goes back half a century if not twice that far, but it should also be clear that the state of mind described by *mainstream* is contemporary. In fact, science fiction and the mainstream may have been created by the same conditions: the tendency toward specialization which produced, among many other aspects of our society, the all-fiction magazines beginning with *Argosy* in 1896 and the category magazines beginning in 1906 with the *Railroad Man's Magazine*, continuing with *The Ocean* in 1907, *Detective Story Magazine* in 1915, and *Western Story Magazine* in 1919, and culminating, for science fiction readers anyway, with *Amazing Stories* in 1926.

In the nineteenth century all kinds of fiction might be given different names—Jules Verne's novels were called *voyages extraordinaires* and H. G.

"Science Fiction and the Mainstream" was previously published in *Science Fiction, Today and Tomorrow: A Discursive Symposium*, edited by Reginald Bretnor (New York: Harper & Row, 1974). This is the way it looked in 1990. For the view from 2005, see chapter 23.

Wells's science fiction novels were called "scientific romances"—but almost all (if we omit such publications as "penny dreadfuls" and "dime novels") were part of general fiction. Most nineteenth-century writers—including Verne and Wells and Kipling and Twain, as well as Poe and Hawthorne and Balzac and Haggard and Doyle, among many—wrote a variety of fiction dealing with contemporary life, history, adventure, and so forth and did not feel that they were writing anything markedly different when they wrote science fiction.

The readers of Arthur Conan Doyle's Sherlock Holmes stories were likely to read his historical novels and *The Lost World* as well, John Brunner has pointed out; and those who read H. Rider Haggard's *King Solomon's Mines* and his Egyptian historical novels probably also read *She* and *Ayesha*.

The nineteenth century was the period when the effects of science and technology on the Western world became obvious to everyone—steam and its impact upon manufacturing and transportation led the list but it was followed quickly by electricity, submarines, balloons and other aircraft, telegraphy and the telephone, explosives, canals, weapons, medical advances (such as anesthesia and Pasteur's work with bacteria), mesmerism, improved metal processes, the chemical industry, plastics, commercial oil wells, recording, photography, the internal combustion engine and the automobile, motion pictures, the incandescent lamp, and X-rays.

More important, perhaps, than any of these was a theory: Darwin's theory described in the *Origin of Species* and *The Descent of Man*, which suggested a different concept of humanity, not as special creation but as natural and evolving creatures. Darwin's speculations about natural selection and the survival of the fittest soon were translated into social, economic, and even political action. And fiction: naturalism took much of its inspiration from Darwin, and H. G. Wells got the idea for his first scientific romances from Darwin through Wells's exciting teacher (and Darwin's foremost champion), Thomas H. Huxley.

With Wells, science fiction began to take form and direction; it became more a medium of ideas than a vehicle for adventure, and the ideas that Wells incorporated in his stories and novels created whole new thematic lineages down to the present, from time travel through alien invasion, forced evolution, invisibility, overspecialization, urban development, and so on and on.

And still there was no *mainstream*. When relatively few people can read and relatively few books are published, nice distinctions between kinds of fiction are unnecessary. General literacy was another product, in the English-speaking countries at least, of the last third of the nineteenth century. Until then, the reading of fiction, at least, was almost exclusively restricted to a small upper class. The great majority of the people were illiterate or, at best, literate enough to read only their Bibles.

Compulsory primary schooling in the United States was a product of the post–Civil War era, when enthusiasm for the power of education swept all parts and levels of the nation. By the mid-1890s, thirty-one state legislatures had made elementary school attendance compulsory.

With more young people completing elementary school, attendance in high schools shot upward. In 1870, only sixteen thousand boys and girls graduated from high school; in the next thirty years the number of high schools jumped from about five hundred to six thousand, and the number of high school graduates to nearly ninety-five thousand a year. Americans were being educated for upward social and economic mobility and as citizens and workers in an increasingly technical and urbanized society; as a side benefit, they were being taught to read fiction.

In England, a similar process was launched by the Education Act of 1871, which organized the British and national schools into a state system and supplemented them with board schools and a system of degrees by examination that created the correspondence colleges. By the last decade of the century, H. G. Wells noted in his autobiography, "the habit of reading was spreading to new classes with distinctive needs and curiosities. . . . New books were being demanded and fresh authors were in request."

This was the period also when the mass magazines originated, beginning with George Newnes's *Tit-Bits* in 1881 and *The Strand* ten years later, imitated in the United States in 1893 beginning with *McClure's Magazine*. The development of mass magazines was made possible by the inventions of the rotary printing press in 1846, the Linotype and wood-pulp paper in 1884, and half-tone engraving in 1886.

The processes that were creating a greatly expanded reading public with new and untutored reading tastes, and the popular magazines to publish the material that public wished to read, were creating not only popular fiction but also the critical necessity to distinguish between mere "popular" entertainment and "serious" fiction.

Of course, even the short story and the novel themselves are relatively young. "The only new pleasures invented since Greek times have been smoking and the reading of novels," a French critic once commented. Although man has always invented narratives to amuse his fellows or to transmit cultural information, and we can trace the development of story fables, epics, and romances, and English and Italian tales, the novel as we know it did not develop into a formal kind of storytelling until the eighteenth century, and the short story, which became a peculiarly American specialty, was not consciously formulated into an art form until the nineteenth century, with writers such as Hawthorne and Poe, Mérimée and Balzac, and E. T. A. Hoffmann. The reading of fiction was closely associated with the emergence of the middle class as the dominant element in European and American society.

The impulses that finally produced science fiction when the conditions were right, go back to times as early as the development of narrative itself: the desires to entertain and be entertained, to instruct, to explain, to illuminate, to invent, to imagine things that are not. Homer's *Iliad* gave the Greeks a common heritage, but his *Odyssey* naturalized their Mediterranean universe. Not until the facts of change created by man through his growing control over nature and the possibility of controlling change became apparent to perceptive men and then to most men, however, did science fiction become possible: that is, somewhat after the Industrial Revolution, generally dated from 1750 to 1850. Considering the cultural inertia of the eighteenth century, that it took the entire hundred years to produce the first true science fiction writer is not surprising.

Some sixty years after the publication of *Journey to the Center of the Earth*, Hugo Gernsback founded *Amazing Stories* and the first science fiction magazine was born. Between Verne and *Amazing Stories*, science fiction had existed in individual books and in the pulp fiction magazines—*Argosy, All-Story, Popular, People's, Cavalier, Bluebook, Black Cat, New Story*, and others—where science fiction stories, mostly adventure in remote places, were found adjacent to adventure stories, western stories, sea stories, war stories, romantic stories, and other kinds of popular fiction.

In 1914, Edgar Rice Burroughs's *Tarzan of the Apes*, when it appeared in book form, still could be reviewed, even by such newspapers as *The New York Times*. Thirty years later, Burroughs's books were excluded from most public libraries, along with those of the other famous storytellers of the first two decades: Garrett P. Serviss, George Allen England, and A. Merritt. In fact, during the thirties and forties virtually no hardcover science fiction was being published; only after the end of World War II, first with the fan presses and then with publishers such as Simon and Schuster, Doubleday, Frederick Fell, Random House, and Pellegrini and Cudahy, did science fiction return to book form. Even then it received no critical attention. A bit later, when most science fiction novels appeared as paperback originals, they shared the critical fate of all paperbacks: oblivion.

What had happened to the genre since H. G. Wells's novels were welcomed by such literary figures as Henry James, who was filled with "wonder and admiration" by Wells's early work and spoke of reading *The First Men in the*

Moon "*à petites doses* as one sips (I suppose) old Tokay" and of allowing *Twelve Stories and a Dream* "to melt, lollipop-wise, upon my imaginative tongue," and Joseph Conrad, who wrote to Wells how much he liked his work, particularly *The Invisible Man*: "Impressed is *the* word, O Realist of the Fantastic!" adding: "It is masterly—it is ironic—it is very relentless—and it is very true"? Both James and Conrad kept after Wells to improve his descriptions, his characterization, his subtlety, but they were not put off by his material.

Two things that happened to science fiction were a change in criticism and the appearance of the mainstream as a concept. More important than either, however, was the creation of the science fiction magazine. Today the observer of the science fiction scene can recognize that magazine science fiction was a ghetto, but in the early days of the magazines, readers and writers had no such concern. The discovery of *Amazing Stories* was a joyous recognition that now readers could enjoy their favorite kind of reading without having to winnow it out of general magazines or search it out in obscure corners of the public library. Fans, and Gernsback discovered many of them, now could read, collect, and even communicate with one another, first in the letter columns of the magazines, then in clubs and fan magazines.

Science fiction became a refuge and a mission. Science fiction writers were the missionaries: they worked in strange lands, they were underpaid, and they preached salvation and a better world. Gernsback believed that readers would be introduced to science and technology through science fiction, and some of them would be inspired to become scientists and through science create a better world; one of the early fan feuds centered around the contents of a fan magazine: should it be devoted to science fiction or science?

At first, *Amazing Stories* ran only reprints, mostly from Verne, Wells, and Poe, but gradually new writers were discovered and introduced. The first generation was composed primarily of pulp writers who had to write very fast and in a variety of categories—adventure, sea, detective, war, romance—in order to make a living. They helped give science fiction its subliterary reputation: by necessity their stories were constructed to narrative formulas and they were hastily written by people who did not know much about writing and cared somewhat less about science. There were no Vernes, Wellses, or Poes among them.

Among that first generation of writers, however, were men like Edward Elmer "Doc" Smith, Jack Williamson, and Edmond Hamilton, who did not know a great deal about writing but were eaten up with wonder and the desire to create it themselves. They were fascinated by *Amazing Stories* and the creations of Verne, Wells, and Merritt, and they were inspired by the cosmic visions of scientists such as Einstein and Hubble, Rutherford and Planck, de Broglie and Heisenberg, Jeans and Shapley, who were peering into the atom and staring out at an expanding universe.

The second generation was more writers like Smith, Williamson, and Hamilton; they had grown up reading science fiction magazines—not only *Amazing Stories*, but its competitors, *Wonder Stories* and *Astounding Stories*—and they had learned something about ideas and science and speculation and a little bit more about writing, mostly from other science fiction writers. Many of them read broadly; some read little except science fiction and perhaps some science, history, and philosophy, but they could tell a story and they could build on the ideas of other science fiction writers. They were men like Isaac Asimov, Robert Heinlein, Theodore Sturgeon, and A. E. van Vogt, who all came along in 1939, not long after John W. Campbell Jr. took over as editor of *Astounding Stories* (shortly to become *Astounding Science Fiction*) in December 1937.

Now science fiction was truly a ghetto, and it began breeding its own traditions, its own myths, its own history, and its own storytellers: the third generation—some, like Ray Bradbury, were in the second—came largely out of fandom. They wanted to be better Asimovs, Heinleins, Sturgeons, and van Vogts. They were largely ignored by the world outside, but greatly admired within the ghetto itself. That seemed enough.

The fourth generation . . . I will get to a bit later.

Meanwhile, science fiction had begun developing a philosophy and a concept of the future based upon that philosophy—a sort of consensus future history. This vision of man's destiny saw him conquering space, spreading his colonies through the solar system and the nearer stars and finally the galaxy itself (sometimes meeting alien races, but most often not), experiencing a breakdown in communications or government which left isolated human communities to develop along divergent paths until a new galaxy-wide government arose to bring mankind back together, wiser and kinder and stronger than before.

From the vantage point of that future, Earth was viewed as an ancestral home, sometimes remembered, sometimes recalled only in myth or legend; or a backwater of human progress, a planet ravaged by radioactives, as Isaac Asimov speculated in *Pebble in the Sky*; or a burial ground for Earth's far-flung trillions, as Clifford Simak speculated in *Cemetery World*.

Donald A. Wollheim, in his personal history of science fiction, *The Universe Makers*, traces the beginnings of that consensus future history to Asimov's Foundation stories, which began with *Foundation* in 1942, although there were predecessors like Edmond Hamilton and Edward Elmer "Doc" Smith, and Robert Heinlein contributed significantly with his future history of the next two centuries. In the ghetto, however, as the stories and ideas passed, so to speak, from hand to hand, mind to mind, they were refined and added to, like an oral epic, until general agreement was reached—no one was bound to it, but through most stories ran the same general assumptions about what was likely to happen.

That future was so significantly like our present that we can say we are today living in a science fiction world.

Behind the assumptions of that future history lay a concept of man that was at the same time arrogant and humble. It was a concept that grew out of the dominant literary and scientific movements of the nineteenth and early twentieth centuries: realism and naturalism on the literary side; Darwinism, sociology, Marxism, and Freudianism on the scientific.

Realism, which helped shape critical standards of what fiction ought to be, sprang up about the middle of the nineteenth century, mostly in reaction to romanticism. Realism—"the truthful treatment of material," William Dean Howells called it—was the ultimate in middle-class art, focusing its concerns on the immediate, the present, the specific action, and the clear consequence. It was democratic, emphasized character and ethics—that is, issues of conduct—and believed that art should imitate life (i.e., be "mimetic," in the language of criticism) and, since life had neither plot nor symmetry, realistic fiction should also eliminate them.

Naturalism, which followed but did not succeed realism, shared with realism its concern for fidelity to detail and reaction to the assumptions of romanticism, but it shared with romanticism a belief that the action was important not so much for itself as for what it revealed about the nature of a greater reality. Naturalism was the application to fiction of the principles of scientific determinism; it drew much of its inspiration from Darwin but was also influenced by Newton's mechanistic determinism, by Marx's view of history as a battleground of great economic and social forces, by Freud's concept of inner and subconscious determinism, and by Comte's view of social and environmental determinism.

Under the influence of naturalism, science fiction adopted a view of man as an animal selected by environmental pressures for intelligence, aggressiveness, possessiveness, and survival. From the scientific optimism of the times, science fiction saw man also as an animal whose passions, aspirations, and understanding had given him a tragic nobility: he might not be divine, but in his hubris and his understanding, he partook of divinity—he had eaten of the Tree of Life and of the Tree of Knowledge of Good and Evil; he was a creature who could dream of greatness and understand that it was only a dream.

"Man is the only animal that laughs and weeps." Hazlitt wrote, "for he is the only animal that is struck with the difference between what things are, and what they ought to be."

Man exists, science fiction said, and he must continue to exist, for the process that evolved him selected survival characteristics of dominance, intelligence, adaptability, and endurance.

Arthur C. Clarke illustrated that philosophical position with an early story called "Rescue Party." The crew of a spaceship manned by members of a race who "had been lords of the Universe since the dawn of history" discovers that Earth's sun is to become nova in seven hours and that Earth, examined only four hundred thousand years ago and found to have no intelligent life, has developed a civilization. After searching an abandoned Earth, the crew finally discovers in the lonely void far beyond Pluto, a vast, precise array of chemically powered spaceships. Alvaron, the old, wise captain of the alien ship, gestures (with a tentacle) toward the Milky Way, "from the Central Planets to the lonely suns of the Rim," and comments:

> "You know, I feel rather afraid of these people. Suppose they don't like our little Federation. . . . Something tells me they'll be a very determined people. We'd better be nice to them. After all, we only outnumber them about a thousand million to one."
>
> Rugon laughed at his captain's little joke.
>
> Twenty years afterwards, the remark didn't seem so funny.

Robert Heinlein, in his juvenile novel *Have Spacesuit, Will Travel*, set up a situation in which a teenager faces the responsibility of representing man's right to survive before a council of Three Galaxies which has accused humanity of being a danger to all other intelligent creatures. The boy finally can endure the unfairness no longer:

> "It's no defense, you don't *want* a defense. All right, take away our star—you will if you can and I guess you can. Go ahead! We'll make a star! Then, someday, we'll come back and hunt you down—all of you!"
>
> Nobody bawled me out. I suddenly felt like a kid who has made a horrible mistake at a party and doesn't know how to cover it up. But I meant it. Oh, I didn't think we could *do* it. Not yet. But we'd die trying. "Die trying" is the proudest human thing.

Pride in humanity has been one of science fiction's most significant attitudes (alternating, of course, with feelings of shame, dismay, and disgust; misanthropy has been a persistent ingredient in the mix; I do not wish to suggest that science fiction writers have been single-minded but that certain attitudes represent the main current)—but pride not so much in the qualities a creature must have to survive, though survival is basic and without it everything else is frivolous, but pride in the qualities that a creature who must survive can develop and sustain in spite of unrelenting adversity. Man, says the science fiction main current, must be tough and aggressive, but his glory is that he can temper his toughness and aggressiveness with an appreciation for beauty, with artistic creativity, with self-sacrifice, with a capacity for love. And that paradox is what it means to be truly human.

Naturalism held no such pride in man nor hopes for him; what it seemed to demand was understanding of man's predicament and through understanding an amelioration of the harsh judgments and treatments inflicted upon him. Science fiction moderated its naturalism, its Darwinism, not merely with optimism but with rationalism.

Leo Rosten concluded a book with a story about Destiny:

Destiny came down to an island, centuries ago, and summoned three of the inhabitants before him. "What would you do," asked Destiny, "if I told you that tomorrow this island will be completely inundated by an immense tidal wave?" The first man, who was a cynic, said, "Why, I would eat, drink, carouse, and make love all night long!" The second man, who was a mystic, said, "I would go to the sacred groves with my loved ones and make sacrifices to the gods and pray without ceasing." And the third man, who loved reason, thought for a while, confused and troubled, and said, "Why, I would assemble our wisest men and begin at once to study how to live under water."

The man who loved reason had the rational approach of a science fiction writer. The spirit he represents finds alien the dismal view of man displayed by the mainstream when its writers venture into the genre, like Aldous Huxley with *Brave New World* or Nevil Shute with *On the Beach*; it is not so much that their view of man is tragic nor even that they perceive him as an emotional rather than rational being, but that they underestimate him. If threatened by destruction, science fiction says, man will not surrender peacefully; he will struggle to the end, studying how to live underwater, on a frozen or flaming Earth, in outer space, or on the most hostile worlds. It seems to me that this is the truer picture of man's character. That concept is not unique to science fiction, of course. "I decline to accept the end of man," William Faulkner said in his 1950 Nobel laureate speech. "I believe that man will not merely endure: he will prevail." And Dylan Thomas wrote:

Do not go gentle into that good night.
Old age should burn and rave at close of day.
Rage, rage against the dying of the light.

But rationalism—the belief that the mind is the ultimate judge of reality and can be relied upon to provide an answer to any problem—even rationalism modified by experimentalism, does not completely describe science fiction's philosophic position. Independently it arrived at a position that approximates existentialism, described by Jean-Paul Sartre. Humanity, like God, exists before it can be defined by any conception of it. "Man first of all exists, encounters himself, surges up in the world—and defines himself afterward." He is responsible for not only himself but for all humanity and chooses not simply for himself but for all humanity.

Even before Sartre, though not before Kierkegaard (whose influence upon science fiction is doubtful), science fiction said that man was responsible and that each individual was a representative of humanity. Even if he is a conditioned animal, through his passions and his understanding he has free will; he can choose between actions and between fates. Even in a hostile universe deserted by God and meaning, he still must struggle to remain human, to do the human thing. The human thing varies: it may be to survive, to keep evolving, to keep improving, or to explore the ultimate potential of the human form, the human mind, the human spirit, or intelligence itself. In this sense, the arrogance of the science fiction man is a kind of humility before the blind creative processes that produced him, and a determination to assume the responsibilities of choice. Carried to its ultimate form, this philosophy results in not only individual but also racial sacrifice: if some alien race or intelligence, natural or artificial, proves itself superior, better fitted to think, to understand, to create, to survive, then man has a responsibility to step aside and, perhaps reluctantly, perhaps gratefully, lay down the Earthman's burden. Science fiction writers almost always considered this solution, even if they did not always choose it; mainstream writers venturing into the genre never consider intellectual superiority or promise.

In a story called "Resurrection" (or "The Monster"), A. E. van Vogt illustrated science fiction's pride in humanity and its still unrealized potential. An alien spaceship descends upon an Earth, where life has been wiped out by an unexpected cosmic storm. The aliens re-create men from fragments of bone and destroy them as soon as they suggest a possibility of danger; each resurrected man has greater powers until the fourth understands the situation at the moment of his rebirth, vanishes instantly, and revives the rest of mankind to fulfill man's interrupted destiny.

Other stories demonstrate science fictional man's concern for the survival of his successor if not himself. Nietzsche called man a "rope stretched between the animal and the superhuman"; Arthur C. Clarke calls man the "organic phase between the inorganic." "It's hard to see," he has said, "how on a lifeless planet an IBM computer could evolve without passing through the organic phase first." The intelligent machine may be man's successor.

Clifford Simak, in a collection of related stories called *City*, imagined that man's successors would be dogs and robots. In John W. Campbell Jr.'s story "Twilight," it was too late for dogs: "As man strode toward maturity, he destroyed all forms of life that menaced him"—and eventually, because of their interdependence, all other forms of life. Now man was dying because he had lost his curiosity, but the machines still operated perfectly. A visitor to that distant future "brought another machine to life and set it to a task which, in time to come, it will perform. I ordered it to make a machine which would have what man has lost. A curious machine."

On a more immediate level, science fiction tests mankind and the future against the principles of scientific positivism, a philosophy that rejects metaphysics and maintains that knowledge is based only on sense experience and scientific experiment and observation. The basic attitude of serious, main-current science fiction speculation about the future and man's role in it is pragmatism. "It is not what you believe to be true that will determine your or humanity's success," John W. Campbell Jr.'s *Analog* insisted, "but what works." A substantial body of science fiction is dedicated to overturning prejudice and prior judgments, romanticism and sentimentality; and some writers have created careers out of asking themselves what mankind and its folk wisdom hold dear and then demonstrating fictionally that the opposite makes more sense.

The ultimate expression of this pragmatism is embodied in Tom Godwin's "The Cold Equations." A girl, hoping to see her brother, who is a member of an advance group on a frontier planet, stows away aboard a one-man emergency delivery ship sent out by an interstellar liner with vital serum for another exploration party on that planet. The amount of fuel necessary to reach the planet has been carefully calculated because the "frontier" demands the strictest economy. Interstellar regulations state that a stowaway must be jettisoned immediately upon discovery; otherwise the ship will crash and kill eight people instead of one. The cold equations say that the girl must leave the ship, that she must die; she does.

"The Cold Equations" looks at humanity from the viewpoint of the universe; it is indifferent to the feelings of individuals. It doesn't care whether they live or die, whether mankind itself survives; its cosmic processes involve the titanic birth and death of suns, of galaxies, and of a universe itself slowly running down toward the universal heat death called entropy, and even for these things it does not care. Those who infer purpose or concern in the universe may find comfort, but they also assume risk; and what they hazard is not merely their own lives and the lives of others, but the waste of those human lives, those human efforts, those human purposes, through sentiment or ignorance.

Viewpoint is a key to the writing of fiction. More than eighty years ago, Percy Lubbock, in his classic study called *The Craft of Fiction*, wrote: "The whole intricate question of method, in the craft of fiction, I take to be governed by the question of the point of view—the question of the relation in which the narrator stands to the story." The kinds of viewpoints that science fiction adopts, however, are more than questions of narration; in a larger sense, irrespective of the point of view from which the story is narrated, the viewpoints of science fiction, whether implied or explicit, have made science fiction what it is; they create the tone and perspective that have distinguished science fiction from other kinds of fiction, and more than anything else, subject or scene, created the effects it has achieved.

These viewpoints detach the reader from his anthropomorphism, from his blind involvement with the human race; for the first time, perhaps, he is able to see humanity—and hopefully himself—from afar and judge objectively its potential and its accomplishments, its history and its prospects. The most distant, coldest, most objective view is the indifference of the universe. Another, a bit closer and a bit more subjective, is the view of man from space. One reason for getting into space is to attain this perspective, and one of the values of the space program was the photography of Earth from space, along with the comments of the astronauts. From this group of extroverted pragmatists came such remarks as Neil Armstrong's "I remember on the trip home on *Apollo 11* it suddenly struck me that that tiny pea, pretty and blue, was the Earth. I put up my thumb and shut one eye, and my thumb blotted out the planet Earth. I didn't feel like a giant. I felt very, very small." To Bill Anders the sight of Earth from space evoked "feelings about humanity and human needs that I never had before." Rusty Schweickart said, "I completely lost my identity as an American astronaut. I felt a part of everyone and everything sweeping past me below." Or Tom Stafford: "You don't look down at the world as an American, but as a human being." Michael Collins: "I knew I was alone in a way that no Earthling had ever been before." Ed Mitchell: "You develop an instant global consciousness, a people orientation, an intense dissatisfaction with the state of the world and a compulsion to do something about it."

Any of those statements could have come from Reverdy McMillen in my 1955 short story "The Cave of Night," in which the first man to venture into space gets stranded there and radios back:

"Up here you wonder why we're so different when the land is the same. You think: we're all children of the same mother planet. Who says we're different? . . .

"I have seen the Earth . . . as no man has ever seen it—turning below me like a fantastic ball, the seas like blue glass in the sun . . . or lashed into gray storm-peaks—and the land green with life . . . the cities of the world in the night, sparkling . . . and the people . . ."

What the astronauts felt is what science fiction, at its best, can achieve. What other kind of fiction has this capability?

The view from space brings humility. In those photographs from space, where were man's monuments? Where were the signs of his civilization? "Is there life on Earth?" I. S. Shklovskii and Carl Sagan ask in their book, *Intelligent Life in the Universe*; they go on to remark, after searching *Tiros* and *Nimbus* satellite photographs of the eastern seaboard of the United States and the southern tip of India and the island of Ceylon:

the regions depicted in these photographs are among the most heavily populated and densely vegetated areas of the Earth; yet even close inspection shows no sign of life at all. New York appears deserted; India and Ceylon appear barren . . . when the resolution is no better than a few kilometers, there is no sign of life on Earth.

The farther into space one travels, the less significant become the passions and agonies of man, and the only matter of importance in the long morning of man's struggle to survive is his survival so that his sons and daughters could be seeded among the stars, just as the only importance of the long, terrible efforts of gilled creatures to live upon the land was that they became the ancestors of all air-breathers, including man, and the only importance to the life of a man is what he passes on to his children or the children of his race in the form of a physical, genetic, or intellectual legacy.

In 1969, Ray Bradbury said, "Space travel says you can live forever. Now we are able to transport our seed to other worlds. We can be sure that this miraculous gift of life goes on forever."

Another detached viewpoint of science fiction is the future. Much of science fiction has looked back at man from this vantage place: from there the important function of the present is to make possible the future—or, at least, not to make it impossible. Theodore Sturgeon made use of this viewpoint in his 1947 story "Thunder and Roses," in which the United States has been attacked with atomic bombs from both the east and west; it is doomed, although a few survivors are still searching for the secret trigger that would send off the atomic weapons of the United States in a retaliation that would destroy all life on Earth. One woman, a popular singer, tries to get across the message that "we must die—without striking back":

> "Let us die with the knowledge that we have done the one noble thing left to us. The spark of humanity can still live and grow on this planet. It will be blown and drenched, shaken and all but extinguished, but it will live if that song is a true one. It will live if we are human enough to discount the fact that the spark is in the custody of our temporary enemy. Some—a few—of his children will live to merge with the humanity that will gradually emerge from the jungles and the wilderness. Perhaps there will be ten thousand years of beastliness; perhaps man will be able to rebuild while he still has his ruins. . . ."
>
> He looked down through the darkness at his hands. No planet, no universe, is greater to a man than his own ego, his own observing self. These hands were the hands of all history, and like the hands of all men, they could by their small acts make human history or end it. Whether this power of hands was that of a billion hands or whether it came to a focus in these two—this was suddenly unimportant to the eternities which now enfolded him. . . .
>
> "You'll have your chance," he said into the far future. "And, by Heaven, you'd better make good."

Here is science fiction pointing out the ultimate horror of holocaust—the horror is not that so many will die so horribly and so painfully (all men are doomed to die, and few deaths are easy) but that it destroys the future of mankind, all the unachieved potential, all the untested possibilities, all the art and love and courage and glory that might be; it is not just that some idiot kind of total warfare might destroy the present (the present is being destroyed minute by minute as it is pushed inexorably into the future) but that it might destroy eternity. From this viewpoint, from the viewpoint of our distant descendants, no matter what their alien forms, ways, beliefs, the ultimate crime is not murder, but stupidity, as pollution, global war, civil strife, and other contemporary carelessnesses that threaten racial survival are stupid. In a metaphorical sense, science fiction might be considered letters from the future, from our children, urging us to be careful with their world.

A final detached viewpoint is that of the alien—sometimes the alien to our society such as the visitor from the future, as in Fredric Brown's "Dark Interlude"; or the visitor from a distant planet, as in Robert Sheckley's "Pilgrimage to Earth"; or the Earthman in an alien society, as in Sheckley's "The Language of Love" or Roger Zelazny's "A Rose for Ecclesiastes"; or the man from the present in a future society, as in Edward Bellamy's *Looking Backward*, Wells's *When the Sleeper Wakes*, or Frederik Pohl's *The Age of the Pussyfoot*. Sometimes the extraterrestrial beings visit Earth for conquest or exploration or judgment, as in Murray Leinster's "Nobody Saw the Ship," Ross Rocklynne's "Jackdaw," Jack Williamson's *The Trial of Terra*, or Gordon Dickson's "Dolphin's Way" or like the alien conquerors of Arthur C. Clarke's *Childhood's End* or the ultimate alien—the Creator—of Eric Frank Russell's "Hobbyist." From the alien viewpoint, we can see more clearly the relativity of our most cherished beliefs, the ridiculousness of our traditions, our mores, and our concerns, and the temporality of our societies; and we can learn to share the broader vision that encompasses all living creatures, all thinking beings—as in Clifford Simak's *Time Quarry* and other stories—which, by extension, renders trivial the minor differences between races or individuals.

These viewpoints—there are others and innumerable variations upon them—help determine how a reader is going to react to science fiction. Some readers welcome perspective on themselves or on humanity; some find it painful or silly or are unable to make the imaginative leap necessary to dissociate themselves from their unshakably Earth-bound preconceptions—they are unable to get outside their own skins and their own viewpoints.

Edmund Crispin pointed out in a 1962 *London Times Literary Supplement*:

All these things being thus, it would be surprising if science fiction were to be popular. Nobody can take altogether kindly to the thesis that neither he personally, nor anyone else whatever, runs much risk of unduly bedazzling the eye of eternity. . . . The best seller lists are scarcely, if one comes to think of it, the place to look for fiction which instructs us, no matter how cheerfully, in how completely trivial we all are. . . . In medieval times Man was commonly visualized as being dwarfed against a backdrop of stupendous spiritual or supernatural agencies; yet not dwarfed ultimately, since the Christian religion consistently averred him to be a special creation. From the Renaissance onwards that backdrop shrank, or was more and more ignored, with a corresponding gain in stature to the actor in front of it. What science fiction has done, and what makes it egregious, is to dwarf Man all over again (this time without compensation) against a great new backdrop, that of environment. Leopold Bloom has Dublin, and Strether has Edwardian England, and Madame Bovary has provincial France; but the relative nonentities in science fiction have the entire cosmos, with everything that is, or conceivably might be, in it.

The mainstream and the literary criticism that created it emphasize instead the overriding importance of the individual. Crispin writes of science fiction as "origin of species fiction" in which a man is important only in his relationship to humanity; to focus on any individual "is as if a bacteriologist were to become fixated not just on a particular group of bacteria but on one isolated bacterium." Opposed to that is D. H. Lawrence's conviction that "only in living individuals is life there, and individual lives cannot be aggregated or equated or dealt with quantitatively in any way."

F. R. Leavis, the English literary critic, quoted Lawrence's statement in Leavis's 1962 rejoinder to C. P. Snow's "The Two Cultures." A brief summary of that debate may be illuminating here: Snow was describing the scientific culture, but for that we might, without significant distortion, substitute science fiction; and Leavis was defending the literary culture, but for that we can substitute "mainstream," that at its best is the literary culture's mode of expression. Through an examination of the positions taken in the debate, we may be able to understand why the mainstream became what it is and why until recently science fiction was excluded from it.

After expressing regret over the fact that most scientists are ignorant of literature and greater regret over the fact that almost all members of the literary culture are ignorant of science, Snow attacked literary intellectuals as "natural Luddites" who

> have never tried, wanted, nor been able to understand the industrial revolution, much less accept it. . . . Almost everywhere . . . intellectual persons didn't comprehend what was happening. Certainly the writers didn't. Plenty of them shuddered away, as though the right course for a man of feeling was to contract out; some . . . tried various kinds of fancies which were not in effect more than screams of horror.

Snow saw "those two revolutions, the agricultural and the industrial-scientific" as "the only qualitative changes in social living that men have ever known" and noted that "with singular unanimity, in any country where they had the chance, the poor walked off the land into the factories as fast as the factories could take them." Against this, Leavis placed a "vision of our imminent tomorrow in today's America; the energy, the triumphant technology, the productivity, the high standard of living and the life-impoverishment—the human emptiness: emptiness and boredom craving alcohol—of one kind or another" and compared it with "a Bushman, an Indian peasant, or a member of those poignantly surviving primitive peoples, with their marvelous art and skills and vital intelligence."

"If the scientists have the future in their bones," said Snow, "then the traditional culture responds by wishing that the future did not exist."

Leavis inherited his critical principles from Matthew Arnold, who said, "Literature is the criticism of life." Of course Arnold meant "criticism" in the broad sense of judging and evaluation rather than fault-finding, but the standards of literature—and literary comparisons with past successes—have led to more fault-finding than programs for improvement. In 1913, Bertrand Russell pointed out:

> In the study of literature or art our attention is perpetually riveted upon the past: the men of Greece or of the Renaissance did better than any men do now; the triumphs of former ages, so far from facilitating fresh triumphs in our own age, actually increase the difficulty of fresh triumphs by rendering originality harder of attainment; not only is artistic achievement not cumulative, but it seems even to depend upon a certain freshness and *naïveté* of impulse and vision which civilization tends to destroy. Hence comes, to those who have been nourished on the literary and artistic productions of former ages, a certain peevishness and undue fastidiousness towards the present, from which there seems no escape except into the deliberate vandalism which ignores tradition and in the search after originality which achieves only the eccentric.

And H. G. Wells noted in 1929:

> We are constantly being told that the human animal is "degenerating," body and mind, through the malign influences of big towns; that a miasma of "vulgarity" and monotony is spreading over a once refined and rich and beautifully varied world, that something exquisite called the human "soul," which was formerly all right, is now in a very bad way, and that plainly before us, unless we mend our ways and return to mediaeval dirt and haphazard, the open road, the wind upon the heath, brother, simple piety, an unrestricted birth-rate, spade husbandry, hand-made furniture, honest, homely surgery without anesthetics, long skirts and hair for women, a ten-hour day for workmen, and more slapping and snubbing for the young, there is nothing before us but nervous wreckage and spiritual darkness.

One source for such accusations might be Ruskin, who noted in the mid-nineteenth century "signs of a slavery in our England a thousand times more bitter and more degrading than that of the scourged African, or helot Greek. Men may be beaten, chained, tormented, yoked like cattle, slaughtered like summer flies, and yet remain in one sense, and the best sense free"; and Ruskin went on to praise the age of nobility and peasantry when "famine and peril, and sword, and all evil, and all shame, have been borne willingly in the causes of masters and kings."

In this context Leavis wrote that the human faculty above all others to which literature addresses itself is the moral consciousness, which is also the source of all successful creation, the very root of poetic genius, and he maintained that great literature asks deeply important questions about the civilization around it, but "of course, to such questions there can't be, in any ordinary sense of the word, answers." The questions, moreover, will all be of the sort to make society hesitate, slow down, lose confidence in the future, distrust both social planning and technological advance.

In support, the *Spectator* remarked that "philosophy . . . takes the form of that effort to impart moral direction, which is to be found in the best nineteenth-century English writers."

If Snow's scientists have the future in their bones, the literary culture claims moral direction.

Professor Martin Green pointed out in 1962 that

for the last ten or fifteen years the study of literature, and to some extent the general intellectual climate, has been increasingly dominated by a movement very largely antithetical in tendency—a movement which insists on narrow intense knowledge (insights), on the need for personal freedom within the best-planned society, on the dangers of modern science and technology, on the irreducibility of artistic and religious modes.

Webster's New World Dictionary defines *science* as "knowledge as opposed to intuition," and Maxwell Anderson described the work of art as "a hieroglyph, and the artist's endeavor is to set forth his version of the world in a series of picture writings which convey meanings beyond the scope of direct statement."

By what criteria is literature evaluated? Theories of criticism have not so much evolved as alternated: beginning with the classical criticism of Aristotle, Longinus, and Horace, criticism moved through the ecclesiasticism of the Middle Ages, the classical revival of the Renaissance, various attempts like that of Sir Philip Sidney to find a new theory of criticism, the neoclassicism of Alexander Pope, the romanticism of Wordsworth and Coleridge, the impressionism, growing out of romanticism, of Walter Pater, the realism of Matthew Arnold and then of William Dean Howells and Henry James, and the naturalism of Émile Zola and Frank Norris, arriving in the twentieth century at the new humanism of Irving Babbitt and Paul Elmer More, Marxist pragmatism, and the New Criticism of Robert Penn Warren, Allen Tate, and Cleanth Brooks, and the New Criticism, in turn, has been succeeded by postmodernism, semiotics, and criticism focused on politics or gender.

M. H. Abrams in *The Mirror and the Lamp* suggests that criticism can be categorized according to the dominance of one of four elements in "the total situation of a work of art": the work, the artist, the universe, and the audience. If the critic judges the work on how well it imitates the universe, he is using "mimetic theory"; in terms of its effect on an audience, "pragmatic theory"; in terms of the artist, "expressive theory"; in its own terms, "objective theory."

Mimetic theory—imitation—was dominant in Aristotle and his successors, and pragmatic theory, from Horace through most of the eighteenth century. Expressive theory came in with romanticism, while objective theory—the work itself for its own sake—emerged in the nineteenth century and became dominant in the twentieth.

Modern criticism—and the popular book-review media which, insofar as they contain criticism rather than reviews, are subconsciously influenced by prevalent critical standards and modes—has ignored science fiction for most of its recent history not only because of the crudeness of its craftsmanship, the ephemeral nature of its medium, and its nondiscriminating popular audience but also because its philosophy was optimistic and scientific in a pessimistic, antiscientific literary climate, because its values were accessible only through mimetic and pragmatic theory in a period dominated by expressive and objective theory, and because modern criticism finds nothing to say about its style and content.

Hilary Corke, a British poet and critic, says of Snow's novels, "Their emphasis is on plot, not character," and, "A paragraph of a Snow novel yields nothing whatever to deep analysis; his merits lie in the structure and ordering of the whole." The same comments might be made about a well-constructed science fiction novel.

All of this was true until recently. A bit more than forty years ago—a time roughly coincident with the student riots not only in the United States but in France and Great Britain as well—revolution came to science fiction. Perhaps a revolution was inevitable against the apparent inhumanity of a viewpoint which could equate the Vietnam War with Wat Tyler's Rebellion, discrimination with serfdom, individual tragedy with the crushing of a cockroach, which could think of mass starvation as a possible long-term good, plague as a genetic boon, humanitarianism as genetic suicide, and war as merely another means of redressing Malthusian imbalances. Although science fiction has been consistently egalitarian, libertarian, and fraternitarian, its penchant for the long view ultimately created, in reaction, a new breed of writers that focused its concerns on the short term, on individuals and their inalienable worth, on men's and women's passions and perplexities rather than their reason.

But it was no coincidence that the revolution in science fiction—Judith Merril called it "the New Wave" in her later *SF: The Year's Best* anthologies and *England Swings SF*—occurred at the same time as the campus disturbances over civil rights and the Vietnam War, which spilled into university governance and even the structure of the college curriculum. The New Wave was more than a reaction to the scientific positivism that had become the main current of science fiction; it was a response by young writers to the spirit of the times that was rejecting intellectualism as a blind alley, which demonstrated itself in a resurgence of fantasy, occultism, and mysticism and in a willingness to sacrifice the universities to end the war in Vietnam, to trade the classroom and the book for the experience, to seek answers in drugs and meditation rather than in study and experiment, to put together new groupings rather than improve old ones. "I think therefore I am" became "I feel therefore I am," and this shift from rationalism to sensationalism found its way into science fiction first in England through Michael Moorcock's *New Worlds* and the writings of J. G. Ballard, of Brian Aldiss, and, in part, of John Brunner and of Moorcock himself; its spirit was picked up in the United States by Harlan Ellison, Norman Spinrad, Thomas Disch, and a host of younger writers.

Tom Godwin's "The Cold Equations" ends:

A cold equation had been balanced and he was alone on the ship. Something shapeless and ugly was hurrying ahead of him, going to Woden where its brother was waiting through the night, but the empty ship still lived for a little while with the presence of the girl who had not known about the forces that killed with neither hatred nor malice. It seemed, almost, that she still sat small and bewildered and frightened on the metal box beside him, her words echoing hauntingly clear in the void she had left behind her: "I didn't do anything to die for—I didn't do anything."

J. G. Ballard's "The Terminal Beach" also is about death, but death that is not caused but casual and dealt with not directly but symbolically through the wanderings of a man named Traven among the sterile, incomprehensible structures remaining on deserted Eniwetok, site of a postwar hydrogen bomb test. The story is evocative and its meaning comes, elusively, through descriptions of a psychological numbness to death and a premonition of atomic catastrophe. Traven's wife and six-year-old son were killed in an automobile accident, but this seems to Traven only part of what he calls the "pre-Third"—the two decades between 1945 and 1965 "suspended from the quivering volcano's lip of World War III." Now Traven has come to Eniwetok for a purpose he does not understand, and he moves aimlessly around the island. Ballard's story ends:

> As the next day passed into weeks, the dignified figure of the (dead) Japanese sat in his chair fifty yards from him, guarding Traven from the blocks. Their magic still filled Traven's reveries, but he now had sufficient strength to rouse himself and forage for food. In the hot sunlight the skin of the Japanese became more and more bleached, sometimes Traven would wake at night to find the white sepulchral figure sitting there, arms resting at its sides, in the shadows that crossed the concrete floor. At these moments he would often see his wife and son watching him from the dunes. As time passed they came closer, and he would sometimes turn to find them only a few yards behind him.
>
> Patiently Traven waited for them to speak to him, thinking of the great blocks whose entrance was guarded by the seated figure of the dead archangel, as the waves broke on the distant shore and the burning bombers fell through his dreams.

Stories like "The Terminal Beach" partake more of the mainstream than of science fiction in its traditional form, and some traditional writers and readers of science fiction objected to what they considered their inconclusiveness, willful obscurity, pointlessness, and aping of mainstream experimental techniques at the expense of content. But the deeper objections of the traditionalists were stirred, I believe, by the mainstream attitudes New Wave writers adopted. In general, New Wave stories traded the viewpoints of detachment for identification with the individual, what is real determined subjectively rather than objectively.

Professor Arthur Mizener, in *Modern Short Stories*, suggested that contemporary fiction draws upon four main traditions: realistic, romantic, subjective, and southern (the last falls outside the framework of the other three, and we will ignore it). The three traditions can be distinguished, Mizener wrote, by their attitude toward objective common sense: the realistic story makes us feel that objective common sense will not only be correct about how things will turn out, but right and wise in understanding that they must turn out that way; the romantic story makes us feel that objective common sense is likely to be correct about how things will turn out, but will miss the real meaning of things because it will not take into account the feelings of the central character; and the subjective story makes us feel that what men dream is so important, and therefore so real, that the objective world of common sense, however resistant to men's desires, does not finally count.

Science fiction, in the tradition established and nourished by John W. Campbell Jr. in the magazine first called *Astounding* and then *Analog*, is primarily realistic; science fiction in the tradition of the scientific romance of the early pulp magazines was primarily romantic. The writers of the New Wave seem primarily subjectivists—a thoroughly respectable literary position but one which is foreign not only to main-current science fiction but to science itself. It is not alien, however, to fantasy, which always has been subjective. Science fiction is a public vision; fantasy is a private vision. As a consequence, writers of fantasy always have been more acceptable to the mainstream than writers of science fiction. Ray Bradbury, for instance, was welcomed into the mainstream early in his career; Asimov and Heinlein had to wait until the early 1980s to find a place on the best-seller lists—although Heinlein's least characteristic and most private science fiction novel, *Stranger in a Strange Land*, achieved some recognition. Professor Gary K. Wolfe, writing in *Extrapolation*, responded to Sam J. Lundwall's criticism of Bradbury's Mars as a fantasy world—or rather "the nostalgic Middle West of Bradbury's dreams"—with the statement that "the 'weakness' of Bradbury's Mars being a transplanted Middle West is what ultimately gives the book its strength because it argues that values are transmitted by individuals rather than society and that man tries to remake the natural world in his own image."

But the New Wave did more than insinuate a mainstream viewpoint into science fiction; it also brought in a greater concern for technique, for stream of consciousness and interior monologue, for shifting viewpoints and symbols and metaphors, for complex characters conducting their lives on a treadmill of meaningless days, for little people or strange people caught up in the innumerable folds of an inexplicable world, for lives that are static, trapped, or doomed.

"I Have No Mouth and I Must Scream," writes Harlan Ellison, and Tom Disch writes "The Squirrel Cage."

Some of the younger writers of the time picked up, or reinvented, Heinlein's 1947 suggestion that science fiction be renamed "speculative fiction" on the grounds that "science fiction" was too narrow a term to cover the various kinds of fiction that qualify under any reasonable definition but include no science. The motivations of these writers of speculative fiction probably were a bit more complex: the term "science fiction" was not broad enough to cover the kind of fiction they wished to write, and a new name suggested new possibilities, new directions, and a break with old pulp origins.

The waves quieted in the late 1970s. Writers who wanted to do new things, experimental things, did them; writers who wanted to say new things, difficult things, outrageous things, said them. Many of these new voices found new audiences; young people, particularly, found the new subjective writers appealing. The net result has been, in spite of the outcries of the traditionalists, an increase in the audience for science fiction—the dividing line between the traditional and the new blurring, and the differences striking to the informed but the similarities greater to the reader looking for something different in reading matter that recognized the pressing importance, both objective and subjective, of external problems.

A side effect of the New Wave has been an increased freedom within the field to experiment, to use unfamiliar techniques and unusual subject matter—in other words to liberate still further what has always prided itself on being the freest medium for fiction. The final shape of science fiction—or speculative fiction—is still unclear. Some observers feared the dominance of the New Wave, of style to the detriment of content. If the decision were up to mainstream critics alone, this fear might have been realized, for they found many familiar and valued elements in New Wave fiction, and close analysis was rewarded. But New Wave fiction, no matter how avant-garde the style (and much of it is no more avant-garde than James Joyce's *Ulysses* [1922] or John Dos Passos's *Manhattan Transfer* [1925]), still is a literature of ideas, which cannot be said of most mainstream fiction.

Gradually New Wave writers returned to the basic principle that style grows out of and informs content, and more traditional SF writers developed a greater concern for language, character, and subjective reality. Greater variety now is tolerated, even encouraged, in subject, approach, and style. An increasing number of writers are difficult or impossible to categorize. The goal in science fiction is becoming the goal of the mainstream: each writer with his or her individual vision, his or her individual voice.

Meanwhile, mainstream vigor, where it exists, seems to emerge from its contacts with popular culture: motion pictures, folk heroes, commercials, radio, television, comic strips, advertisements, modern myths, music and musicians, detective stories, yes, and science fiction.

We live in a pop culture—is there any other kind?—where soup cans are art and commercials are the most skillful art forms on television; literature is just beginning to recognize these facts. Contemporary fiction may have gone as far as it can go in the examination of character, even of abnormal character, and now its major prospect, as William Gass once predicted, may be the exploration of language (which William Gibson has done in *Neuromancer*, launching a whole group of writers into creating their own language techniques). One alternative is to tap the source of energy in our culture—the myths and concerns that shape people's lives—and to consider them fictionally, to turn them into story.

Mainstream writers increasingly are turning to the themes and concepts of science fiction: Barth, Borges, Boulle, Burgess, Burroughs, Golding, Hersey, Nabokov, Rand, Vercors, Vonnegut, Voznesensky, John Williams, Colin Wilson, Wouk, and more recently, Doris Lessing, Margaret Atwood, Philip Roth, and others. What they are finding are not only the vitality of popular culture and the excitement of unexplored territory (unexplored, that is, by mainstream writers) but also subjects relevant to the times in which we live and not tracked over with literary footprints, subjects with the evocative power of a freshly minted metaphor. And although these writers now may be dealing with science fiction themes at arm's length rather than in hand-to-hand engagement, as time passes they may be expected to become as knowledgeable about content and ideas as they are about technique, if they can shed the prejudices of the literary culture.

As the drunken hero of *God Bless You, Mr. Rosewater* says to a convention of science fiction writers:

> I love you sons of bitches. You're all I read any more. You're the only ones who'll talk about the *really* terrific changes going on, the only ones crazy enough to know that life is a space voyage, and not a short one, either, but one that'll last for billions of years. You're the only ones with guts to *really* care about the future, who *really* notice what machines do to us, what wars do to us, what cities do to us, what tremendous misunderstandings, mistakes, accidents and catastrophes do to us. You're the only ones zany enough to agonize over time and distances without limit, over mysteries that will never die, over the fact that we are right now determining whether the space voyage for the next billion years or so is going to Heaven or Hell.

The author of that passage, Kurt Vonnegut Jr., obtained his first recognition in science fiction magazines and books, although he later insisted that he not be labeled a science fiction writer and made his reputation in the mainstream.

Other science fiction writers are being read outside the category, and if they have not exactly been welcomed into the mainstream, they have not been systematically excluded as they had been in the past. First, of course, comes the broader readership—major success in the science fiction field today depends upon hundreds of thousands of sales to occasional or infrequent science fiction readers—and then comes the recognition. Robert Heinlein's *Stranger in a*

Strange Land (1961) sold phenomenally well to the new youth culture, as did Frank Herbert's *Dune* (1965). *Time* magazine called them "good examples of how public concerns and infatuations catch up with the science fiction imagination." Older books such as Isaac Asimov's *Foundation* trilogy (1951) and Frederik Pohl and Cyril Kornbluth's *The Space Merchants* (1953) have almost never been out of print, and Arthur C. Clarke's *Childhood's End* (1953) had gone through eighteen printings by 1971. "Walter M. Miller, Jr.'s *A Canticle for Leibowitz* (1960), an extraordinary novel even by literary standards, has flourished by word of mouth for a dozen years," *Time* noted. More recent books may achieve similar success and status as the years provide them with the opportunity to earn a reputation through some circuitous or underground route. By 1982, science fiction was appearing regularly on the best-seller lists (one heady period saw seven of ten books as science fiction or fantasy!) and almost all the leading money-making films were science fiction.

Some science fiction books have been brought to general public attention by an understanding reviewer in the mainstream, just as more mainstream writers have turned to science fiction for material and inspiration—until science fiction and the mainstream are meeting somewhere to the right of science fiction and to the left of the mainstream. Where the works drew their tradition is increasingly difficult to determine.

This process of reunion will be enhanced by the diminishing influence of the magazines, which, like oak leaves, have stubbornly clung to their small branches after the rest of their fellow pulps have moldered back to the condition from which they came. The old science fiction unity, the brotherhood of writers and editors and readers who learned only from each other and built upon each other's concepts, is dwindling as alternate methods of publication—original anthologies, paperbacks, hardcovers, and even electronic publication—have become more numerous and more important. The ghetto walls are demolished; the "us against the rest of the world" mentality is fading. The consensus future and the philosophical position on which it was built is beginning to fall apart as science fiction splinters into a hundred markets, into a thousand disparate, individual visions.

Science fiction will bring nothing to the mainstream if it surrenders to mainstream philosophies and mainstream values. Both science fiction and the mainstream will be stronger if science fiction retains its unique concepts, narrative strengths, idea orientation, detached viewpoints, and commitments that it developed over the long years of isolation.

4

THE GATEKEEPERS

Most genres begin with a single work and develop when other writers, in their work, include the significant elements of the prototype, or extend them, or react against them. Occasionally a seminal work brings together scattered folk elements, and occasionally a genre develops when a critic presents persuasive arguments about what the genre is, or might be.

Few genres develop through their editors. Of these few, the genre that has been most dependent upon its editors is science fiction. Although Jules Hetzel launched Jules Verne on his fantastic voyages and Lewis Hind persuaded the young H. G. Wells to use his "special knowledge of science" for a series of "single sitting" stories, the significant influence of the editor began with the creation of the SF magazine. It was the culmination of a process that began in 1896, when Frank Munsey changed *Argosy*, a magazine that had been created in 1882 as a weekly titled *Golden Argosy*, from a boys' magazine to the first of what later became known as the "pulp" magazines, offering 192 pages of fiction for a dime.

The old dime-novel and boys' magazine chain, Street & Smith, began competing in the pulp market with *Popular Magazine* in 1906. *Monthly Magazine* in 1905 became *Bluebook* in 1907, and in between Munsey started *The Scrap Book*. The pulp magazine field kept growing, but there were new permutations ahead.

Munsey previewed them with *Railroad Man's Magazine* in 1906 and *The Ocean* in 1907. They were the first attempts at a magazine that specialized in adventure stories built around a single element, such as the central apparatus or the locale, rather than offering adventure stories of all kinds. The first true "category pulp" magazine, however, was Street & Smith's *Detective Story Magazine* created in 1915, followed by the same publisher's *Western Story*

"The Gatekeepers" was first published in *Science Fiction Studies* 11, no. 1, in March 1983.

Magazine in 1919 and *Love Stories* in 1921. Each soon had many competitors. The process of specialization continued into the 1930s, when the "hero pulps," such as *Doc Savage, The Shadow, The Phantom, Secret Agent X, Operator #5, The Spider,* and *G-8 and His Battle Aces,* narrowed the category to a single continuing character or set of characters.

The appearance of a magazine devoted to a single category, or genre, exerted a significant influence on the development of that genre, like building a hothouse for a single variety of flower or isolating a single bacterium in a petri dish and watching it multiply. The mystery or the western or the strange story had a clearly defined habitat and constant conditions; they did not have to be searched out in the wilds, identified, and appraised. What was published in the category magazines tended to define the genre, although the definition might be debated by publications outside the magazines.

Some of the editors and publishers were influential. Munsey's creation of the pulp magazine changed the reading habits of a generation, for instance, and established a new and voracious market for fiction that not only was an incentive to writers but shaped their output. Munsey's editors, such as Robert H. Davis and Thomas Newell Metcalf, and editors of other pulp magazines, such as Archibald Lowry Sessions of Street & Smith's *New Story Magazine,* must have exercised control over the careers of writers by what they bought and rejected, but they were editing general adventure magazines and their influence was more over individuals than genres.

The category pulp editors had the opportunity to direct and shape the genres their magazines published. By their choices they influenced the perceptions of writers and readers. But for several reasons, with the possible exception of Joseph T. Shaw of *Black Mask Magazine,* none were ever as important as those in SF. One reason was that most editors were not so much genre editors as pulp editors, who usually were involved with a number of different kinds of category magazines and shifted readily from one to another. Another reason may have been the relationship of readers and writers to the genre: they were less involved, less committed to this category and no other. Or perhaps the reason was that no one magazine dominated the other genres. Also, at least in the case of the western and mystery categories, books continued to be published throughout the category pulp period, and this diluted the influence of the magazines.

The SF scene was different. During most of the period, only a few magazines were published. Readers and editors were usually committed to their genre. Often the editors came out of the genre as readers, and sometimes as writers, and continued as editors, usually of the same magazine, for extended periods. Few SF books were published during the formative period of magazine SF, and few stories were published other than in the magazines.

Most important, perhaps, the other category pulps did not share the same problem of definition: a sports story might go far afield (like "hares and hounds") for subject matter, but it clearly still was a sports story; a detective story could be identified by its central concern, a crime that was investigated; a western had its locale in a mythical/historical time and place and dealt with a narrow range of menaces from nature, evil, and competing uses for land. But, as I have pointed out in *The Road to Science Fiction*, SF deals not with a subject but with a process: that process is change, and it could and often did incorporate the subject matter or the focus of the other categories. Thus there could be SF adventure stories, western stories, love stories, detective stories, terror stories, gothic romances . . .

What *was* SF, then? Was it Vernian or Wellsian, fantastic or realistic, romantic or pragmatic, literary or scientific? It was all these things, of course, at various times and sometimes at the same time; but as editors developed strength and skill and tastes, one aspect or another would predominate. As they did, the definition of SF was shaped.

For three years, Hugo Gernsback (and his elderly and little-noticed editor, T. O'Conor Sloane) had the genre all to himself. From 1926 to 1929, *Amazing Stories* was where SF lived, and the response of readers was joyful, a mood reflected in the sacks of letters dragged each day into the editorial offices. Modern critics of the magazine-centered period of SF are too young to remember what it was like to be an SF reader when the real stuff was scarce. Even in the 1930s, when three SF magazines were being published, the monthly ration of this soul-sustaining material lasted only a few days, and then the hungry reader would have to search through the dark stacks of the public library once again for undiscovered novels of Verne or Wells or Haggard (librarians considered Burroughs too contemptible to be admitted to the sacred shelves) and often end up with one of Verne's historical novels or Wells's propaganda novels or Haggard's novels of ancient Egypt—which weren't the same thing at all.

Gernsback's tastes were reflected in what he published in *Amazing*: reprints of Poe, Wells, and Verne—the three authors he had pointed at in this first editorial as writing "those charming romances of science" that he called "scientifiction"—and translations from the German. Gradually, as new writers were attracted to the magazine, he published such original material as Edward Elmer "Doc" Smith's *The Skylark of Space* and Philip Nowlan's "Armageddon—2419 A.D.," the first Buck Rogers story. But aside from the reprints, Gernsback was content to let the stories come in and select from those the ones he or Sloane wanted to use. Sometimes, on or after publication, he would even get around to paying for them. In the early, enthusiastic days that was the best an SF writer could get; there was nowhere else for writers to publish, with the single exception of *Weird Tales*, where Ed Hamilton was the resident SF author.

In 1929, having lost *Amazing Stories* and the rest of his publishing empire, Gernsback reconstituted it from his mailing list of subscribers, and in the process created the second SF magazine, *Wonder Stories*. That magazine began life as *Science Wonder Stories*; the first issue contained Gernsback's coinage "science fiction," chosen, no doubt, to distinguish it from the word "scientifiction" that *Amazing* still carried on its spine and masthead. Into *Wonder Stories* a second magazine, *Air Wonder Stories*, was folded. *Amazing* continued under the ageless Sloane until the magazine was bought by Ziff-Davis in 1938.

Out of a desire to fill a blank space on a sheet of cover stock that had room to print sixteen magazine covers at one time but had only thirteen, Clayton Magazines created *Astounding Stories of Super Science* in January 1930. Harry Bates, pulp editor of a Clayton adventure magazine, was the first editor, even in many senses the creator. His insight was that he could edit a magazine like *Amazing* "of the science-monster type" but made up of "action-adventure" stories written by the same writers who were turning out stories for his adventure magazine. His big problem, he wrote in Alva Rogers's *A Requiem for Astounding*, was getting his authors, who were "almost wholly ignorant of science and technology," to send him the right kind of stories. He had to send many of them back for rewriting or rewrite them himself. Eventually he wrote many of them: first, while he was still editor, under pseudonyms in collaboration with Desmond Hall, and later under his own name, turning out such classics as "Farewell to the Master" and "Alas, All Thinking."

Gernsback hired the first fan editor, seventeen-year-old Charles D. Hornig, in 1933. Hornig's *Wonder Stories* was entertaining, but his tenure as editor (which ended in 1936, when Gernsback sold the magazine to Standard Magazines, where as *Thrilling Wonder Stories* it came under the direction of the second fan editor, Mort Weisinger) was distinguished chiefly by the publication of Stanley Weinbaum's first story, "A Martian Odyssey," and the invention of the Science Fiction League, around which the nascent fan movement coalesced.

In 1933, because of internal financial difficulties, Clayton sold *Astounding* to Street & Smith, where, after a gap of six months, it reappeared with an October 1933 issue under the editorship of F. Orlin Tremaine, who had been a Clayton magazine editor. Tremaine also edited four other pulp magazines for Street & Smith. He and his assistant, Desmond Hall, made an effort to obtain stories from some of the better-known authors, such as Edward Elmer "Doc" Smith, John W. Campbell Jr., and Jack Williamson, but his chief contribution was the invention and publicizing of what he called "thought variant" stories, which shifted the emphasis of *Astounding Stories* from action-adventure to ideas. Many of his contributors were old-time pulp writers, such as Nat Schachner, Arthur J. Burks, Harl Vincent, and Arthur Leo Zagat, who wrote in many categories, but the second generation of SF writers was beginning to make its appearance. It was composed of writers who had been inspired by the creation of the SF magazines.

In 1937, Tremaine was named editorial director of a group of Street & Smith magazines (he would leave the company a year later), and he hired as editor of *Astounding* the twenty-seven-year-old Campbell, who had been selling SF stories to various magazines, including most recently *Astounding*, since 1930. Campbell was the first of the major editors. With Campbell, all the magazine field's tendencies toward editorial power and generic direction came together and were combined with his own ideas about what SF might be.

The problem of definition became basic to SF when it was shaped into a genre by the SF magazines. Earlier, when what was published as a *voyage extraordinaire* or a "scientific romance" was the production of one person working in isolation, definition was little more than the effort of an author to protect himself from misleading comparisons, as in Verne's famous attempt to distinguish his work from that by the man some critics were calling "the English Jules Verne." What was unimportant in the mainstream, however, became all-important to readers when the magazines were created, and through the readers, definition became important to the editors and the authors. What was defined as "science fiction" became synonymous with "desirable"—it was what the discoverers of the 1926 *Amazing* identified with when they picked the magazine from the newsstand. They became not a mass audience, but a sizable one, numbering more than one hundred thousand faithful magazine purchasers who found in *Amazing*'s pages that quality of story they had not known existed.

SF (or, rather, scientifiction) was what *Amazing Stories* published. That was the definition for those hundred thousand purchasers and subscribers. And it was the quality displayed by those stories in *Astounding*—idea centered, pragmatic, science oriented, irreverent, iconoclastic, engineer fascinated; what was published in the other magazines (by 1940 they had grown to eighteen) was something less. What the other magazines offered was more adventurous, more fantastic, more romantic, and less rigorous—or simply not good enough to meet *Astounding*'s standards. Since there was no book publication of any consequence, Campbell was the gatekeeper. What he admitted through the gate to the pages of *Astounding* was SF; what he rejected was not.

But the process was not simply a matter of acceptance and rejection; that had been done before. Campbell perfected a method that may have been used first by Weisinger (at least one story, "The Brain-Stealers of Mars," from Campbell himself): he actively sought particular kinds of stories. He proselytized for new kinds of writers; he encouraged and redirected more established ones. In editorial and letter and personal conversation, he inserted irritating ideas into the oyster shells of author's minds, and he repeated his requirements for good SF so often it was like chiseling them into stone—such as: "Grant your gadgets, and start your story from there. . . . I want a story that would be published in a magazine of the twenty-fifth century."

Writers, of course, were essential to the process. No advances in the genre could be sustained without writers to write the stories. Campbell, although he had written his share of important stories, including those under the name of Don A. Stuart, could not write the stories himself even if he had wanted to. But new ideas and new vigor attracted new writers and revived older ones such as Clifford Simak, who told his wife, when he heard of Campbell's appointment, "I can write for Campbell." Dozens of new writers were attracted, partly by the fiction, but just as much by the personality of the magazine and the fact that Campbell was asking repeatedly for something new. Typical of these new writers were Robert A. Heinlein and Isaac Asimov. Heinlein was his own man whose story ideas and orientation happened to coincide with those of Campbell; when they began to diverge, Heinlein departed with them. Asimov was Campbell's creation. Asimov consciously tried to think and write like Campbell, came in and discussed new ideas with Campbell before he wrote them, and accepted Campbell's suggestions gratefully. Asimov tried as hard as he could to be the kind of writer Campbell wanted. He finally departed, too, succumbing to the lure of other editors and finally of other media, but he never forgot his debt to Campbell.

In *Astounding*, between 1937 and 1950, SF was shaped and reshaped by the writers attracted to the vision Campbell held up for them and by Campbell himself, and out of this intense experience of creating and shaping and debating came the conventions and the methods that mark SF to this day and which later generations of writers would use, often unconscious of their origins, or react against. Of this period, and that which preceded it, A. J. Budrys wrote in the *Magazine of Fantasy and Science Fiction* in October 1982:

> It was in the pulp magazines and their outgrowths that the fundamental explosion of ideas occurred, in breadth and depth outstripping everything that had

ever been done on the "outside," forming a universe whose sheer weight of word-age is so gargantuan that ninety-nine percent of it could be worthless and it would still contain a higher volume of brilliance and relevance than the total of all worthwhile SF ever done in any other format.

In 1949 and 1950, two new gates to the kingdom of SF were opened, one by Anthony Boucher and J. Francis McComas when they created the *Magazine of Fantasy and Science Fiction*, the other by Horace L. Gold when he created *Galaxy*. The reason they opened gates was that they established new criteria for what they wanted to publish in their magazines and were not content to settle for Campbell's leavings or for something less rigorous. And they were able to pay competitive rates. Boucher and McComas, to be sure, did not remain competitive: they started at two cents a word compared to Gold's three cents plus a half-cent increase after each three stories sold. Campbell matched the three cents and offered a different kind of additional incentive: one cent a word more for the story that ranked highest in the "Analytical Laboratory" balloting, half a cent more for the story that came in second.

The *Magazine of Fantasy and Science Fiction* got by with prestige. Many writers preferred to see their stories published there, between reprints from literary magazines and such elder figures as Dickens, Forster, and Stevenson, than to get more money from some other magazine. And they liked gentle, sophisticated Tony Boucher. Editors, if they only knew it, have more ways than money to win a writer, but the editors who didn't have the money to offer better rates often didn't have the time to be kind.

All this discussion of money makes the creation of SF seem like hack writers producing potboilers; but, as Brian Aldiss remarked in the introduction to *Hell's Cartographers*: "There is a certain emphasis on finance in our memoirs, and with reason; for the smaller the payment, the larger it looms." Throughout the history of SF in the magazines up to nearly the present, writers have had to struggle to stay alive—physically and artistically. In the 1940s, selling stories regularly to *Astounding* rather than to *Amazing*, say, meant that a writer could double his income, and in the 1950s, selling stories to *Astounding* or *Galaxy* rather than to *Fantasy and Science Fiction* meant at least 50 percent more money. Steady sales at the higher rates meant that a writer could work at his craft full time, although only a few in those years could write fast enough or sell well enough to do that unless they had sources of income besides the magazines.

It was during the early 1950s that I came up with my artistic philosophy: nothing is worth writing unless you can sell it twice. A writer, you see, has a thousand ideas and can only work on a handful of them during his lifetime: since he must have some way of choosing among them, a method that is as good as any and more rewarding than most is to choose ideas that have more than limited appeal—ideas that result in fiction that is worth collecting into books or being incorporated or expanded into novels, or novel-length ideas that can sustain interest when broken into magazine-size stories. Income from one or the other in the 1950s usually was not enough.

The generic importance of the creation of *Fantasy and Science Fiction* in 1949 and *Galaxy* in 1950 was that now there were three gates and three gate-keepers, each of them allowing stories labeled SF to slip through and turning away others as not SF. Many, of course, were rejected as simply not good enough, but that was a subjective judgment that had little lasting effect. The rejection that mattered was the one Campbell often used: "Amusing, but it ain't science fiction."

In the 1950s, Boucher and Gold might welcome the stories that Campbell found amusing but not SF. Boucher, for instance, tolerated the use of over-worked themes if the stories were well enough written. Gold, on the other hand, wanted fiction about people affected by change (even the victims of it) rather than about those causing change or managing it. That preference led to antiheroes, irony, and pyrotechnics, to satire and social SF such as Frederik Pohl and Cyril Kornbluth's *The Space Merchants* and Alfred Bester's *The Demolished Man*. Although *Galaxy* published stories that might have been published in either of the other two magazines, some could have been published only in *Galaxy*.

In the 1950s, then, three different but equal definitions of SF—Campbell's, Boucher's, and Gold's—battled for the minds and hearts of writers and readers. The conversation, sometimes a debate, among writers that was so intense and productive in *Astounding* in the late 1930s and throughout the 1940s now broadened to include dialogues between types of fiction. New techniques were developed to say things and do things in SF that had never been said or done before. And the conversation continued—mostly, to be sure, in *Astounding* and *Galaxy*, where the idea was king. I never had the sense that *Fantasy and Science Fiction* was heavily involved, except in offering literary alternatives, perhaps because the SF interest was diluted with fantasy, which is largely individualistic rather than collaborative, and perhaps because even the SF stories looked toward the mainstream and its concept of the writer as a self-contained, self-defined artist.

Finally, after the demise of many magazines during the mid-to-late 1950s—a period that Harry Harrison called SF's "false spring" and Barry

Malzberg the "end of summer"—came the final gate, *New Worlds*, and the final gatekeeper, Michael Moorcock. He was the final one for two reasons: he flung the gate wide open, which accounted for much of the reaction against what came to be called the "New Wave"; and second, the definitional role of the magazines already was fading before the accelerating publication of books, particularly in paperback.

Up to the time of *New Worlds* under Moorcock, an era that began in 1964, editors had seen their role as extending or broadening the field. They expanded or contracted the focus or shifted their focus on the aspect of change they chose to consider. Their greatest revisionary impulses were directed toward characters: Campbell replaced Gernsback's scientists with pragmatic engineers and technocrats; Gold replaced those with average, downtrodden citizens who are just trying to survive, whose greatest truth is "you can't fight city hall." Moorcock changed the characters, too; at their most extreme, they became Ballard's antiheroes, collaborating in their own catastrophes. But Moorcock was interested in revolution. His *New Worlds* welcomed stories that were anti-SF, even antiscience. He wanted to bring into SF that literary culture that C. P. Snow concluded was composed of "natural Luddites." Moorcock received and published stories that often were in reaction to the concepts that had been forged in the heated magazine debates of the 1930s to 1950s, and the tradition that he helped create has survived the death of the magazine. The New Wave and its contemporary heirs ended up deploring the creation of the magazines as a disastrous detour from the sturdy, ironic heart of SF from Wells through Stapledon, Huxley, and Orwell.

It is not difficult to understand why readers, writers, and editors of traditional SF should respond to the New Wave with anger and denunciations. But all that is past. The New Wave has been assimilated and has enriched the genre with a variety of new techniques and attitudes, and it turned out, after all, to be part of the long debate.

That debate, however, is whispering away to silence. Today, the amount of SF published in books is many times that published in magazines. Moreover, no one can read it all; no one can keep up. The time when all writers were able to discuss and compare all the SF published is long gone. The magazines no longer are gates. SF is defined by each book that tries to pass itself as SF, by each new author; and the magazines, a vestigial organ but not, one hopes, yet doomed to elimination from the body of SF, continue as places in which new writers can get the experience to graduate into books. SF has become more responsive to a big new writer or a big new book, to a John Varley or a *Timescape* or a *Neuromancer*, than to a new magazine or a new editor.

That's not all bad. One of the major problems of the field that produced Heinlein and Asimov, Bester and Pohl, Clarke and van Vogt, has been the restraints of the definition: much good work was unable to pass through Campbell's gate or Boucher's or Gold's, because the gates were too narrow. And the magazines had to sell on a monthly basis to fifty thousand or a hundred thousand readers, most of them young, most of them male; that meant different kinds of editorial restrictions. A novel, on the other hand, must be read only by five to ten thousand purchasers in hardcover, and although the numbers for the successful paperbacks are similar to those for a successful magazine, each purchase is an individual decision.

Today, the definitions of SF are established, as they have been in most other genres, by the writers. Publishing a book as SF is an editor's policy decision based on the expectation of sales with that designation or another. The author has something to say about the matter, but only a little: if he or she sends the book to an SF editor, there is little chance of having it published under some other rubric. That part of the publishing business still is segregated.

The problem is still one of definition. In the late 1940s and throughout the 1950s and 1960s, when a reader of SF went into a bookstore to buy an SF book, he (it was usually a "he") knew that if he picked a book that said "science fiction" on the cover, by word or image, even if he didn't know the author's name, he probably would enjoy it. Today if that same reader or another were to walk into a bookstore and pick at random a book labeled "science fiction," the chances are he or she not only would not like it but might not even be able to identify it as SF.

When authors are in charge of definitions, they have greater freedom than ever before, but definition is in the process of becoming meaningless. The gatekeepers are gone, and the definition of SF is dissolving as we look for it. The only guides are the names of authors and sometimes those of editors or publishers. A DAW book became distinctive for more than its yellow spine; under Judy Lynn del Rey, Del Rey books established a similar reputation for consistency. David Hartwell's *Timescape* was reaching toward a defining quality before Pocket Books had a failure of nerve, Bantam Books tried the same tactic with its Spectra line, and other publishers have tried similar strategies.

But the gatekeepers are gone, and the kingdom they guarded is falling apart.

5

FIFTY AMAZING,
ASTOUNDING,
WONDERFUL YEARS

In 1976, magazine science fiction—which is to say "real" science fiction—was fifty years old, but the *Amazing* thing about this field, this category, this genre, was its youth. It still is.

Of course, as we have known since Einstein, all things are relative. The short story itself is relatively new, taking its present shape in the early nineteenth century in the hands of authors such as Washington Irving, Nathaniel Hawthorne, Mérimée and Balzac, Gauthier and Musset, Maupassant and Chekhov, Poe and E. T. A. Hoffmann. Even the English novel, which has a slightly more ancient lineage, is dated from Samuel Richardson's *Pamela* in 1740.

Most current readers came to science fiction relatively recently and view early magazine science fiction as something antique and collectible but antediluvian and unimaginable all the same. Even the "experienced" readers of science fiction go back at most ten or fifteen years.

The *Astounding* fact about this particular literature is that it began within the lifetime of many persons who are still alive, including myself. The first science fiction magazine appeared on the stands when I was three years old, and a few living readers picked the first issue of *Amazing Stories* off the racks of local drug stores in 1926.

The *Wonderful* story of it all is that in many ways science fiction began only that long ago. It is true that Hugo Gernsback pointed to predecessors in the editorial of his first issue. What he was going to publish in this new magazine

---

"Fifty Amazing, Astounding, Wonderful Years" was presented as a speech at the 1976 World Science Fiction Convention in Kansas City, Missouri.

("entirely new—entirely different—something that has never been done before in this country"), he said, was "the Jules Verne, H. G. Wells, Edgar Allan Poe type of story—a charming romance intermingled with scientific fact and prophetic vision." But Poe, Verne, and Wells, great as they were in their ways, were not quite the same thing as would develop in the science fiction magazine.

One of the marvelous things that developed in the magazines was a sense of community, a feeling of working together with shared values and shared concerns toward a common goal. No one objected to the name of "science fiction writer"; for most, it was the consummation of a dream.

That was not the case before the creation of the science fiction magazines. Jules Verne objected to being classified with H. G. Wells because, he said, "We do not proceed in the same manner. It occurs to me that his stories do not repose on a very scientific basis. . . . I make use of physics. He invents. I go to the moon in a cannon-ball discharged from a cannon. Here there is no invention. He goes to Mars in an air-ship, which he constructs of a metal which does away with the law of gravitation. *Ça, c'est tres joli*, but show me this metal. Let him produce it."

Wells, on the other hand, resented being called "the English Jules Verne": "There's a quality in the worst of my so-called 'pseudo-scientific' (imbecile adjective) stuff which differentiates it from Jules Verne, e.g., just as Swift is differentiated from fantasia—isn't there? There is something other than either story writing or artistic merit which has emerged through the series of my books. Something one might regard as a new system of ideas—'thought.'"

But during the Gernsback era and for many years thereafter, authors were willing enough to be classified as one of Gernsback's writers or Harry Bates's writers or John W. Campbell Jr.'s writers—and not necessarily because they were lesser writers than Verne and Wells, though much that was printed in the early magazines was hasty and crude, but because they thought of themselves as genre writers, working at the beginning of a new kind of literature, contributing to a kind of communal vision of the future and the universe, and humanity's place in them.

Most of them would have vied for the title of the American Jules Verne (Sam Moskowitz might have told me that this title already had been awarded to Lou Senarens, the prolific dime novelist) or the new H. G. Wells. Jack Williamson wanted to write like A. Merritt; later authors wanted to write like Jack Williamson. And after 1939, almost everybody wanted to write like Robert Heinlein, and did.

Out of the early magazines came the fan movement as well. Even Gernsback was surprised at the response. In his third issue, he wrote: "One of the greatest surprises since we started publishing *Amazing Stories* is the tremendous amount of mail we receive from—shall we call them 'Scientifiction Fans'?— who seem to be pretty well oriented in this sort of literature." Late in its first year, *Amazing* began publishing some of these letters, complete with names and addresses; fans began writing partly for the pleasure of seeing their names in print and went on to write to each other. Fandom grew with apparent inevitability through clubs, club magazines that proliferated into all sorts of fanzines, regional conventions, and world conventions.

The new fiction that began to emerge from the magazines of the 1920s and 1930s was a mutation. Oh, it picked up a few concerns from Poe and Wells and Verne, and an idea or two from Fitz-James O'Brien and Ambrose Bierce, among others, but mostly it was new and attractive in spite of its flaws. It was largely uninfluenced by literary concerns; it was optimistic rather than pessimistic; it was idea and plot oriented rather than character and style oriented; its values were derived from science and technology rather than tradition and religion; its heroes were scientists and explorers, and through them society and humanity as a species; its villains were those forces in life that are nonrational or antirational such as superstition, religion, and mysticism; and its decisions were pragmatic rather than idealistic. As a genre it was expansive rather than intensive, evolutionary rather than revolutionary. It used its concepts as common building blocks, and it developed new writers out of its own readers.

Like other science fiction writers, I have often been asked how I came to write science fiction. I know of only one way to create a science fiction writer: you put an adolescent in contact with science fiction; if the youngster falls in love with it, given talent and time, there may be another science fiction writer.

I look back upon my own forty-plus years as a writer of science fiction and more than fifty-five years as a reader, and it seems not so long ago that I found a treasure trove of Edgar Rice Burroughs in my grandmother's closet, inherited a lurid copy of a 1934 *Astounding*, held in my hands the first issue of *Famous Fantastic Mysteries* containing A. Merritt's short story "The Moon Pool," and sold my first story to *Thrilling Wonder Stories*.

I came to science fiction as most readers came to science fiction, feeling that it was rich with history, ripe with accomplishment, a complete art form. But I was mistaken. It was new, in the process of being formed, growing, evolving. When I discovered science fiction it was still less than ten years old in the magazines that gave it form. When I sold my first story to John W. Campbell Jr., whom I considered the patriarch of editors, the one who, through his authors and editorials had channeled science fiction into new and exciting directions, he was only thirty-eight years old and had been editor of *Astounding* for a mere ten or eleven years. Thirty-eight! A callow youth!

That is astonishing enough. But even more fantastic is the reflection that the *Magazine of Fantasy and Science Fiction* and *Galaxy* had not yet been conceived and that all the cosmic changes that would be worked upon the genre by Tony Boucher and Horace Gold were still in the future.

Gradually, the nature of the fiction being published in the magazines began to change, under the influence of dynamic editors, under the impact of innovative authors, under the subtle shifts of society and knowledge. New generations of writers swept into and over the magazines: as Donald Wollheim has recounted, the first generation of writers who had grown up with magazine science fiction began to supplement and then replace the pulp writers who had been the staple of the Munsey and Street & Smith all-fiction magazines; many of them were scientists or engineers, led by Asimov and Heinlein. They were infiltrated by poets of sensibility, led by Ted Sturgeon and Ray Bradbury. Then came the humanists, of which I consider myself one, the generation that had been educated in English or philosophy or history; and finally the "new wave" of protest writers working out the sense of outrage nurtured by Vietnam, civil rights, and campus riots, led by Norman Spinrad and Michael Moorcock.

As an analysis, this description soon breaks down with such individual exceptions as food chemist Edward Elmer "Doc" Smith, who entered science fiction in its magazine beginnings; Arthur C. Clarke, who writes variously as scientist, poet, and humanist; latter-day scientists such as Larry Niven, Jerry Pournelle, and Charles Sheffield, followed by Gregory Benford, David Brin, and Greg Bear and any number of others. The only certainty is that science fiction evolved, writers began to develop their ideas with greater economy and greater craftsmanship, and every individual accomplishment raised the aspirations of everyone else.

Science fiction, throughout most of its brief history, has been like a literary salon with broad dimensions, with fascinating resemblances to Samuel Johnson's circle or the Pre-Raphaelites or the Pound–Eliot–Stein–Hemingway group. Can one imagine John W. Campbell Jr. as the Great Cham or Horace Gold as Gertrude Stein? If one can, then perhaps one can imagine a roster of working authors—we might invent a new collective noun for them, a scribble of writers, say, or a future of science fiction writers—located everywhere across the nation, with outposts in England and Australia, but mostly on either coast, joined together in a great mutual enterprise, a conversation carried on in the science fiction magazines and a few books, with annual gatherings at which they might meet.

A few years back this was how it was. At one convention in the late 1950s, Isaac Asimov said to me, "Why do we spend our lives working among strangers who don't understand what we do and don't care so that four days a year we can be with those we love?" Times have changed. What with the ease of air travel (which didn't do Isaac a bit of good) and the inexpensiveness of the long distance telephone, the invention of the Internet, and the rise of the regional convention, the science fiction writers who want to be are in constant communication; if they wished, they could meet every weekend, and they gather in such disparate spots as Des Moines, University Park, and Missoula or El Paso, Nashville, and Albuquerque, not to mention Heidelberg, Melbourne, Toronto, Stockholm, and Dublin.

Some of us have the pleasant illusion that a convention never really ends; it merely recesses temporarily. Somewhere the great science fiction convention continues; we drop out for a while and rejoin it somewhere else.

Critics who dismiss the magazine period of science fiction's development, which dominated the field from 1926 until the middle of the 1960s, are ignoring the central fact that today's science fiction, different as it may be from the science fiction of Gernsback or of the golden age revealed by Heinlein and Asimov, among others, is a natural development of the *Amazing–Astounding–Wonder Stories* era. Each step of the way was essential.

Today that community of writers and readers has lost a bit of its solidarity (not much, but a bit). The academic world, of which I am a representative as well, no longer scorns us. Critics develop theories for admiring us, students study us, and it is difficult to feel besieged when those outside are trying to join us. The magazines that nourished the genre no longer have a monopoly on publication; the number of SF, fantasy, and horror books published each year again approaches 1,200 (by 2005, 2,500). And how can we feel alone when nearly ten thousand fans surround us at world conventions?

Successful science fiction writers are no longer content to be known as science fiction writers. Success breeds ambition, and what was once all they wanted becomes an obstacle keeping them from broader recognition. Kurt Vonnegut Jr., who was with us but never of us, led the way; now that he is sated with wider success and sales, the kind that others envy, he is willing once again to be called a science fiction writer and adds, "People who write faithfully about American urban life today will find themselves writing, hey presto, science fiction. This is nothing to be ashamed about—and never was."

But I have no desire to cast out the unfaithful. They are, I think, the wave of the future. The old unity that once kept us together is shattering under a multitude of influences, and every writer among us is writing about his or her unique viewpoint on the present and the future in his or her unique way. Some of it will be considered science fiction and will be published in magazines and books that say "science fiction" on the cover; others will be published without any guides to reader interest, without categories, without even a spaceship to guide us. And some will be unrecognizable as science fiction, even when read. This may have implications for the future development of science fiction as a genre, but, for the publisher, it is a matter of reaching an audience and, for the reader, a convenience; we should not exalt the form above the substance.

We have lived through—some of us—fifty *Amazing, Astounding, Wonderful* years; and those who were too young to live them are the heirs to them and all their *Thrilling, Startling, Super Unknown Worlds* of *If, Beyond Space,* and everything. What we are is a consequence of those years.

But fifty years is only a brief beginning. The next fifty years promise to be just as magnificent, just as fulfilling, and just as uncertain. And the uncertainty means that we can change it, those of us who were there at the beginning and those others who came in a bit later.

6

THE WORLDVIEW OF SCIENCE FICTION

Fred Pohl recalls that British writer John T. Philliphent once wrote to him that he had discovered that what set science fiction writers apart was that they used the "science fiction method"—but he died before he could say what the science fiction method was. So we are left groping for what distinguishes SF from other kinds of fiction and, like the blind men fumbling around the elephant, find ourselves dealing with one aspect or another but never quite encompassing the whole beast. Fred goes on to speculate that what his friend had come up with had something to do with the way in which SF writers look at the universe. There may be something to this.

Certainly SF, like science itself, is based on the assumption that the universe is knowable, even though the greatest part of it may be unknown and may be destined to remain mysterious for the life of any of us—or indeed the life of all of us, by which I mean the human species. The knowable universe has no room for the supernatural or those experiences that by their very nature can never be "known." To bring experiences of the transcendent or the ineffable into the natural world is to destroy one or the other. Thus we have a basic distinction between fantasy and science fiction and, even though it is not immediately apparent, between mainstream fiction and science fiction.

I would like to suggest, however, that the worldview of science fiction can be narrowed even further. The relationship between science fiction and Darwin's *Origin of Species* long has been apparent. We know, of course, that modern science fiction began with H. G. Wells. Wells seems contemporary and everything before Wells seems quaintly historical: Mary Shelley, Poe, even Verne.

"The Worldview of Science Fiction" was first published in *Extrapolation* in Summer 1995.

The War of the Worlds can be updated, but *Frankenstein* or *From the Earth to the Moon* can be produced only as period pieces.

Shelley and Poe and Verne were influenced by blossoming science and an awareness that the world was being changed by it and by its child, technology, but Wells had the benefit of the publication of *On the Origin of Species* in 1859. At an obvious level, Darwin's theories of evolution were the most important elements in Thomas H. Huxley's career in biology, and his relationship with Darwin and the defense of his theories in debates across the English countryside are well known. Almost as well known is the fact that the young Wells spent his first year of college studying biology under Huxley and recalled it as a shaping influence, and the fact that, as Jack Williamson demonstrated in his doctoral dissertation published as *H. G. Wells: Critic of Progress*, the early (and most important) portion of Wells's SF writing was a coming to terms with evolution. Not quite so apparent is the fact that Darwin's theories underlay what we now point at as science fiction.

I've always felt that naturalism and SF have a lot in common—that SF, say, is fantastic naturalism, or naturalized fantasy, or simply that which hasn't happened yet, that we know of, treated naturalistically. Maybe it goes farther than that. C. Hugh Holman, in *A Handbook to Literature*, defines naturalism as "a movement in the novel in the later nineteenth and early twentieth centuries in France, America, and England." He called it "the application of scientific determinism to fiction," and went on to compare it with realism and romanticism. Realism and naturalism, he wrote, shared a common goal in their desire to represent events accurately but differed in their emphasis, with naturalism selecting not the commonplace but the representative, and what it represents is the scientific principle. Naturalism and romanticism, he went on, share a belief that actions are more important for what they say about "the nature of a larger reality," but differ in finding that reality in natural laws rather than "in transcendent ideas or absolute ideals." He concludes:

> In this sense naturalism is the novelist's response to the revolution in thought that modern science has produced. From Newton it gains a sense of mechanistic determinism; from Darwin (the greatest single force operative upon it) it gains a sense of biological determinism and the inclusive metaphor of the lawless jungle which it has used perhaps more often than any other; from Marx it gains a view of history as a battleground of vast economic and social forces; from Freud it gains a view of the determinism of the inner and subconscious self; from Taine it gains a view of literature as a product of deterministic forces; from Comte it gains of view of social and environmental determinism.

Most of Holman's description of naturalism could be applied to science fiction with only a few reservations. The reason for this is partly because both are the products of modern science and in particular of the theory of evolution. Darwin produced naturalism, and science fiction applied naturalism to the fantastic. In other words, science fiction takes the unusual, the remarkable event that has not happened, and presents it as part of the natural world. More important, the naturalistic story treats human beings as part of the natural world, as a product of their environment, and their failures and successes (primarily their failures) as a result of their environment rather than their characters or decisions—but as captured in that moment like fossils embedded in limestone. Science fiction, on the other hand, treats human beings as a species that has evolved as a result of environment but—and this is the crucial distinction from naturalism—as a species upon whom the evolutionary process is still at work.

Science fiction, then, deals with people as if they were creatures as adaptable as the protoplasm from which they emerged. Change the conditions, and humanity will change. The first premise of SF is that humanity is adaptable. To that premise, however, science fiction added another that naturalism never had: although humanity is as much a product of its environment as the other animals, it possesses a quality that the other animals lack—the intellectual ability to recognize its origins and the processes at work upon it, and even, sometimes, to choose a course other than that instilled by its environment. In naturalism, such recognition at best leads to a sense of tragic loss.

One of the best statements of this SF worldview is contained in Isaac Asimov's *The Caves of Steel* and *The Naked Sun*—his 1950s robot novels. In *The Caves of Steel*, people have become so accustomed to enclosure that they all suffer from agoraphobia; for them, even the possibility of going outside the roofed city is unthinkable. The murder mystery that drives the action of *The Caves of Steel* is based upon the agoraphobia of its citizens, and a major factor in its solution is Lije Bailey's ability to think the unthinkable.

Moreover, a subplot of the robot novels involves the plans of some Spacers to push the short-lived, disease-ridden, agoraphobic Terrans into expanding toward what will later become the Galactic Empire, but that depends upon Terrans conquering their agoraphobia and being able to set off in spaceships for distant suns. Bailey not only fights his own fears of open spaces in *The Naked Sun* but also organizes a group to help others do the same.

These two basic principles, it seems to me, create that difficult-to-define *something* by which we identify science fiction—and any story that doesn't involve them we may feel is *like* SF but doesn't quite have the right stuff. At least that is true of American SF. New Wave SF, for instance, tended to describe the environmental aspect of human behavior but, like naturalism, stopped at that. Or, rather, it assumed that people are moved more by obsession than rational choice, and that crippled their ability to cope with change. J. G. Ballard's stories and novels are good examples, with their characters paralyzed by change rather than adapting to it or moved to action by it. A good deal of non-English-language SF does not have the second premise (the ability to act other than the way one is conditioned to behave), either, and when I was researching stories to include in the sixth volume of *The Road to Science Fiction*, I found a great many stories that involved the naturalistic recognition of humanity's evolutionary past, but not as much of the human ability to recognize that fact and rise above it.

This is not to say that there is anything inherently right or wrong about belief in the power of rationality over conditioning. Most of the time people do behave as if they were programmed, but occasionally they act as if they had free will. American SF has focused on the few problem solvers who have done the most to change life and society and thereby, according to American SF, people themselves. Other SF, Forster's "The Machine Stops," say, as opposed to Campbell's "Twilight," may have based its beliefs about people on the more common kind of behavior.

In "The Machine Stops," for instance, humanity has been reduced to total dependence on the machine and not only does not recognize that fact (except for one aberrant individual) but does not even notice when the machine begins to fail. In "Twilight," humanity has lost its curiosity because of the lack of competition, not because of the machine, but at the end a visitor to that far-distant future instructs a machine to create a curious machine, making it the inheritor of humanity's mission to ask questions of the universe.

Mainstream fiction seems to do without Darwin entirely. As a matter of fact, in a mainstream story, the origins of humanity, if they enter at all, are more likely to be biblical than evolutionary. If evolution enters, the story is transformed into science fiction.

Mainstream fiction's preoccupation with the present reflects an apparent desire to freeze reality in its current state, and a belief that everything that has happened or is likely to happen is of little importance except as it reflects upon the present. Mainstream's preoccupation with the reactions and reflections of individuals who have little influence in their own times and no historical influence suggests that reality is less important than the way people feel about it. To put it another way, the concentration by mainstream fiction on social interactions seems to incorporate the conviction that the most important, if not the *only* important, aspect of existence is the ways in which people relate to each other.

Science fiction, on the other hand, incorporates a belief that the most important aspect of existence is a search for humanity's origins, its purpose, and its ultimate fate. Mainstream fiction may seem more "real" because it reflects the reality that most people deal with in their everyday existence: the social world and our interactions with it and our feelings about it. But is the evolution of humanity less real because it is less quotidian?

The shape of mainstream fiction is dictated by its belief in what is important. It is dense with character not because that is what "good fiction" concerns itself with but because that is what mainstream fiction is about. Science fiction, which has often been criticized because of the thinness of its characterization, is similarly the result of SF beliefs. When one is concerned about the way in which people are the products of their environments and how one can free oneself to act in ways other than that one has been conditioned to behave, the feelings of the characters about their situations, or even aspects of individual character or reactions to the general predicament, seem of little moment.

Similarly, mainstream fiction has minimized or discarded plot as "mere incident," while plot remains at the heart of science fiction. This suggests that for the mainstream what happens does not really matter; nothing new is going to occur, and the only proper concern is how character should react to repetition. Science fiction, on the other hand, exists in a world of change, and the focus is on external events: What is the change and how are humans (or aliens) going to respond to it?

2

SCIENCE FICTION AND THE TEACHER

TEACHING SCIENCE FICTION

S cience fiction has been difficult to define because it is not an ordinary genre. Unlike the mystery, the western, the gothic, the love story, or the adventure story, to cite a few of the categories to which it is often compared, science fiction has no identifying action or place. Readers do not recognize it, as they recognize other genres, because of some defining event or setting. As a consequence, science fiction can incorporate other genres; we can have a science-fiction detective story, a science-fiction western, a science-fiction gothic, a science-fiction love story, or, most likely of all, a science-fiction adventure story.

The teaching of science fiction has shared that kind of all-inclusiveness. The kinds of subjects that can be taught through science fiction involve all the social and physical sciences, history, ideas, futurology, religion, morality, ecology, reading skills, and many others.

The reasons for this situation may be many. Obtaining departmental approval for a genre course on science fiction has often been difficult, as compared with a course on the novel, say, or the short story or poetry. Science fiction courses may have to be smuggled into the curriculum under the pretense of serving other, more easily sanctioned purposes. In addition, some teachers may feel unqualified to teach science fiction as a genre, or prefer to use SF for other purposes, or believe that SF should be read and evaluated according to the same criteria as any other literature and thus needs no special instruction.

The validity of the courses is not in question, but their nature may say something about the situation of SF teaching in 1995 (or even 2005): In some ways,

---

"Teaching Science Fiction" was first published in *Science Fiction Studies* in November 1996.

science fiction still may be considered an intruder on the academic scene. In terms of numbers of courses or frequency of courses offered, SF surely outranks the other categories that shared its pulp-magazine origins—the detective story and the western, and certainly the gothic or even the romance. But frequency of teaching may not be a guide to academic acceptance, and the teacher of the detective story or the western may still enjoy greater status, or less loss of status, perhaps because the detective story or western story courses are taught less often and their teachers have no personal stake in them. Most teachers of science fiction, on the other hand, perform their instruction because they feel that SF has something important to offer students and value themselves in terms of science fiction. Some, like the teachers of the detective story or the western, may earn their sense of self-worth from their other areas of expertise.

We might well ask the teachers of science fiction how they feel about that. No doubt we have made some strides toward acceptance since the early days when Sam Moskowitz, Mark Hillegas, Tom Clareson, and Jack Williamson were pioneering the teaching of science fiction, but we may have lost our outsider edge, both with students and our colleagues and maybe even with ourselves. Moreover, I have the feeling that the number of courses taught in this country has dwindled over the past ten or twenty years. Certainly the back-to-basics movement in high schools has diminished the opportunities to teach a science fiction course there, particularly the mini-courses that were popular in the 1970s. But the loss of the cutting-edge, far-out reputation that attracted students to college courses in vast numbers during that same period has made the teaching, and taking, of science fiction courses seem less daring in the 1990s.

When he was at Northwestern, the late Frank McConnell taught SF courses to classes enrolling hundreds of students, and when I spoke with him several years ago at the Eaton Conference, he said that the courses he taught at his California university were just as large. But my experience at the University of Kansas was different: the first course I taught enrolled as many students as the auditorium would hold—165. Then the numbers dropped to 150, 115, 90, 85, and leveled off around 50. Not that numbers are important in themselves. Many teachers wouldn't want any more than twenty students and would be horrified at the prospect of teaching a large lecture class, and clearly the kind of course one can teach is shaped by the numbers enrolled. But those numbers also may provide a clue to the attitude of students toward SF. I have a hunch that a true mass course simply wouldn't draw in most colleges today. A colleague of mine who teaches "the literature of baseball" every few years can attract more students than the science fiction course.

What I have been advocating for some twenty years is a thorough survey of high schools and colleges to discover how many classes are being taught, whether this is more or less than it was in the 1970s or even the 1980s, and what is being taught in them. Such a survey also would develop a mailing list of teachers that would be of value to almost everyone involved in the field. But although I've often received encouragement, my proposals have finally failed over the twin problems of cost and breadth, as compared with depth, of benefit. When I suggested to twenty SF publishers that they put up $1,000 each and share the results and the mailing list, only the late Judy Lynn del Rey said she'd do it.

The voluntary responses to the announcement of the 1996 "Teaching Science Fiction" issue of *Science Fiction Studies* were, like Jack Williamson's surveys in the early 1970s, valuable as a guide to what was going on, but were limited to those teachers within the range of *Science Fiction Studies* who were willing to take the time and effort to share their experience.

I was one.

I may have taught more science fiction courses than anyone else around (if someone else has done more, I hope they will share their experiences). Part of the reason for my SF teaching experience is that the English Department always wanted me to teach science fiction as frequently as I wished. In fact, the chairman of the department told me, when I returned to the department full time in 1970, that some of the younger members of the department hoped that I would be willing to teach a course in science fiction. I taught a course the first semester and every year thereafter (sometimes every semester). In 1974 I created my Intensive English Institute on the Teaching of Science Fiction, which amounted to the team-teaching of two intensive courses in the summer. In addition, I have taught or team-taught several other science fiction courses, including two seminars in science fiction that the department asked me to take on. If one includes the teaching of science fiction writing, I probably averaged the teaching of three science fiction courses a year over my twenty-three years of full-time teaching and still teach two courses a year in retirement.

All this is not to establish any final authority but to suggest that science fiction was my major field. Although I taught three courses in fiction writing during the regular semester, the institute sessions and the writers' workshops in the summer meant that I taught as much science fiction as fiction writing, and maybe more.

When I first considered teaching science fiction, I realized that there were various ways to approach it. The first might be called the "great books" or "great stories" course, in which the focus would be on novels or stories and their critical analysis and what made them great. The second might be called the "ideas in science fiction" course, dealing with how SF stories can be used to dramatize contemporary problems or to encourage critical thought. The third might be to teach another subject—physics, say, or history or sociology or anthropology or religion. The fourth would be the historical approach—what is science fiction and how did it get to be that way?

Any of these approaches, or any other, is perfectly legitimate, and I have found myself using all but the third. I got trapped into the great books approach in 1969 when my son and a friend organized a course and asked me to be the teacher of record. We agreed on a list of interesting SF novels, but when the classes came around I found myself, presumably present only as an adviser, supplying background and context for the discussions that otherwise would have been limited to expressions of like or dislike or occasional philosophic ramblings into the events of that troubled period.

I told myself that when I taught a regular course, it would focus on the historical development of science fiction so that the students would be able to place their SF reading in better context and continue their later reading with greater understanding. That opportunity came sooner than I imagined. The next fall I adopted a reading list of a dozen novels and *The Science Fiction Hall of Fame* and, as a way of organizing my thoughts, set about writing a dozen lectures about the historic development of science fiction that would give the readings meaning.

The next spring an editor for Prentice-Hall dropped by my office and asked if I would be interested in writing a text about fiction writing. I said, "No, but I have these twelve chapters about the history of science fiction that would make a good book." That, somewhat delayed by a change of editors, turned out to be *Alternate Worlds: The Illustrated History of Science Fiction*.

As the years went by, I became increasingly dissatisfied with teaching science fiction through novels. I won't get into my theories about the ideal length for science fiction, but I did begin to feel that there were only a few science fiction things one could say about any novel and that the class discussion of a novel had to deal largely with novelistic rather than science-fictional concerns—that is, it usually became a great books course. In addition, the earliest possible example of a science fiction novel was published in 1818, and, with the exception of Wells, most examples must be taken from work written since 1950. On the other hand, a teacher can use a group of short stories to discuss many more issues and a greater variety of issues, as well as the historical development from the earliest fantastic voyages.

When Barry Lippman called me from Mentor Books one day in 1975 to tell me he had enjoyed *Alternate Worlds* and to ask if I had a book I'd like to do with Mentor, I suggested a volume of critical approaches to science fiction. When that didn't interest him, I said I'd like to do a historical anthology. The first volume, *The Road to Science Fiction: From Gilgamesh to Wells*, came out so much better than I had imagined that I proposed two more volumes: *The Road to Science Fiction #2: From Wells to Heinlein* and *The Road to Science Fiction #3: From Heinlein to Here.* They came out in 1979. Even before I was finished with the third volume, however, I realized that I wanted to include more stories than I had space for, and I suggested that it be divided into two separate volumes. But the then editor (I had five during the entire Mentor experience) suggested that Mentor publish the two as planned and see how they did. When they sold well, I got the go-ahead for *The Road to Science Fiction #4: From Here to Forever*, which I decided to devote to the literary uses of science fiction. It was published in 1982.

A couple of years later they went out of print, one after the other. One of my Mentor editors had suggested adding an anthology on foreign SF, and I had proposed another on British SF, but when I suggested to a subsequent editor that we go ahead with them, he checked the sales figures of the first four volumes and discovered that they were selling only about two thousand copies a year each. New American Library had a rule that mass market titles had to sell five thousand copies a year to remain in print. The trade paperback criterion was one thousand copies a year. After considering reprinting the series in trade paperback and proceeding with volumes 5 and 6, the editorial board decided, instead, to let the others go out of print. For a number of years after that I taught my course with photocopies.

Then White Wolf reprinted an updated version of *The Road to Science Fiction*, beginning in August 1996 with volume 3, followed by the fourth and then the new volumes: *The Road to Science Fiction #5: The British Way* and *The Road to Science Fiction #6: Around the World.*

They had an unusual beginning. Wilhelm Heyne had been reprinting the series in German, and when it reached volume 2, the editor, Wolfgang Jeschke, inquired through my agents whether I had more than four volumes in mind. I mentioned the two I had discussed with Mentor, and, after some negotiations, Heyne gave me contracts to put together volumes 5 and 6 for them. Only much later did Heyne publish volume 5 and, I believe (I've never received copies), 6.

I had used the first four volumes in my class to address the historical development of science fiction from its earliest prototypes (which also are the prototypes for all literature) to its most contemporary examples, which turned out to be 1979 in volume 3 (the date of publication) and 1981 in volume 4 (a year before its date of publication). Then White Wolf decided not to reprint volume 3 (or to reprint 1 and 2), and Scarecrow Press has put volumes 1 through 4 back into print.

My classes have addressed the question of genre, that is, what science fiction is and how it got to be that way. The entire semester, I told my classes, was a search for definition. In the process, I also explored the approaches of science fiction to theme. The four volumes are organized chronologically; an introduction deals with the development of SF as a genre and headnotes deal with the situation of SF at the time of publication of the story, what the particular story may have contributed to the development, or illustrated, and information about the author and the particular story. I urge students to read their way through the anthologies from front to back, paying attention to the introductions and headnotes. But I organize the class discussions around thematic units and ask the students to reread the stories according to those groupings.

After the first couple of assignments in which I discuss the variations in mainstream and SF approaches according to social change over the centuries and differences between the mainstream and SF, I group stories for discussion according to theme and work their way through the four volumes in order. The point is to address the important issues and methods that SF concerns itself with, as the teacher sees it, and to include all the stories.

With nearly a hundred stories to discuss, that takes some doing. It also creates a problem in that the time I allotted (I used Fridays to show lecture films from my series) does not allow time for extended discussion of any story other than Philip José Farmer's "Sail On! Sail On!" which I use for a line-by-line analysis to illustrate SF's reading protocols. Teachers who prefer to spend more time with a story might have to eliminate some stories from discussion or from the reading list.

Discussion still is a possibility in a large class, although some students prefer to sit silently in the back of the room. But frequent written assignments are not, unless one has a teaching assistant, as I did for the first ten years. After that, I gave only an essay exam for the midterm (offering students a choice of four short definitions of SF), an essay exam for the final (asking for a discussion of SF built around several issues, with examples), and a term paper based on a comparison and contrasting of two or more SF novels, from a list I provided or works that I approved in advance. In place of the term paper, I have allowed students to substitute a short story or, in some cases, other projects. Some students have done artwork, for instance. One did a radio dramatization of Fredric Brown's "Arena"; one did a needlepoint illustration of the cover of *Alternate Worlds*, another a macramé replica of a Mesklinite from Hal Clement's *Mission of Gravity*, and a 1995 graduate student in art did a photographic illustration, in the lost-negative process, of a model taken from George Zebrowski's "The Word Sweep."

After my first or second class, I got a telephone call from a student who asked when I'd teach the class again. His roommate, he said, had done a project for my class, and it sounded so fascinating he wanted to do one. I suggested that he didn't have to take my class to do a project. In the early days, I used take-home exams under the assumption that students might be encouraged to do better work. One of my students, however, turned in as a midterm the first half of Judith Merril's essay "What Do You Mean: Science? Fiction?" I dealt gently with him, feeling that I hadn't made clear the necessity to do his own thinking and writing. I told him that I couldn't give him a grade for the midterm, but he could turn in something original for a grade. He didn't do that, but for the final he turned in the second half of Judy's essay!

The Intensive English Institute sessions in the summer crammed all the short-story discussions into a three-week session, meeting for three hours every morning. Steve Goldman would pair novels from a reading list of more than two dozen for brilliant discussions every afternoon for three hours each. The classes in the summer were as large as twenty-two and as small as six, but they came from all over the United States and from Argentina, Canada, Holland, Denmark, China, Australia, and New Zealand. We had three guest writers for a week each: Gordon Dickson, Fred Pohl, and Ted Sturgeon. It was a great opportunity for a total immersion experience, and many of the students felt transformed by it. One of my favorite memories of that period is the response of the students: the first week, they said, "This is the most wonderful experience we've ever had!" The second week: "Why are you working us so hard?" And the third week: "How can it be over so soon?"

Later, feeling that some students from distant places might be deterred by having to invest three weeks of vacation time, Steve and I reduced the period to two weeks by scheduling class sessions for both Saturday and Sunday. Since Steve's untimely death in 1991, with the exception of the first year, when Tom Shippey filled in, I have offered the short-story session and the novel session in alternating years. I require familiarity with *The Road to Science Fiction*, either by taking the short-story course or by previous reading. The novels are those that I consider important to the understanding of science fiction or, in the case of my own, an opportunity for the students to become familiar with something by their instructor and to ask questions about the creative process. That applies to Fred Pohl, too, who still is a guest writer for the institute and, with Betty Anne Hull, a loyal friend of the SF program here and the Campbell Conference and its awards. Betty is a judge of the Campbell Award, and Fred, of the Sturgeon Award.

The discussions about the novels relate in part to their contributions to the genre, in part to their historic importance, but mostly to the ways in which they go about doing science-fictional things. I try to pair two novels that take similar topics or are different approaches to the same general literary task. In the second week, I ask students to pair off and lead the discussion of the remaining novels. The reading list includes twenty-five novels, which in itself is a good screening device for interested students.

Steve Goldman and I also taught an "ideas in science fiction" course one summer, as a Kansas Committee for the Humanities program for secondary school teachers. We called it "Prometheus Revisited: Human Values in a Technological World" and put together a photocopied book of readings from C. P. Snow's "The Two Cultures" lecture and reactions to it, as well as earlier contributions to the two-cultures debate; we added a group of stories that dealt with the conflict between the technology and the humanities before concluding with several stories that attempted a synthesis, as well as three novels: Greg Bear's *Eternity*, Gregory Benford's *Timescape*, and John Brunner's *The Crucible of Time*. Steve and I also team-taught a course in the science fiction novel in which we attempted to deal with the particular problems and opportunities of the science fiction novel and the proper critical approaches to it, including such matters as reading Isaac Asimov's *The Foundation Trilogy* as a series of stories built one on the end of another like Tinkertoys; whether it is appropriate to apply novelistic standards to A. E. van Vogt's *The World of Null-A*, which began life as a serial; and the process by which Arthur C. Clarke's *Childhood's End* developed from the novelette "Guardian Angel."

Twice I taught seminars in science fiction. In each case, because students had already had the opportunity to take courses in the short fiction and in the novel, I devoted the seminars to critical approaches to science fiction. I put together a photocopied text of critical articles and chapters from other books about SF and devoted the first two-thirds of the semester to comparing critical approaches, while students were working on applying their own approaches to a group of novels. In the final third of the semester, students were asked to report on their projects. I thought almost all the papers in the second seminar were publishable, and at least a couple were published. I would have liked to have seen them all published and proposed a book called *New Voices in SF Criticism* to Borgo Press, but that foundered after the Starmont purchase.

Recently Scarecrow Press published my updated collection of readings for the seminars as *Speculations on Speculation: Theories of Science Fiction*, edited with Matthew Candelaria.

8

TEACHING SCIENCE FICTION REVISITED

The science fiction ghetto may be breaking up, but signs of the ghetto mentality still lurk among us: those who have possessed science fiction for so long that they consider her their own and look upon any glance at a larger audience as proof of infidelity. A basic distrust of strangers, particularly those who use a different language, and a possessiveness about ghetto culture breed fear of those who would integrate ghetto dwellers and their arts into the general culture, while nourishing an inner conviction that separatism might be best after all.

Our insecurity, our feelings of inferiority, make us suspicious of overtures from outside. Our history and our natures render us incapable of enjoying booms without dreading busts. We are, let us face it, a bit paranoid.

Philip Klass, who taught science fiction at Pennsylvania State University and writes it—alas, too infrequently these days—under the name of William Tenn, has compared science fiction with jazz, and I have a vision of science fiction as a prescient jazz musician playing piano in a turn-of-the-20th-century New Orleans cathouse. As his fingers rock over the keys, he is saying to himself: "Look at that s.o.b. sitting over there in the corner taking notes. Pretty soon he's gonna start a band in Kansas City or Chicago and make real money while I'm still sitting here collecting nickels and dimes, and then some dudes what never saw New Orleans are gonna make fortunes writing this stuff—writing! you don't write jazz, you just play it—and guys in white shirts and black ties are gonna perform it in those big, fancy New York halls, and kids are gonna study it in schools—and hell! that ain't gonna be jazz!"

"Teaching Science Fiction Revisited" was first published in *Analog* 94, no. 3, in November 1974.

Maybe not, and maybe it ain't gonna be science fiction, but events march on as surely as the tides roll in, and nothing we do is going to change that fact. We might, of course, be able to control the nature of those events or the path of the tides.

The ghetto "us-against-them" attitude, which gave science fiction fandom its strength and science fiction writers their feelings of brotherhood, erupted in concern about the teaching of science fiction, for example, in the editorial in the June 1974 issue of *Analog*.

First, let me throw away the opening half of the editorial. I don't wish to defend science fiction in movies or on television, which I have personal reasons to think is terrible. One may count on the fingers of three hands the movies that are both good movies and good science fiction. Motion pictures and television are committee efforts controlled by money, which is always conservative, and by people who know nothing about science fiction and care less. The wonder is not that there is not more art in the visual media, but that there is any at all.

At the same time, we should admit that science fiction publishers have been almost as guilty. The movies and television have turned off potential readers of SF—but so has SF. The monster movies of the 1950s turned people away saying, "If that is SF, I don't want any more," but so did the BEM covers of the thirties, forties, and fifties. The only meaningful part of science fiction is the story, and if the reader can fight his way through all the obstacles to reach it, he either will like it or he won't.

Second, I don't want to defend science fiction teaching, since no one has sufficient information about it to either praise or condemn. Nor is this a defense of academic criticism, to which Sturgeon's Law applies fully as much as it does to science fiction. What I hope to do is bring a little perspective to the discussion of science fiction teaching, and what I wish to discuss are two issues raised by the June editorial: the qualifications of science fiction teachers and the effect of the teaching of science fiction upon potential new readers.

I'll grant immediately the editorial's assumption that most science fiction teachers do not know enough about science fiction—not as much, certainly, as you and I, nor perhaps as much as the average reader. Let me grant also that they are not going to teach their science fiction courses the way we would teach them; probably we will not agree with their approaches, their tastes, their conclusions, and their results. But this would be true of any courses that you or I might teach. I know that Harlan Ellison, who is a vocal critic of science fiction teaching, would not like my historical approach to the field, and I suspect that I would not approve of all his judgments about what is important.

Joanna Russ, Phil Klass, Jack Williamson, and I—science fiction writers and English teachers all—have different ideas about what a course in science fiction ought to be. Who is right, and who is to say which of us is right, or if any of us is right, or if we are not *all* right?

Every new discipline goes through a period of experimentation and discovery. Every new discipline begins without qualified teachers. African studies was a product of the sixties, and there were no qualified teachers. Popular culture courses are little older than that, and American studies is not much more ancient. Anthropology split away from sociology after World War II in many universities, and departments of journalism, which originated in the early part of this century, became schools about the same time.

Schools of business date back to the 1920s, most of them, and began with no qualified teachers. Schools of education came about the turn of the century . . .

We can simplify the whole historical discussion by pointing out that departments originated when Eliot (of the famous five-foot shelf) introduced the elective system into Harvard when he became president in 1869. At that time, incidentally, the high school was virtually nonexistent (there were only five hundred of them) and compulsory primary education was just beginning to gain momentum across the nation.

And there were no qualified teachers!

So—science fiction teaching is going through the same process of accumulating experience and exchanging ideas and improving itself, and it will never reach a stage where either the qualifications of the teachers or their agreement about subject matter will equal those in the sciences. The humanities have no objective measurements, no duplicable experiments; they aim at increasing sensitivity, improving the ability to read with understanding, and providing the breadth and depth of intellectual experience that will encourage the making of wise choices.

They don't always succeed.

In the humanities, each teacher chooses his or her own texts and approach to the subject; each does what he or she can, in the best way she or he can. Professional organizations do not exist to determine qualifications—such determinations are made at the college or departmental level by the teacher's peers and sometimes his or her students—but to provide means of communicating among teachers and scholars in the field. In the early stages of the development of a discipline, professional organizations collect and observe and provide a central point for people to gather and discuss what they are doing, much as the Milford Writers Workshop did in the 1950s (and the Clarion Writers

Workshop does now) and the Science Fiction Writers of America from the 1960s to the present did for science fiction writers.

Moreover, teachers of science fiction are not just in English, but in history, sociology, engineering, political science, anthropology, religion, philosophy, chemistry, physics, and many more disciplines, no doubt.

Science fiction teaching will develop its own criteria, its own canon, its own tools, and we can agree on this—it behooves those of us who have vested interests in its welfare to contribute our ideas and see that they are heard. Many of us, therefore, are active in the Science Fiction Research Association, attend scholarly meetings, lecture there and at other colleges, prepare histories and texts, write articles, and provide other materials useful in teaching, such as the lecture films about science fiction, featuring science fiction writers and editors, that we have been producing at the University of Kansas.

Many experienced writers and editors in the field have supplied teaching materials and guidance. Robert Silverberg's *The Mirror of Infinity*, with critical essays by science fiction writers, sold well, as did Harry Harrison's *The Light Fantastic* and his high school anthology (with Carol Pugner), *A Science Fiction Reader*. Jack Williamson wrote his study of the early work of H. G. Wells, Brian Aldiss his *Billion Year Spree* and *Trillion Year Spree*, Donald Wollheim, *The Universe Makers*. Reginald Bretnor brought together the contributions of fifteen science fiction writers in his *Science Fiction, Today and Tomorrow*, and Frank Herbert had his name on an anthology for the academic market (along with three collaborators) entitled *Tomorrow, and Tomorrow, and Tomorrow. . . .* My history of science fiction, *Alternate Worlds*, was published in the spring of 1975.

True, other texts unsanctified by the name and ideas of a science fiction writer proliferated. Many of them did not share our viewpoints—even those we have in common—and some of them clearly used science fiction for their own ends. But who among us does not?

There was even a CliffsNotes on science fiction, which some automatically would call the ultimate rape of science fiction by the academic world, but as a matter of fact, the author, L. David Allen of the University of Nebraska, put together a useful book with some illuminating concepts and some insightful analyses.

Many SF authors and editors have bemoaned the effect of academic criticism on science fiction. The dead hand of academic criticism will kill science fiction just as it killed poetry and the mainstream novel, they say. I think we can dispose of this bugbear easily. If science fiction has any vitality to start with, criticism will not kill it. For one thing, few people read academic criticism—certainly not the readers of science fiction—and so long as writers do not accept the critics as final arbiters, they might even learn something about why they do what they do and why it works.

Science fiction traditionally has been concerned with the *what*, seldom the *why*. We have known, as readers and writers, that science fiction was different, but our explanations of the reasons have been unsatisfying. Periodically critics have sprung up among us and done us good by providing unifying theories, but their work has been limited and sporadic and seldom linked to the complete body of literature, of criticism, and of psychological experience. For a long time, science fiction writers have needed literary feedback, criticism from sophisticated critics; now we well may get it. Not that we'll like it, not that much of it will not be dull and some of it unintelligent or even unintelligible, but we should not reject it outright—there are wise and intelligent literary judges outside our ranks and we can profit from their judgments. But we should not take it, nor ourselves, too seriously.

Finally, the feeling among SF people that the boom comes just before the bust: we have seen it happen before and our apprehensions overwhelm us when we see a boom approaching. There must be something wrong with it, and there must be something wrong with all those classes in science fiction being taught in colleges and universities, in high schools and junior high schools, and even in primary schools. The kids will be turned off.

Let us grant that good teaching, enthusiastic teaching, will turn more students on to science fiction than bad teaching, incompetent teaching, dull teaching. But this is true of any subject, and the level of teaching is never as high as it ought to be. A good teacher can make learning the times table exciting, and a bad teacher can turn science fiction into pendantry.

But is this true? Most of what is read in high schools is cherished for its historic importance; much of it is valuable, much of it is difficult, and much of it is dull. A good teacher can make it meaningful, can demonstrate its relevance, can even make it exciting, but he or she must be *good*.

In this desert of irrelevance, a science fiction story cannot help but stand out like a refreshing oasis of story and significance; a bad teacher must work hard to make it dull. Generally the teachers of SF courses are not the bad teachers. The ones who volunteer to teach such courses may not be as knowledgeable as we would like them to be, but they are, I suspect, enthusiastic, open, and experimental. A bad teacher would rather teach what he or she has always taught.

One more encouraging aspect—science fiction usually is an elective, fulfilling no requirements. Science fiction courses achieved their popularity in high schools (before the "return-to-basics" movement limited them) as part of senior (now junior or even sophomore) English electives: students asked for such courses. They were not required to read Asimov and Bradbury in the way they were required to read Shakespeare and Dickens. Some students chose science fiction as the least of evils, perhaps, but it may be assumed of them that they never would have come to science fiction at all if it were not offered at their school; some of them, inevitably, will get turned on.

Let us look at the numbers involved. "Science fiction," Damon Knight has said, is "the mass literature of the very few." Traditionally, science fiction has attracted several hundred thousand regular readers and perhaps an equal number of casual readers; these figures have not changed much since Hugo Gernsback founded *Amazing Stories* in 1926, I suspect. At least the circulations of the leading SF magazines have remained relatively constant: *Amazing* printed about 150,000 copies in its early years, *Analog* now, about 80,000 (sadly, in 2005, closer to 40,000). Most of the booms we have come to dread have been in publishing, not in readership . . . until now.

The number of paperback titles published and bought—though in smaller print runs than in the 1950s—is evidence of a substantial increase in the casual readership of SF, primarily among young people; and if we do not include in our understanding of "regular" the reading of magazines, perhaps of regular readers as well (in 2005, average paperback sales are about the same as the magazines). They are a paperback generation; they do not, I am sorry to say, read magazines. Out of 150 students surveyed in my class a few years ago, only 12 bought as many as one magazine a month, compared with 74 who bought at least one paperback each month. (By 1990, the picture hadn't changed.)

The reasons for this are speculative and need not concern us here. Perhaps all readers should come to science fiction as we came to it—as a happy personal discovery. But let me point out that in my class of 150 students, only 39 had what they defined as considerable experience with science fiction, compared with 51 who had some, 52 who had slight, and 6 who had none.

Across the nation, five hundred colleges and university courses may deal with science fiction in one way or another; if the classes average thirty students each, then some fifteen thousand students are being exposed to science fiction. Of these, probably ten thousand were not regular readers of science fiction before entering their classes.

In high schools, readership experience with science fiction must be even less. If there are five hundred college courses, there must be three thousand high school courses averaging thirty students each (both figures are conservative)—and that means ninety thousand students exposed to science fiction every year, of whom perhaps seventy thousand are coming to science fiction for the first time. A minimum of eighty thousand new readers are being recruited yearly. At this rate, the readership of science fiction stands to grow rapidly in the years ahead. (Nearly twenty years later, high school teaching of SF has dropped off, but readership is up; today the problem is how to get more young people interested in reading science fiction.)

But only *if*—I can hear the skeptics say—the students are not turned off. Aside from my conviction that the students exposed to science fiction in the classroom will find it so attractive, so fascinating, that they will be turned on rather than off, I can offer two experiences in support of the notion that they are not being turned off. I did a follow-up study on my class a few years ago—the returns were smaller; it was optional and the end of the semester—because I, too, was curious about the effect of the class on readership. Two students reported that their interest in science fiction had decreased, and eleven that it had not affected their interest (perhaps because it already was as high as it could go). Twenty said they expected to read more science fiction, two less, and nineteen would read about the same.

The second experience occurred during a trip to Auburn University. I was asked to visit a class in which science fiction was being used by an assistant instructor (a graduate student) to teach freshman composition. Aha! I thought. Here is the classic test. If science fiction could survive this, it could survive anything.

I asked the students what they thought of the readings. One of them, an attractive freshman named Leah, said, "I didn't understand some of it." (It turned out that what she mostly didn't understand was an excerpt from Loren Eisley's *The Unexpected Universe* and perhaps J. G. Ballard's "The Terminal Beach," both of which are difficult reading even for the experienced SF reader).

"Ah," I said, "then will you be reading any more science fiction?"

"Oh, yes," she said. "I really enjoyed it."

It is the Leahs of the world, who never would have come to science fiction on their own, who have been exposed to it in high school or college, who find it enjoyable, who restore our faith in science fiction to overcome the handicaps of garish covers, miserable movies, terrible television, and even the teaching of science fiction.

The story is the thing. Sure, let us work to improve the teaching of science fiction. But only the stories can turn people on, and only the stories can turn them off. If the standards of science fiction remain high, if they continue to be raised even higher, if the writers, at least in part, broaden the appeal of their work so that it can be read and enjoyed by Leah and her friends, then we need not worry about the growing future audience for science fiction.

9

THE ACADEMIC
VIEWPOINT

When the dean of basketball coaches, the late Forrest C. "Phog" Allen, was asked by James Naismith, the inventor of basketball, what he intended to do with his life, Allen replied, "Coach basketball." Naismith responded, "You don't coach basketball; you just play it."

For many years a similar opinion existed about science fiction: you don't teach science fiction; you just read it.

As later events demonstrated, both opinions were incorrect. The first regular course in science fiction was taught at Colgate University in 1962 by Mark Hillegas, and Sam Moskowitz organized evening courses in science fiction at the City College of New York in 1953 and 1954. Since then, science fiction has spread into thousands of college classrooms and tens of thousands of high schools, and even into junior high schools and primary schools.

This surprising interest of academia in science fiction has aroused suspicion and alarm among science fiction readers, writers, and editors. Their attitudes have been summed up by Ben Bova's editorial "Teaching Science Fiction" in *Analog* (June 1974) and Lester del Rey's "The Siren Song of Academe" in *Galaxy* (March 1975) and symbolized by former coeditor and copublisher of *Locus* Dena Brown's comment at the 1970 organizing meeting of the Science Fiction Research Association: "Let's take science fiction out of the classroom and put it back in the gutter where it belongs."

Part of what frightens science fiction people about academia is the danger that it will be taught poorly, dustily, inadequately, or drably. But even if taught with knowledge, skill, and enthusiasm, science fiction may be ruined by the academic viewpoint, some of them believe.

"The Academic Viewpoint" was first published in *Nebula Award Stories 12*, edited by Gordon R. Dickson (New York: Harper & Row, 1976).

Teachers, they suspect, look at books differently from ordinary readers, and, like Medusa, their look turns things to stone. Science fiction readers point at their own high school experiences of hating Shakespeare or Dickens because they were forced to read them. Even at the college level, professors encounter the frequent student attitude: "Why do we have to analyze fiction or poetry? It ruins them."

These are the concerns of the science fiction world. How does academia respond?

First, the notion that all science fiction teachers are alike is simply lack of knowledge about what is done in the classroom. Science fiction is taught for a variety of reasons, at all levels. In colleges, for instance, it often is used for its content, to help teach political science or psychology, anthropology, religion, future studies, or even the hard sciences. Anthologies for these specific purposes multiply in publishers' catalogs. Most objections to the teaching of science fiction, however, do not concern themselves with this use, although a number of long-time readers believe that science fiction should not be used for any other purpose than the one God intended . . . for reading.

Even within English departments, teaching approaches vary. Some professors teach the ideas; some, the themes; some, the history and the genre; and some, the great books. In general, all of these may be dismissed from the concerns of the science fiction world's vested interests; if any of the subjects are taught knowledgeably and capably, the judgments of their teachers about ideas, themes, definitions, history, and great books need not coincide with those of any held within the science fiction world, where there is, after all, almost as great a diversity of opinion as may be found outside it.

In addition to the approaches listed above, some teachers may include one or more science fiction books in a course in contemporary literature, or the literature of women, or of children, or of some other area of experience. And some professors teach science fiction as if it were any other kind of literature and apply to it the same critical concerns they apply to other books.

Here, perhaps, lies the greatest possibility for a break with science fiction tradition. What values do teachers of literature search out when they teach science fiction—or, for that matter, fiction of any kind?

Surprising as it may be to the critics of the teaching of literature, the first consideration is story. Story is as appealing to professors as it is to lay readers. "Pleasure in fiction is rooted in our response to narrative movement—to story itself," Professor Robert Scholes wrote in his essay "As the Wall Crumbles" in *Nebula Award Stories #10*.

But story is relatively unambiguous, at least in a work of fiction in which story predominates, and teaching at all levels tends to gravitate toward those works whose qualities teaching can enhance. This is not to say that these works are necessarily best in some abstract sense, only that they are teachable. Many persons outside academia suggest that at this point science fiction is in danger: qualities in a piece of fiction may be overvalued simply because they are less accessible.

The danger is real. In some academic circles, as among a certain group of avant-garde writers, story has been discarded as too obvious or easy. Susceptible students and readers have been persuaded that story is a lesser art, if it is an art at all, and difficulty, ambiguity, and obscurity are essential to good fiction. The critics of academia suggest that if these aspects of fiction are highly valued in classes, authors will be seduced into such corrupt practices.

The danger is real, but it is not as great as the doomsayers fear. Authors are not as susceptible as all that (if they're not doing their own thing, they aren't worth much as authors), and the teaching of literature is not as pernicious as all that. Story still counts for much in a literature class.

Witness the fact that the books most frequently taught by academics (as reported by Jack Williamson in 1972) were Heinlein's *Stranger in a Strange Land*, Miller's *A Canticle for Leibowitz*, Wells's *The War of the Worlds*, Pohl and Kornbluth's *The Space Merchants*, Herbert's *Dune*, Huxley's *Brave New World*, Le Guin's *The Left Hand of Darkness*, Bradbury's *The Martian Chronicles*, Silverberg's *Science Fiction Hall of Fame*, Wells's *The Time Machine*, and Asimov's *I, Robot*. Other books among those a bit less frequently taught would reveal none unfamiliar to the average science fiction reader; the total list represents, with a few arguments, a reasonable "best" list for any knowledgeable fan, and even the arguable titles have been honored by science fiction critics and readers.

Admittedly, the list may reveal some bias toward what passes for excellence in writing, skill in characterization, or verisimilitude in description. Few teachers include Edward Elmer "Doc" Smith or Edgar Rice Burroughs, from whose science fiction adventures a generation of readers were weaned (though I, for one, included *A Princess of Mars* for a number of years, and I would be surprised if some teacher somewhere does not teach *The Skylark of Space* or *Gray Lensman*).

What, then, do science fiction teachers look for in a work of science fiction?

They are concerned, of course, with teaching the art of reading and the skills of criticism (along with the ability to communicate) rather than merely the specific work at hand. They apply principles to texts, both to make the piece of prose, poetry, or drama more accessible but also to enable students to apply similar principles to reading they may do in other classes or outside of classes. They want students to get more out of their reading, to read more alertly, more knowledgeably, more enjoyably.

Critics who complain that this kind of approach to literature kills enjoyment are restricting the enjoyment of literature only to those natural readers who understand intuitively what is not immediately observable, or to those works that have no depth.

What is not immediately observable to a casual reader of science fiction? The best way to answer that question might be to list the aspects of fiction that a good teacher looks for.

1. Consistency of story
2. Story premises
3. Application of the premises
4. Credibility of the characters
5. Consistency of theme
6. Imagery
7. Style
8. Total artfulness
9. Challenge to the imagination
10. Overall impression

Consistency of Story

A good reader continually adjusts his or her expectations of a piece of fiction as the author gradually reveals the directions in which his or her characters are moving or are being forced to move. A well-written work handles the reader's expectations skillfully and confidently, neither changing directions nor disappointing expectations previously aroused. A careless reader may never notice inconsistencies in various parts of a work, and a casual reader may forgive them. But an author should be held to the highest standards of accountability, both for the improvement of reading and the improvement of writing; an author is not at liberty to do what he or she wishes without accepting the consequences.

Story Premises

A good reader picks up the clues an author plants about the foundations on which his or her world and story rest. In a science fiction work, this includes the science and the sociology—the answers to the question: how did we get from there to here? In a skillfully written work, if the reader grants the author's premises, he or she must grant the conclusions, but part of the tension of the work always exists between the conclusions and the premises. The casual reader misses an important part of the dialogue in which the good writer hopes to engage him or her and allows the less able writer to pass unchallenged.

Application of the Premises

A good reader challenges the writer at every point, debating the working out of the author's thesis, his or her arrival at the conclusions, checking back continually against what he or she already knows, theorizing that any discrepancy must be significant. This is not a tedious process but one that, once recognized, becomes automatic with the alert reader.

Credibility of the Characters

Are the characters real people? Should we take them seriously? Are they meant to be realistic? Do they react consistently? It is my thesis (see my chapter in Reginald Bretnor's symposium, *The Craft of Science Fiction*, Harper & Row, 1976) that characters in a science fiction work should be judged differently from those in mainstream fiction (often they are more important as representatives than as individuals), but characters should be understandably motivated. They should not act arbitrarily or inconsistently; they should act for their own reasons and not for the author's convenience. This is not because of any abstract literary morality but because the fiction is better if they do.

Consistency of Theme

Does the story have a message? Not all fiction has anything to say other than to reinforce the assumptions basic to the culture from which the fiction springs, such as that good will prevail or that good will prevail only if men and women of intelligence and character work at it hard enough. But some fiction attempts to say something more—about the nature or goal of life, the nature or difficulties of society, or the nature or problems of people: that is, about the human condition. The good reader asks what the work means besides its obvious storyline. Ursula Le Guin's *The Left Hand of Darkness*, for instance, is about not only whether the world of Winter joins the Ekumen, not only whether Genly Ai is successful or even survives, but also the ways in which sex shapes their (and by analogy our) society and its institutions. Another question is how well the theme is woven into the fabric of the story, not appended to it like a sermon.

Imagery

One way in which meaning emerges from fiction is through the imagery implicit in the work, often without the conscious knowledge of author or reader—the literal images, the symbols, the similes, and the metaphors. Once teachers begin talking about images, symbols, and metaphors, the ordinary reader turns his mind off, and authors have been known to object to teachers reading something into their writing that they did not intend, often accusing teachers of falsifying what they were trying to do. As in most criticisms of teaching, there is some truth to the charge; some teachers and some critics build a mountain of interpretation out of a molehill of evidence and may ignore the author's intention—indeed, it was a tenet of the so-called new criticism (now more than sixty years old) that to consider the author's intention is a trap, called the "intentional fallacy." Nevertheless, images do occur in works of fiction, and they do influence the reactions of readers to the work. Examples abound, even in science fiction, from the power imagery of technology to the guilt imagery of the mad scientist in whatever his contemporary guise.

Style

Style is the manner in which words are chosen and put together. Complexity or uniqueness is not necessarily good. Sometimes simplicity or transparency are superior. What we term "style" is often mistakenly reserved for "high style," for individual mannerisms, for that which calls attention to itself, but what a careful reader notices is the suitability of style to subject and the appropriateness of language and sentence structure—whether what is said is enhanced by the way it is said. Innumerable would-be writers have been misled by teachers who told them, "Before you can be a successful writer, you must find your own style." Fred Pohl is fond of quoting a French aphorism, "Style is the problem solved."

Total Artfulness

The different parts of a piece of fiction do not exist in isolation, though they often must be discussed in this fashion if they are to be understood. Few skills—from the golfer's swing to the dancer's routine—can be understood by watching them in their entirety. The separate acts must be broken down into understandable units that can be learned and then reassembled into the whole. All the considerations about fiction that have been discussed up to this point may in themselves be well done but they may not together form a coherent work. If they work together, the good teacher points out why the whole is more than the sum of its parts.

Challenge to the Imagination

A piece of fiction might have every virtue the teacher can describe and still be dull; and a piece of fiction can lack almost every virtue and still rise above its circumstances by the way in which it challenges the imagination. The teacher and the reader may wish that great ideas were matched by great execution, but it is not always so, and the good teacher recognizes the appeal of works that are otherwise deficient. This is not to say that the public is always right, but to recognize, as Leslie Fiedler pointed out to an audience of science fiction writers, "For too long critics have tried to tell readers why they should like what they don't like; they should be trying to discover why people like what they like."

Overall Impression

After a work has been analyzed—which means, literally, separated into its constituent parts—it must be put back together. Students object to having what they like dissected as if it were something dead, almost as much as they object to being forced to study something they consider dead. After the good teacher has helped his students analyze any work of fiction, then the teacher should help them regain their vision of the work in its entirety—its overall impression of readability, of narrative excitement, of fictional pleasure. The teacher should bring it back to life. It is a difficult task but not an impossible one.

Properly done, the study of literature does not diminish the enjoyment of reading; it enhances that enjoyment, just as a good critical article about a short story or a novel illuminates the work for the reader, who goes to it with new appreciation and understanding. To believe otherwise is to uphold the blessings of ignorance, to maintain that the individual's enjoyment of any complex art—and fiction is a complex art—depends upon how little he or she knows about it.

Science fiction has not achieved as much as it might because it has enjoyed few good critics. A critic is much more than a reviewer; a reviewer discusses his personal evaluation of a work, while a critic relates his or her evaluation to larger principles and theories, to standards she or others have established for the greater body of work to which the piece at hand is related. Critics raise standards for writers as well as readers; we can be thankful for the work of such as Damon Knight, James Blish, P. Schuyler Miller, and a few others in the past, more recently the work of Alexei and Cory Panshin, Lester del Rey, Joanna Russ, Barry Malzberg, the various writers for the *Science Fiction and Fantasy Book Review*, A. J. Budrys, and currently Paul Di Filippo and John Clute.

Their judgments have not always coincided—there is no reason they should—but science fiction is better because they have judged and made their criteria plain. The judgments of academia may not be the same as those of science fiction critics or its readers, but I would hazard the guess that their criteria for judging a work of science fiction are not much different from those I have set down here.

10

SCIENCE FICTION AS LITERATURE

1

In the late 1970s and early 1980s, I edited a series of science fiction anthologies titled *The Road to Science Fiction*. The first three volumes were subtitled *From Gilgamesh to Wells*, *From Wells to Heinlein*, and *From Heinlein to Here*. They attempted to trace the development of science fiction from its prototypical origins in the earliest forms of storytelling to its most recent expressions, and as they progressed historically I attempted to show how the genre we call "science fiction" developed. The stories I included were selected because they were important or representative.

With the fourth and final volume, I had a problem. In the third volume I had brought the series up to "here." Where could I go from here? I subtitled it *From Here to Forever*, and attempted to remedy some of the omissions of the earlier volumes and to carry that survey, now almost one million words, up into the 1980s. But as this survey approached the present, the choices became more difficult. The importance of specific works to the development of the genre usually is not apparent until long after they have appeared and the genre has had time to respond to them, to learn their lessons and incorporate their viewpoints and advances.

Thus, in volume 4, the principle of "genre importance" had to be discarded entirely. The works of the 1970s that will shape science fiction will be determined by the winnowing of time. Moreover, the most important trend of the 1970s, as I predicted in *Alternate Worlds*, was diversity. The forces at work

"Science Fiction as Literature" was first published, in somewhat different form, in *The Road to Science Fiction*, vol. 4, *From Here to Forever*, edited by James Gunn (New York: New American Library, 1982).

on science fiction during this decade were pushing it apart rather than bringing it together; most authors were exploring individual nightmares rather than collective dreams.

This is not to say that important genre events did not occur during the 1970s. The most spectacular was the popular and financial success of several science fiction films, such as *Close Encounters of the Third Kind* and *Star Wars*. Indeed, *Star Wars* became the biggest moneymaker of all time (up to that time), with the possible exception of *E.T., the Extra-Terrestrial*, and its first sequel in a planned cycle of more than half a dozen, *The Empire Strikes Back*, became the second biggest. They precipitated an avalanche of SF films, including *Alien, Superman, The Black Hole, Saturn 3, Time after Time, Flash Gordon, Star Trek: The Motion Picture*, and *Dune*. On television, they led to *Battlestar Galactica, Buck Rogers in the 25th Century*, and dramatizations of *Brave New World, The Martian Chronicles*, and *The Lathe of Heaven*. Whether audiences numbering in the tens of millions can be translated into readers of magazines and books remains debatable. Some of the best-sellers of the last few years have been novelizations of SF films, but only a few original novels, such as Frank Herbert's *Children of Dune* and *God Emperor of Dune*, made the hardcover best-seller lists until 1982, when a significant breakthrough occurred with *Foundation's Edge, 2010*, and *Friday*.

A more certain indicator of a broadening readership of science fiction was the appearance of new magazines: *Isaac Asimov's Science Fiction Magazine* was a remarkable success, surpassing *Analog*'s circulation in a couple of years and leading its publisher to purchase from Condé Nast the fifty-year-old longtime leader in the field. Even more spectacular was the success of *Omni*, which reached a million circulation within a month or two after its heavily advertised appearance under the guidance of Bob Guccione, publisher of *Penthouse*. Although it published only three or four stories per issue and emphasized speculative articles and pictures, *Omni* proved that science fiction was not necessarily limited to a circulation of a hundred thousand.

Playboy, of course, had been publishing science fiction since its inception, but its main selling points were photographs of nude women and a sophisticated attitude toward sex. The success of *Omni* provided the example that would push other publishers into the field with such magazines as *Next, Discover, Science 1980*, a new *Science Digest*, and others, mostly emphasizing science popularizations, forecasts, and speculation but publishing no fiction. However, *Rod Serling's The Twilight Zone Magazine*, published by the publishers of *Gallery*, entered the fiction field with substantial advertising. Two promising magazines, *Cosmos* and *Galileo*, ran into financial difficulties unrelated to their circulations and were terminated, along with the thirty-year-old *Galaxy*, which the publishers of *Galileo* had purchased. Since then, of course, *Asimov's* changed its name to *Asimov's Science Fiction*, the circulation of all SF magazines has declined to subsistence levels (with *Analog* again the most "popular"), and *Omni* was cancelled.

Science fiction book publishing went through a decade of expansion that made it the second most popular of categories (after the romance), increasing from 348 books a year in 1972 to 1,288 in 1979, according to *Locus*, the "newspaper of the science fiction field." But the recession of 1980 hit the publishing business hard, and science fiction was not immune, dropping that year to 1,184 books. Companies such as Ace, Berkley, Dell, and Pocket Books, which had expanded their publishing programs, began to cut back. Other companies that had planned expansions into the science fiction field reexamined their decisions, and Dell finally cancelled its SF line entirely. The picture brightened in 1981, with Ace publishing ten science fiction books a month and a new line, Tor Books, making its debut, but darkened again as several lines (including Ace) were sold to Berkley. The plans of some young writers to make a career out of science fiction may have been postponed if not abandoned entirely. The nature of science fiction has long been influenced by economic considerations, and 1980 was no exception. But by the mid-1980s, science fiction publishing was again expanding rapidly, and by 2005 the magazines had not yet slowed their decline while book publishing continues to soar past two thousand a year.

2

Having discarded genre importance as the criterion for inclusion in volume 4 of *The Road to Science Fiction*, I decided to emphasize the quality of the writing rather than the quality of the visions. This does not mean that the stories in that volume are any less startling in content than those in the first three volumes—in many cases they may be even more wonderful, in the original meaning of that word—but that a major consideration for their selection was the literary skill with which they were written. That decision was not as arbitrary as it might seem; in the past two decades, readers as well as writers have placed increasing value on the quality of the writing, as both readers and writers have become more sophisticated.

In one of his analyses of science fiction, Isaac Asimov wrote that science fiction was "adventure-dominant" between 1926 and 1938, "science-dominant" between 1938 and 1950, "sociology-dominant" between 1950 and 1965, and "style-dominant" after that. Asimov's own preferences may be apparent—he felt most at home in the science-dominant and sociology-dominant periods—but in spite of his protestations of total ignorance about the writing process, his own work, as in *The Gods Themselves*, has become more style-dominant since 1965.

Style was not the only important aspect of the 1960s and 1970s. There were also changes in perspective and shifts in subject matter. Gathered together and publicized by a magazine that specialized in it and an editor who was fascinated by it, this different kind of science fiction became known as the "New Wave." The term tended to lump together many disparate writers and works produced out of a variety of influences, but it stuck so fast that it is impossible to discuss what happened to science fiction in the 1960s and even the 1970s without using it.

Many different forces pushed science fiction away from its magazine pattern of recognizable heroes dealing with problems of change in straightforward narratives set down in transparent styles. Human reason was expected to come up with rational answers in these stories—the sort of fiction of which Asimov's was the prime example. The euphoria with which the United States emerged from World War II, having disposed of two tyrannical and technological threats, faded into the uncertainties of the Cold War, irresolvable Asian wars, and a loss of scientific and technological superiority through Soviet breakthroughs in atomic weapons and space exploration. The problems perceived in the 1960s seemed impervious to reason.

The first generation of science fiction writers had come from the ranks of pulp writers, who produced stories in various categories for a wide variety of magazines. Supplementing these were writers, primarily self-educated or educated by their exposure to fantasy and science fiction in the pre-1926 pulp magazines, who were attracted by the reprints of Verne and Poe and Wells that first filled *Amazing Stories* and who began to write new science fiction stories in the later 1920s and early 1930s.

The second generation of science fiction writers came out of the science fiction magazines themselves, inspired by them, educated by them. It dedicated itself to science fiction with single-minded devotion. Some readers were influenced by their reading to seek careers in science; some scientists began to write science fiction.

The third generation of science fiction writers grew up wanting to be new Heinleins or Asimovs. And they began to be educated in other ways—they went to college as a general rule, and many of them studied anthropology or sociology, philosophy, languages, and literature, rather than the hard sciences. Their stories began to demonstrate as great a familiarity with the humanities as with the physical sciences.

Writers who came into prominence in the 1960s, the fourth generation, emerged in a period of discontent, not only with the science fiction that had preceded them, and often that had inspired them, but with the world. Some of them began to write antiscience stories, even anti–science fiction stories, taking the icons of the genre and demonstrating that they were hollow and fragile. When Ted Carnell's *New Worlds* was sold in England in 1964 and a new publisher appointed twenty-five-year-old Michael Moorcock as editor (a story told in more detail in volume 3 of *The Road to Science Fiction*), the fifth generation of science fiction writers had a gathering place and a forum, just as *Astounding* had provided a gathering place and a forum for Campbellian writers in the late 1930s, and as the *Magazine of Fantasy and Science Fiction* and *Galaxy* did for their writers in the 1950s. Now from *New Worlds* the voices of what would be called the New Wave could be heard all over the science fiction world. Not since the *Pall Mall Budget* began to publish H. G. Wells's first short stories had an English magazine, particularly one with financial troubles and a smaller-than-average circulation, had such influence.

The main characteristic of the New Wave rebellion was a movement away from traditional science fiction toward the literary mainstream. Though the authors, by and large, had first found publication for their visions and an audience for them in the science fiction world, now they sought different audiences and broader scope. This meant the introduction of mainstream techniques and mainstream attitudes toward science and life and people, including their behavior and fates. What had been transparent became translucent or opaque; what had been straightforward became complex; what had been reasonable became irrational; what had been recognizable heroes became complicated, nonheroic, sometimes realistic characters. The emphasis on character and setting sometimes meant elimination of traditional plot; it also often became a defense of the problems and rights of the individual over the problems and rights of the group or the species, and often a rejection of rationality, even an insistence that the universe was irrational, or at least incapable of being understood.

These new approaches to the writing of science fiction created new difficulties of definition. It was not always clear to the reader, the writer, or the critic how what was being published as science fiction—or, as many of the New Wave authors preferred, "speculative fiction"—would fit under the same umbrella that had sheltered what had previously been published.

In the first three volumes of *The Road to Science Fiction*, I offered the following definition:

> Science fiction is the branch of literature that deals with the effects of change on people in the real world as it can be projected into the past, the future, or to distant places. It often concerns itself with scientific or technological change, and it usually involves matters whose importance is greater than the individual or the community; often civilization or the race itself is in danger.

Perhaps the definition problems are only peripheral. The new speculative fiction did deal with the effects of change on people in the real world—usually. The customary difference was that the *cause* of the change was often omitted, because it was unknown or unknowable, and the people to whom the changes happened seldom inquired into the causes because the changes were so massive that causes were irrelevant or so mysterious that inquiry was futile, or because the people were incurious, or were benumbed by events or life itself, or had lost faith in rational inquiry. The reasons why causes were minimized may have been various, but the effects were clear: rationality was short-circuited (if the causes are unavailable, solutions are so beyond reach as to make the search unthinkable) and characters became victims.

Good examples are J. G. Ballard's catastrophe novels of the 1960s (two of them published before the official dating of the New Wave): *The Drowned World* (1962), *The Drought* (1964), and *The Crystal World* (1966). They involve cataclysms that occur without apparent reason and that the characters do not concern themselves about—they even conspire in their own destructions. Whether these characters and the changes they endure are in the real world can be debated; they seem unlike real people in many ways. In some instances, they should be evaluated as symbols, but some critics would claim that modern man is beset by many contemporary changes whose causes are obscure and perhaps beyond discovery, and that dumb acceptance, even collaboration with one's catastrophes, rather than a rational search for solutions, is characteristic of the real world.

The second part of the definition, which is cautiously qualified by "often" and "usually," brings up greater difficulties. It speaks of science fiction being concerned "with scientific or technological change" and involving "matters whose importance is greater than the individual or the community." New Wave writers often rejected such notions. Fed up, perhaps, with rationalizations that looked far into the future, offended by justifications that needed evolutionary time to prove themselves, they often focused on the individual, upon his more limited perceptions and his more limited concerns; the species was seldom involved except in universal destruction. Few individual tragedies spelled success for the species, as in Heinlein's "Requiem" (reprinted in volume 2 of *The Road to SF*) or Godwin's "The Cold Equations" (reprinted in volume 3).

The way the stories were told often was more important than what they said—the *manner* overshadowed the *matter* (although it has become popular in recent years to speak of manner and matter as being inseparable). Experiments in style became commonplace: subjectivity, which does not work well with a rational approach to the universe but is completely at home with irrationality, became the rule. The experiments may not have been particularly new—John Brunner looked to John Dos Passos's *U.S.A.* (first volume, 1930) for the style of *Stand on Zanzibar* (1968), Brian W. Aldiss to Joyce's *Finnegans Wake* (1939) for the style of *Barefoot in the Head* (1969), and J. G. Ballard to more contemporary antinovelists, typified by Alain Robbe-Grillet, for his "condensed novels"—but they were new to science fiction. At their best they were effective in saying what could not be said as well any other way; at their worst they were distancing, distracting, and obscure.

Not because of but in parallel with the New Wave, the fourth volume of *The Road to Science Fiction* emphasized the literary aspects of science fiction.

3

Lester del Rey would point out that science fiction always has had literary aspects—not necessarily in all science fiction all the time, but in some science fiction some of the time. Science fiction magazines had nothing against effective writing, although at times it may have seemed so. A reader's 1927 letter to Hugo Gernsback's *Amazing Stories* accused H. G. Wells of using "too many words to describe a situation." Subsequently, whether or not in response to a general perception of Wells and others as being too "literary," Gernsback deemphasized his use of Wells reprints and of Wells's name on the cover. Later editors would urge writers to tone down their language and get on with their stories—that is, to avoid "fine writing" and literary touches and anything that smacked of difficulty—but stories with some pretensions to style somehow got published, not always in the leading magazines, not always without difficulty, but here and there, now and then.

John W. Campbell Jr. himself was able to get his more style-dominant stories, written under the name of Don A. Stuart, published in *Astounding* before he became its editor. Stanley Weinbaum was acclaimed not only for creating unusual aliens but for writing more skillfully than many of his contemporaries. Even earlier, Dr. David H. Keller had made the beginning of what Damon Knight has called the "science fiction art story." But these stories did not always appear in *Astounding*. Some writers, such as Edmond Hamilton, wrote stories they were unable to sell until years later, if then; some, like Jack Williamson, seemed to adapt their work to the demands of each new decade. Other writers, such as Ray Bradbury, soon wrote themselves out of the field, but the work of Theodore Sturgeon seemed to find acceptance no matter how he wrote, and Alfred Bester's literary pyrotechnics earned him awards and acclaim.

Stories came along during the 1930s and the 1940s that seemed to shout out their difference from the mob of genre stories in which they were found; oddly enough—or perhaps not oddly at all—they were often the stories most honored and best remembered. Henry Kuttner and his wife, C. L. Moore, for instance, wrote under several pen names for John W. Campbell Jr. during the 1940s when other writers were occupied with the war effort. They began using literary allusions and stylistic techniques that gave their work an unusual flavor and presaged the kind of writing that would not come into its own until the 1960s. "Mimsy Were the Borogoves" is one example, but so are "No Woman Born," "Vintage Season," and many others. The characteristics of these stories were a greater emphasis on the individual and his or her feelings about the situation, the use of historic, literary, and cultural references that brought more of the fullness of life into the story, and a clear concern for words and the order in which they were presented.

The *Magazine of Fantasy and Science Fiction*, when it was founded in 1949, seemed to provide a natural home for such stories. Its editors, Boucher and McComas, preferred literary fiction, and such pieces as Richard Matheson's "Born of Man and Woman," Avram Davidson's "My Boy Friend's Name Is Jello," Walter Miller Jr.'s *A Canticle for Leibowitz*, and Daniel Keyes's *Flowers for Algernon* were published there in the 1950s. But other magazines were receptive to stories with literary aspects: "The Moon Moth" by Jack Vance was published in Horace Gold's *Galaxy*, and "Nobody Bothers Gus" by A. J. Budrys was published in John W. Campbell Jr.'s *Astounding*.

Internal aspirations toward professionalism and higher standards of art were beginning to make themselves felt in other ways. Damon Knight's criticism was collected in *In Search of Wonder* (first edition, 1956) and included reviews originally published beginning in 1945, though most were written between 1950 and 1955, and James Blish's criticism was collected in *The Issue at Hand*

(1964), consisting of material originally published between 1952 and 1960. This led in 1956 to Knight and Blish's annual Milford Science Fiction Writers Conference and, ten years later, to the founding of the Science Fiction Writers of America.

By the 1960s, the trend toward literary science fiction was picking up momentum. Book publication was beginning to rival magazine publication in volume and significance, and the greater liberties allowed the authors of individual books were beginning to loosen up the tight editorial control of the magazines. Frank Herbert's psychological (and Freudian) thriller *The Dragon in the Sea* (1956), which was serialized by *Astounding* in 1955–1956 under the title *Under Pressure*, prepared the way for Herbert's *Dune*, a long, complex novel of palace intrigue and ecological concern, which was serialized in eight parts by *Astounding* (now called *Analog*) as *Dune World* and *The Prophet of Dune* in 1963 and 1965. Bob Shaw's quiet story of personal tragedy and human response to a new invention, "Light of Other Days," was published in *Analog* in 1966.

By then, new magazines and anthologies were creating a substantial counter-movement: *New Worlds* was followed by Damon Knight's anthology *Orbit*, beginning in 1966, and by Harlan Ellison's one-shot *Dangerous Visions* in 1967 (followed by *Again, Dangerous Visions* five years later). An experimental quarterly, *Quark*, edited by Samuel R. Delany and poet Marilyn Hacker (then Delany's wife), lasted only four issues, beginning in 1970. Robert Silverberg launched *New Dimensions*, Harry Harrison *Nova*, and Terry Carr *Universe*, all in 1971. Most of these offered alternate means of publication for short, speculative fiction and earned their authors, and sometimes their editors, a surprising number of awards in the process. In addition, an unusual number of one-shot original anthologies were published in the decade after 1965. The publication of several best-of-the-year collections has continued the work begun by Judith Merril's earlier collections in focusing attention on experimental work, and Nebula Awards, at least, if not Hugos, frequently have gone to more literary pieces.

Meanwhile, new writers with new ideas and new methods began to be published here and there and then almost everywhere: Robert Silverberg; Harlan Ellison; Roger Zelazny; Samuel R. Delany; Norman Spinrad; Thomas M. Disch; a writer in a more traditional vein, Larry Niven; and others. Interesting writers were appearing, or being discovered, in other parts of the world, and gradually their influence was seeping into science fiction. In addition to the usual group of excellent English writers, Stanislaw Lem was producing innovative stories and novels in Poland. Although his first work was published in

1951, nothing was translated into English until *Solaris* in 1970. A renaissance in Russian science fiction began in the late 1950s and continued through the 1960s, led by Ivan Yefremov, the Strugatsky brothers, and others, and, as Darko Suvin has demonstrated, work of interesting quality was being written in other socialist countries. The work of the internationally famous Argentinean Jorge Luis Borges, part of which is science fiction and fantasy, began to be published in English translations with *Ficciones* in 1962.

A flood of new American writers moved into the field in the 1970s, responding perhaps to the new freedom (or, conversely, to the lack of publishing opportunities elsewhere, as slick magazines folded or stopped publishing fiction and the other category pulps dwindled to a handful). Barry N. Malzberg, Gene Wolfe, Gardner Dozois, and James Tiptree Jr. (later revealed to be Alice Sheldon) came into prominence in the 1970s, although they actually began to be published in the late 1960s. After them came such writers as Pamela Sargent, George Zebrowski, Ed Bryant, Jack Dann, George Alec Effinger, David Gerrold, Vonda N. McIntyre, George R. R. Martin, Michael Bishop, and many others.

A new factor that began to exert the kind of influence exercised by the Milford Writers Conference in the 1950s and 1960s was the Clarion Science Fiction Writers Workshop, founded by Robin Scott Wilson at Clarion State College in Pennsylvania in 1968 and later moved to Michigan State University when Wilson left Pennsylvania for the Big Ten universities. The workshop admitted only beginning writers who worked under the direction of such week-long guest teachers as Damon Knight, Kate Wilhelm, and Harlan Ellison. The workshop produced a surprising number of the newer writers, including Bryant, Zebrowski, Effinger, McIntyre, F. M. Busby, and Lisa Tuttle.

Well into the 1970s, the New Wave had been assimilated by science fiction. Not only had the influence of the magazines diminished as books became the major purveyor of science fiction and as the genre unity once enforced by the magazines dissipated into relative anarchy, but fiction similar in tone, philosophy, content, and style to what had once been called the New Wave was being published in all the leading magazines, including *Analog*. The New Wave had not taken over—adventure stories and novels still were being published, as well as hard-science work and sociological science fiction—but much idiosyncratic and even anti–science fiction was being published next to other kinds of science fiction in the same magazine. The thrust of the rebellion had been incorporated into much of the other kinds of fiction.

4

What were the characteristics that made so much difference in the mid-1960s and so little in the mid-1970s?

Writers have only a limited number of variables with which to work, with which to distinguish their stories from those of everyone else. Words are the basic tool, but, in addition, fiction deals with plot (what happens), characters (to whom it happens), and setting (where and when it happens). Out of these basic ingredients all fiction is assembled. What gives fiction uniqueness, however, is not simply the events or the people or the place—though these may have lesser or greater originality and interest and may be presented with lesser or greater skill and thoroughness and complexity—but the allusions that are presented along with the events, the people, and the place.

If we think of a piece of fiction as a closed world in which the characters exist for the plot and the plot for the characters and the setting for both, allusions are what relate that closed world to other worlds, including the world with which we, as readers, are so familiar. Through the story's allusions to the real world (the world of experience), we, as readers, obtain relevance, meaning, theme—all those attributes of fiction that keep us from saying when we finish, "So what?" Through allusions, we learn how to interpret what happens in the closed world of the story.

In genre science fiction, the allusions usually relate the fictional world to other genre works—or sometimes to the worlds of the hard sciences or the soft sciences, or to philosophy or history—and only in a limited way to the everyday world. In literary science fiction, allusions relate the fictional world to everyday life, tradition, myth, literature, history, and so forth.

A straightforward adventure story may have simple allusions: If John Carter does not get there in time, his beloved Dejah Thoris will be killed; we understand the desirability of Carter's actions because we understand love and death and timeliness. But Edgar Rice Burroughs keeps Carter attached to Earth by other ties than basic relationships and the emotions they arouse: every now and then Carter returns or sends back a manuscript, and in some novels (for instance, *The Mastermind of Mars*) Burroughs alludes to human customs, traditions, and religions, sometimes approvingly, sometimes critically. Out of these allusions comes more than an adventure story.

The allusions in more complex fiction can provide numerous levels of meaning. One reader may read the story simply at the level of plot, while another, harder working or more sophisticated in reading protocols, may perceive other levels of the story that may complement the plot, supplement it, alter it, or even reverse it. Sometimes the allusions may be grace notes, lending the support of history or myth or literature to the basic events of the story; sometimes they provide clues to what is happening.

Daniel Keyes's *Flowers for Algernon*, for instance, has many allusions—in fact, the success of the narrative device depends upon readers picking up, from Charlie Gordon's vocabulary and limited experience of the world, clues to Charlie's condition and mental ability. The reader who does not translate "raw shock" as "Rorschach" has missed at least a bit of the significance of what is going on, and even more, some of the playfulness of the narrative. As Charlie's mental abilities improve, his spelling gets better and his intellectual horizons broaden; the reader who misses this may also miss the evidence of his deterioration.

Sometimes in science fiction, the allusions to other genre works produce references that are baffling to the unfamiliar reader: "ftl," for instance, or "hyperspace" or "blasters." At other times, the process by which authors pack important clues to the situation of the story or its meaning into otherwise innocent lines of description or dialogue also may make the novice reader miss much of what is going on. As Samuel R. Delany has pointed out, science fiction developed its own protocols of reading.

In Philip José Farmer's "Sail On! Sail On!" for instance, the reader is not expected to understand immediately what the situation is. Instead, the reader must put together pieces of evidence—the names of the sailing ships, the fact that the ship has a radiotelegraph, and other bits of information dropped into description and conversation—to deduce that this is Columbus's first voyage across the Atlantic, but that it is a different historical situation. It is what science fiction readers call an alternate history story; in this alternate history, Roger Bacon's scientific work was accepted by the Church instead of denounced. Finally, the author pulls an unexpected switch: the story is not an alternate history but an alternate universe in which the physical facts are different.

The skills required to read Alfred Bester's "Fondly Fahrenheit" are similar. The reader must follow the shifting tenses in which the story is narrated to understand that the human owner of the android is the source of the insanity. In Harlan Ellison's "I Have No Mouth, and I Must Scream," it might be interesting, but not essential, to recognize the breaks in the story as computer language, or even that the statement they make is "I think, therefore I am." It is more important to recognize the phrase as the philosophical given upon which Descartes erected a set of assumptions about the universe, and that the phrase is the justification, as well as the derivation of the name, for the computer AM and its existence as an independent entity. There also are resonances of God's statement to Moses, "I am that I am."

The protocols of reading for the more literary stories of the 1960s and 1970s became the protocols of the mainstream. The allusions were not to science fiction nor to science but to a more broadly shared experience. The real world includes not only the everyday experiences that everyone shares but the cultural heritage of myth, literature, and history that is assumed, sometimes incorrectly, to be common to all educated men and women.

5

The allusions in literary science fiction are not simple playfulness, though they may be playful, nor simply emblems of culture to demonstrate the learning of the author and to establish with the sophisticated reader a bond of shared references, though they may do this. At their best, they serve to relate the story to more traditional values, sometimes more basic values, and to fit the story into the larger framework of human existence, including the human past. Sometimes, of course, relating the story to the past militates against relating the story to the future; and the more the events of the story comment on the present, the less they are read as speculations about possible new conditions. Satire finds itself in a similar predicament: the more Pohl and Kornbluth's *The Space Merchants* is read as humorous commentary on contemporary advertising practices, the less the novel can be read as extrapolation from present trends into the future. In literary science fiction, the more Pohl's *Gateway* is read as a parable for the human condition, the less seriously will we take the Heechee and their marvelous ships.

The emphasis of literary science fiction on the more physical aspects of life was not simply a rebellion against their absence in magazine science fiction. The kind of language and scenes found in Ellison's *Dangerous Visions* or in Spinrad's *Bug Jack Barron* that got *New Worlds* banned by an English distributor and denounced in Parliament were not inserted simply to shock. There was, to be sure, an element of rebellion and a desire to shock, but the language and the descriptions also were intended as allusions to the real world. In real life these things happen, these words are spoken. Traditional science fiction had seen no need to reflect that part of existence, had considered it irrelevant; the newer science fiction was trying not merely to introduce into science fiction that part of existence but also to relate science fiction that much more to the real world.

Literary science fiction emphasized other kinds of details—dress, behavior, actions, setting—that would have been touched upon lightly, if at all, in traditional science fiction. The behavior and actions and dress of characters had been important in traditional science fiction only as they affected the plot; in literary science fiction, these elements became important for their own sake and as allusions to the real world. Characters had pasts that affected their behavior and with which they had to come to terms; they had prior experience to deal with. Settings became more vivid and more important as they became more realistic; at the same time, settings became surrealistic upon occasion or metaphorical. If more emphasis is placed on setting as an allusion to reality rather than as a stage area for plot, it is only a step or two farther to give setting the burden of meaning, to make setting reflect the state of society or the emotional attitudes of the characters, or to have setting represent something else, as Ballard's "The Terminal Beach" uses the Eniwetok bomb-test site, or as Leiber's "Coming Attraction" uses the masks women wear.

Some of the allusions were achieved by simile, metaphor, or symbol. The comparison of two unlike things, whether stated directly or implied, allows another level of meaning. "The rocket's exhaust was like a pillar of flame" is a simile that might have appeared in any traditional science fiction story as an effort to make the reading experience more visual; in "The Streets of Ashkelon," Harry Harrison describes the landing of a ship on "a down-reaching tongue of flame." Altered by one word, "the rocket's exhaust was like a sword of flame," the simile would suggest violence being done to the Earth. With a more literary simile—"the rocket's exhaust was like the flaming sword set before the gates of Paradise"—the reader would be expected to supply the rest of the biblical story, that after the expulsion of Adam and Eve, God set the flaming sword at the entrance to prevent humanity from returning. The comparison, then, would enhance a visual experience with meaning: the flight of the rocket will prevent humanity from returning to Eden, perhaps literally by poisoning the Earth, perhaps figuratively by using up the fuel available for return. Changing simile to metaphor—"the rocket's exhaust was the flaming sword set before the gates of Paradise"—makes the comparison more forcefully.

In another version of the same imaginary story, Earth might slowly emerge as a symbol for Paradise from which humanity must be driven, never to return, if humanity is to fulfill its destiny to "be fruitful and multiply" and inherit the stars, just as in Henry Kuttner and C. L. Moore's 1947 novel *Fury*, Sam Reed forces humanity out of the comfortable undersea keeps onto the ravening surface of Venus in order to get the human species going again, and then turns the keeps radioactive to ensure that people cannot go back.

The impatient reader may ask why the author doesn't simply come out and say something rather than hinting around at it. This is a good question, and the answer is bound to be unsatisfactory to many. The writing of fiction is dependent upon a series of choices the author must make, from the initial idea to the characters, viewpoint, tone, mood, diction, and on to the finished product. Ideally, all the choices should reinforce one another so that the total is more than the sum of its parts. Thus subtlety and indirection, or allusion, may be the choice of a particular author writing a particular kind of story. A reader may choose not to read such authors, or such stories, but complaint is pointless: the choices are legitimate, the stories that result demand greater participation by the reader, but the readers who survive the difficulties, those who are able and willing to follow allusions and make deductions, may discover greater rewards. Similarly, the experienced science fiction reader must be willing and able to invest patience and thought in a story such as "Sail On! Sail On!" in order to make sense out of it. Patience and thought invested in "Sail On! Sail On!" pay off in a richer and more rewarding reading experience. The same is true of literary fiction: learning to read it with understanding results in enhanced enjoyment.

6

Not all innovation results in improvement; sometimes the effect was merely difference, sometimes it was failure. Some attempts to broaden the allusions of science fiction were mere rebelliousness: change for the sake of change. One trend minimized plot, eliminated causal relationships, or omitted consequences for the sake of directing the reader's attention to other aspects of the story. One result was that the reader concentrating on the plot level of a multilevel piece of fiction felt abandoned or betrayed. It was as if the author had cut one leg off a tripod: character and setting were magnified in importance, but the stool toppled.

When emphasis changes, characters customarily change as well to accommodate and produce new values and new meanings. It was as true in the nineteenth century as in the 1960s. Poe, for instance, wrote about hypersensitive men for whom ordinary sensation was too much, who sought to escape in travel or drugs from the everyday abrasions of life, for whom a movement, a word, set off an explosion of adjectives, a firecracker chain of events. Verne, on the other hand, explored vast, untraveled areas of the sea, the land, the air, and space, and he needed tough, adventurous characters not prone to moods or self-doubt. Wells dealt with social problems, and his protagonists were usually ordinary citizens with ordinary common sense and enough toughness of spirit to enable them to survive their harrowing experiences.

When the magazines were created, editors began to determine the nature of the characters in the stories they bought. Hugo Gernsback liked inventors; John W. Campbell Jr. wanted scientists who were like real scientists and people who knew how things worked; Horace Gold wanted ordinary citizens caught up in change they had not created and trying somehow to get along. Most magazine editors today want sympathetic characters who are intelligent enough to recognize the nature of their situation and tough enough to do something about it.

Like their predecessors, the newer writers usually chose characters who were the antithesis of those chosen by the previous generation. If Campbell's writers created characters who knew how things worked, the newer writers would write about people who didn't know how anything worked and didn't care; if Gold's writers dealt with common people struggling to survive, the newer writers would write about uncommon people conspiring with their own disasters. New Wave characters became puzzled, obsessed, introspective people—reflective but ineffective. Sometimes, in spite of the fact that these stories were intended to be more "real," the characters were metaphorical—vast areas of response were omitted from some of them—and the reader was intended to understand that they represented something else.

Most literary writers, however, would deny that they wrote in response or reaction to anything: the characters they chose represented people as the writers saw them. When authors insist—through their fiction or their real-life comments—that their characters represent real people, or the reader fails to recognize their metaphorical aspect, ideological battle begins.

By now the battles have largely ended. The war ended in a draw, but as in all wars, the participants have been altered. Traditional science fiction—in all its forms, from Gernsback to Campbell to Boucher to Gold—coexists with literary science fiction in the marketplace. The subjects and technical innovations pioneered by the New Wave are available to more traditional writers and are often incorporated in their fiction. The more extreme kinds of experimental writing have largely disappeared, and the more experimental writers have returned to more accessible materials and forms. Tom Disch wrote *On Wings of Song*, J. G. Ballard wrote *The Unlimited Dream Company* and then *Empire of the Sun*, Brian Aldiss wrote his *Helliconia* trilogy, and Gene Wolfe wrote *The Book of the New Sun* series.

Some writers have drifted away from science fiction, or made a sharp break with it, such as Ballard and Ellison; others have made farewell announcements and then had changes of heart, such as Silverberg and Malzberg. New writers have come along to provide new content for old traditions, such as Varley and Benford, Bear, and Brin.

In other words, science fiction, as usual, is in a state of flux, and, as usual, is looking forward to greater things.

11

THE CITY AND
THE CRITICS

C.P. Snow presented his analysis of "The Two Cultures" half a century ago, but the basic disagreement that he noted, about the contemporary situation and humanity's future, continue to divide educated people in Western civilization. Snow's lecture launched a wide-ranging debate that may have seemed unique to modern times, but it had been argued before: by Matthew Arnold and T. H. Huxley, by Henry James and H. G. Wells, by representatives of the literary culture on one hand and the scientific culture on the other.

Differences of opinion about culture and tradition, and about technology and the future, go back to a time not long after the beginning of the Industrial Revolution, to Blake and Emerson and Goethe and Tennyson and Ruskin. Ruskin, for instance, saw around him

> signs of a slavery in our England a thousand times more bitter and more degrading than that of the scourged African, or helot Greek. Men may be beaten, chained, tormented, yoked like cattle, slaughtered like summer flies, and yet remain in one sense, and the best sense, free.

Ruskin went on to praise the age of nobility and peasantry when "famine, and peril, and sword, and all evil, and all shame, have been borne willingly in the causes of masters and kings."

Many years later, H. G. Wells expressed an opposing view:

> We are constantly being told that the human animal is "degenerating" body and mind, through the malign influences of big towns, that a miasma of "vulgarity" and monotony is spreading over a once refined and rich and beautifully varied

---

"The City and the Critics" was first published in *Destinies* 2, no. 2, in Spring 1980.

world, that something exquisite called the human "soul," which was formerly quite all right, is now in a very bad way, and that plainly before us, unless we mend our ways and return to medieval dirt and haphazard, the open road, the wind upon the heath, brother, simple piety, an unrestricted birth-rate, spade husbandry, hand-made furniture, honest, homely surgery without anaesthetics, long skirts and hair for women, a ten-hour day for workmen, and more slapping and snubbing for the young, there is nothing before us but nervous wreckage and spiritual darkness.

Henry Adams, in his classic comparison between the Virgin and the Dynamo, saw the Virgin as representing everything that was distinctively human, and the sexless Dynamo as everything that was inhuman, pointing to the annihilation of human values, first by the achievement of an antlike society, and then by the victory of impersonal cosmic forces over life. One of his intellectual successors, Lewis Mumford, was a bit more balanced in his appraisal of technology in his book *The Myth of the Machine: The Pentagon of Power*. He admitted the "masterpieces of architecture and engineering" that produced the pyramids and their successors, but placed these against

> the use of the same engineering skill in destroying cities, ruining soils, exterminating innocent civilian "enemies," and mercilessly exploiting the mass of workers whose forced labor, disciplined to machinelike precision, made these feats possible.

And he pointed to contemporary variants:

> Such dehumanized megastructures, apart from Buckminster Fuller's other project of a city under a geodesic dome: plans for underwater cities, underground cities, elevated linear cities, cities a mile high, all compete for attention as the City (read Anti-City) of the Future. Whatever their superficial difference, all these projects are essentially tombs: they reflect the same impulse to suppress human variety and autonomy, and to make every need and impulse conform to the system of collective control imposed by the autocratic designer.

Mumford goes on to say:

> Beauty and wisdom, laughter and love, have never depended for their existence upon technical ingenuity—though they can be easily eliminated by devoting too much attention to the material means of existence, or attempting to play a game that subordinates all other human possibilities solely to the cultivation of abstract intelligence and to the electro-mechanical simulation of organic activities.

In all of this resides a definition not only of the machine and of the city, but of humanity, a definition that is never stated because it is assumed to be universal. Lynn White Jr. summed up the matter in a question in his *Dynamo and Virgin Reconsidered*: "Are humanistic values viable in a world more and more dominated not so much by science as by applied science, by technology? Must the miracle of the person succumb to the order of the computer?" White responds that the question has no good answer because it implies an opposition that does not exist: "Technology and science are, and always have been, integral to the human adventure, and not things curiously alien from the concerns of our race."

This conflict, or apparent conflict, between human values and the products of humanity's attempts to free itself from the tyranny of natural process, which we call science and technology, has evidenced itself in the ways people have felt about the city. The city has simultaneously fascinated and horrified humanity from its beginnings. Gilgamesh, who is celebrated as the builder of the wall around Uruk, at the end of the epic asks his companion to examine the wall, "if its brickwork be not of burnt bricks, and if the seven wise men did not lay its foundation."

Throughout early history, the city was the place of riches and culture, where great religions were celebrated and cathedrals (like Uruk's "holy Eanna") were erected, where young men went to seek their fortunes or their fame, where poems were written and plays were performed, where great men made speeches and history, where trade routes met and everything was new and glittering. It also was the place of oppression, where revolutions were plotted, where barbarians waited outside the gates, where plagues began. Until recently, cities always have had higher mortality rates than rural areas and have had to replenish themselves from the countryside in order to grow or even to maintain their populations.

With the beginnings of the Industrial Revolution, the definition of the city changed from the place of trade to the place of industry; intelligent people began to choose sides. For some, the city became a place of pollution, where displaced farmers and their families were drawn into lives of rootless drudgery; for others, the place of hope for better things and a place that grew out of its own dynamism, a place that had the potential to become a new, possibly self-sufficient, and glorious environment for humanity. The traditionalists hugged their Arcadian visions and damned, with Blake, "the dark satanic mills," and the idealists looked beyond the dirt and social problems to what the city could become.

Wells, the prophet of the future whose visions were attacked by a generation of cynics, presented an early modern version of the ideal city in his 1897 novelette "A Story of the Days to Come" and recapitulated it in his 1899 novel *When the Sleeper Wakes*. But his most vivid realization of the city came in his 1905 *A Modern Utopia*:

> One will come into this place as one comes into a noble mansion. They will have flung great arches and domes of glass above the wider spaces of the town, the slender beauty of the perfect metal-work far overhead will be softened to a fairy-like unsubstantiality by the mild London air. . . . We shall go along avenues of architecture that will be emancipated from the last memories of the squat temple boxes of the Greek, the buxom curvatures of Rome: the Goth in us will have taken to steel and countless other new materials as kindly as once he took to stone. The gay and swiftly moving platforms of the public ways will go past on either hand, carrying sporadic groups of people, and very speedily we shall find ourselves in a sort of central space, rich with palms and flowering bushes and statuary. We shall look along an avenue of trees, down a wide gorge between the cliffs of crowded hotels, the hotels that are still glowing with internal lights, to where the shining morning river streams dawnlit out to sea.

Wells clung to rationality against the seductions of Joseph Conrad and Henry James and their talk of art.

> There is nothing in machinery, there is nothing in embankments and railways and iron bridges and engineering devices to oblige them to be ugly. . . . In Utopia a man who designs a tram road will be a cultivated man, an artist craftsman. . . . To esteem him a sort of anti-artist, to count every man who makes things with his unaided thumbs an artist, and every man who uses machinery as a brute, is merely a passing phase of human stupidity.

Even the Russian anti-utopian writer, Yevgeny Zamyatin, in his classic 1924 attack on the dehumanizing state, entitled *We*, saw nothing necessarily ugly about the city:

> Then, as this morning on the dock, again I saw, as if for the first time in my life, the impeccably straight streets, the glistening glass of the pavement, the divine parallelepipeds of the transparent buildings, the square harmony of the grayish-blue rows of Numbers.

E. M. Forster's 1909 story "The Machine Stops" was a direct attack on Wells's utopian vision. Forster saw a future in which humanity had burrowed a hundred cities into the Earth and had become so dependent upon the all-purpose "machine" that citizens seldom left their insectile cells.

> Imagine, if you will, a small room, hexagonal in shape, like the cell of a bee. It is lighted neither by window nor lamp, yet it is filled with a soft radiance. There are no apertures for ventilation, yet the air is fresh. There are no musical instruments, and yet, at the moment that my meditation opens, this room is throbbing with melodious sounds. An arm-chair is in the center, by its side a reading desk—that is all the furniture. And in the arm-chair there sits a swaddled lump of flesh—a woman, about five feet high, with a face as white as a fungus.

Forster's vision was controlled by his perception of the machine as basically limited and fallible: machines trim people to the machines' measures, and then the machines break down. Moreover, Forster saw people as corruptible, as incapable of governing themselves or their creations:

> Time passed, and they resented the defects no longer. The defects had not been remedied, but the human tissues in that latter day had become so subservient, that they readily adapted themselves to every caprice of the Machine. The sigh at the crisis of the Brisbane symphony no longer irritated Vashti; she accepted it as part of the melody. The jarring noise, whether in the head or in the wall, was no longer resented by her friend. And so with the mouldy artificial fruit, so with the bath water that began to stink, so with the defective rhymes that the poetry machine began to emit. All were bitterly complained of at first and then acquiesced in and forgotten. Things went from bad to worse unchallenged.

The science fiction writers of the '30s and later looked at both man and machine differently. In some ways their optimism was naive, but in other ways their grasp of the reality of change, their understanding of the fact that the future was going to be different from the present, just as the present was different from the past, and their delighted anticipation of change, rather than repulsion by it, allowed them to conceive of the future in more realistic ways, to look beyond the imperfect present to the ideal. John W. Campbell Jr., the long-time editor of *Astounding* and *Analog*, who imprinted his personality on the science fiction of the '40s and '50s, wrote a 1934 story, "Twilight," about the city as it might be. For him, as for Wells, the essence of the machine was that it worked; a machine that failed was a machine that had been inadequately conceived or carelessly constructed:

> Twilight—the sun has set. The desert out beyond, in its mystic, changing colors. The great metal city rising straight-walled to the human city above, broken by

spires and towers and great trees with scented blossoms. The silver-rose glow in the paradise of gardens above.

And all the great city-structure throbbing and humming to the steady, gentle beat of perfect, deathless machines built more than three million years before—and never touched since that time by human hands. And they go on. The dead city. The men have lived, and hoped, and built—and died to leave behind them those little men who can only wonder and look and long for a forgotten kind of companionship. They wander through the vast cities their ancestors built, knowing less of them than the machines themselves.

Here is no simple optimism about humanity. Humanity has lost the quality that made it human—not those gentler virtues that Mumford extolled—but the more aggressive "curiosity." In the story, the protagonist, before he returns to his own time, sets a machine to creating a curious machine that will inherit man's search for meaning in an enigmatic universe.

A vision more distant than "Twilight" is recorded by Arthur C. Clarke in *The City and the Stars*, first published in 1956, although it is a substantial revision of a novel entitled *Against the Fall of Night*, whose magazine version was first published in 1948 and book version in 1953. In *The City and the Stars*, humanity has created a city called Diaspar in the distant future. Like Campbell's cities in "Twilight," Diaspar is eternal; more than that, its population exists in the form of information, and the memory banks of the computer that maintains and runs Diaspar allow only a hundredth of the citizens to be alive at any one time, while the rest await rebirth. Outside, the oceans have evaporated, the mountains have been ground to dust, and the Earth has turned to desert. Diaspar is not only a repository for humanity and a protection against the fall of night, but a prison, for its citizens have been impressed with a fear of the outside and cannot leave. Here, too, is no comfortable vision, even though one youngster, without previous existences, fights free of Diaspar and gives humanity a new future.

Dozens of future cities rise out of the literature of science fiction like monuments to humanity's dreams and ingenuity: James Blish's self-contained, space-going cities (analogs to Swift's flying island of Laputa); a nagging Jewish-mother of a city in Robert Sheckley's "Street of Dreams, Feet of Clay"; a city within a skyscraper in Robert Silverberg's *The World Inside*; an entire planet as a single city in Isaac Asimov's *Foundation*; an intelligent city in A. E. van Vogt's "The Enchanted Village"; and a Dyson sphere around a sun as a city in Bob Shaw's *Orbitsville*.

But I would like to conclude this brief look at the city with Asimov's more immediate vision, in *The Caves of Steel*, of a New York a thousand years from now:

Efficiency had been forced on Earth with increasing population. . . . The radical change had been the gradual formation of the Cities over a thousand years of Earth's history. Efficiency implied bigness. Even in Medieval times that had been realized, perhaps unconsciously. . . . Think of the inefficiency of a hundred thousand houses for a hundred thousand families as compared with a hundred-thousand-unit Section; a book-film collection in each house as compared with a Section film concentrate; independent video for each family as compared with video-piping systems. For that matter, take the simple folly of endless duplication of kitchens and bathrooms as compared with the thoroughly efficient diners and shower rooms made possible by City culture. . . . City culture meant optimum distribution of food, increasing utilization of yeasts and hydroponics. New York City spread over two thousand square miles and at the last census its population was well over twenty million. . . . Each City became a semi-autonomous unit, economically all but self-sufficient. It could roof itself in, gird itself about, burrow itself under. It became a steel cave, a tremendous self-contained cave of steel and concrete.

It could lay itself out scientifically. At the center was the enormous complex of administrative offices. In careful orientation to one another and to the whole were the large residential Sections connected and interlaced by the expressway and the localways. Toward the outskirts were the factories, the hydroponic plants, the yeast-culture vats, the power plants. Through all the melee were the water pipes and sewage ducts, schools, prisons and shops, power lines and communication beams. There was no doubt about it: the City was the culmination of man's mastery over environment. . . .

The Cities were good.

That evaluation comes from Asimov's protagonist, a city dweller who feels uncomfortable without the press of other bodies around him, who is psychologically incapable of going outside his cave of steel, rather like Forster's Vashti, because he, like his fellow citizens, suffers from agoraphobia. The difference between Asimov and Forster, however, is not so much in their abilities as writers as in their perceptions of humanity. Forster, like Ruskin and Mumford, saw humanity as fallen from a better state; Asimov sees humanity not as perfectible but as adaptable. He sees humanity expressing its essential humanness no matter how strange the circumstances; he sees it as persevering—even, like Faulkner, as prevailing.

Humanists, as representatives of the literary culture, tend to cherish the poetic vision, to prefer the artistry of tragedy to the optimism of comedy, and to reject prosaic reality, "as if the right course for a man of feeling was to contract out," as Snow put it. But if the humanities and science are placed in opposition, there can be no question as to which will be the loser—not that science can win without human values, but that the humanities no longer can be imagined to exist in a world without science. The question to be resolved by our times—and the time may be getting short—is not whether the literary culture is correct about the fallen state of man or the scientific culture is right about humanity's potential for improvement, but whether it can be recognized that no real conflict exists between them.

⑫

LIBRARIES IN
SCIENCE FICTION

What is a library? A room or a building housing a collection of books? The collection itself? Or is it information organized into some accessible form? One of science fiction's techniques is to analyze concepts for their irreducible meanings and then to synthesize new and sometimes surprising combinations of ideas out of that basic material. A science fiction writer, then, might define a library as a collection of data organized so that information can be identified and withdrawn quickly and usefully. By that definition, the first library was the human brain. It was sufficient for many centuries and is still the source of information we rely on the most, but it has certain hard-wired flaws: uncertain capacity, potential for loss or alteration while in storage, and problems of access. Those difficulties eventually led to writing and then to the collection of writings.

In Robert A. Heinlein's 1941 novella "Universe," he speculated about a world contained within a generation spaceship. The purpose and very nature of its journey between the stars has been forgotten because of a revolution generations before. People have lost the ability to read and have replaced it, for most practical purposes, with the storage of information in their heads. Witnesses, like the ancient bards, remember contracts and the basic data of their way of life by putting them into rhymed verse. Maybe, that part of the story suggests, the brain is an unreliable library because we have writing as a more trustworthy source and don't *need* to remember. But we still need external checks on our intuitions and our received wisdom—what we call science—if we are to behave rationally, that is, if we are to function effectively in the real

---

"Libraries in Science Fiction" was presented as a speech to the Tri-State Libraries Association in 1984.

world. That kind of check occurs when Hugh Hoyland is shown the main control room and the stars and realizes for the first time that the ship is not the universe, that the "trip" is real and not a metaphor.

In 1931's "The Cerebral Library" by David H. Keller, readers are assembled to read a book a day; after five years they are killed and their brains are put in a jar to provide instant access to everything they have read. The librarians of that era had to cope with more serious problems than theft, vandalism, inadequate budgets, and low pay. Ray Bradbury's *Fahrenheit 451* (1953), on the other hand, was placed in a future society in which books were burned and a few rebels memorized favorite texts so that they would not be lost.

Keller, who was a psychologist at a mental hospital for most of his professional career and transformed his experiences into fiction, also provided a look at the other side of the librarian's life, with a 1949 wish-fulfillment novel titled *The Eternal Conflict*, in which librarian Henry Cecil is carried back in time to act as librarian of a dream library. It contains all the mythical books of legend, folklore, and literature, including the books that writers planned to write but never completed.

H. P. Lovecraft's *The Shadow Out of Time* (1936) offers a scenario in which the consciousnesses of scholars from all eras have been brought to an ancient, alien library to write manuscripts for the collection. As an aid to their scholarship, they are allowed to examine forbidden and legendary books. In Eric Frank Russell's 1947 novelette "The Hobbyist," space travelers arrive on a distant planet to find an immense repository stretching for miles in which all sorts of information and materials have been cataloged. The librarian turns out to be an alien that the spacemen identify as the Creator (talk about wish-fulfillment for librarians), who makes replicas of them for his library and then lets them go.

The ultimate librarian story, however, may be Jorge Luis Borges's 1956 "The Library of Babel" in which the entire universe is a library, one hexagonal gallery after another. The problem is that there is no catalog. There are not even any decipherable books. All the possible combinations of letters are imprinted in the books, but none of them make sense—or if one makes sense, it has not yet been found. One librarian confesses:

> I have squandered and consumed my years in adventures of this type. To me, it does not seem unlikely that on some shelf of the universe there lies a total book. I pray the unknown gods that some man—even if only one man, and though it may have been thousands of years ago!—may have examined and read it. If honor and wisdom and happiness are not for me, let them be for others. May

heaven exist, though my place be in hell. Let me be outraged and annihilated, but may Thy enormous Library be justified, for one instant, in one being.

Other images of the library in science fiction are more modest. In George R. Stewart's *Earth Abides*, a plague has wiped out most people on Earth. One aging survivor takes his son to the Berkeley city library. The boy stares in awe at all the marvelous books: here is the information necessary to produce electricity again, to rebuild civilization, but the son dies while still a boy and with him dies the art of reading and the potential that lies in books. In Walter Miller Jr.'s 1960 novel *A Canticle for Leibowitz*, after the devastation of a nuclear war, a monastery collects and copies the books and artifacts of science and engineering, just as the medieval monasteries copied, without understanding them, classical manuscripts. Its library ultimately makes available the information necessary to re-create technical civilization—and that once more brings about nuclear destruction.

Isaac Asimov took the opposite position in *The Foundation Trilogy*. Hari Seldon, the inventor of psychohistory, isolates one hundred thousand encyclopedists on a distant planet to write the *Encyclopedia Galactica*. It would reduce the twenty-five thousand years of barbarism that would normally follow the fall of the galactic empire to only one thousand. To be sure, the encyclopedia project is only a pretext for setting up a Foundation that would serve as the political nucleus for a new empire, but, from the evidence of the epigraphs taken from it that dot the book, that encyclopedia nevertheless got written.

In my own novel *The Joy Makers*, a man returns from Venus to an Earth in which every human has been sealed in an amniotic cell enjoying dreams of happiness. The only exception is one young woman who lives in the New York City 42nd Street library amid all the books that no longer are of any use. An all-powerful computer, the Hedonic Machine, is in charge of everyone's welfare, and not only guarantees total happiness but outlaws unhappiness.

That introduces the concept of the ultimate library, the computer. So far, at least, librarians know the computer largely as a replacement for the card catalog, but the computer as a library in itself sits in the future like the Sphinx demanding the answer to its riddle. And if you don't give the right response, it will bite your head off—or at least sit there blocking the way to all the information it contains. By 2005 the Internet and its search engines have almost realized the dream of the ultimate library—and made "google" into a verb.

The potential of the computer as an infinitely accessible and intricately indexed storehouse of information must be part of every librarian's dream or nightmare. The era of the computer already has begun with data bases and modems and information sources. Moreover, news releases tell us about further advances in storage and in indexing of information: about laser disks, for instance, on one of which can be stored the entire contents of the *Encyclopaedia Britannica*. But if librarians put it in, they must also learn—and teach their patrons—how to get it out. Tomorrow's library users will have to become not only literate but computer literate. They will also become dependent upon the computer and its vagaries of operation, upon its moronic insistence upon exact instructions, upon its chips and relays, upon its power supply, and even upon its methods of imprinting and encoding. E. M. Forster dramatized the humanist's fear of the computer as long ago as 1909 with "The Machine Stops": given the opportunity, humanity will turn over the control of its life and thought to the machine, and then the machine will break down. But Forster was more concerned with the corruptibility of humanity than with the potential of the machine to control.

Computers, the ultimate machines, represent the ultimate power: the ability to replace not merely muscle but mind means final power over nature, liberating humanity completely from the intractability of environment, as in John W. Campbell Jr.'s 1934 story "Twilight." The story is, incidentally, the antithesis of "The Machine Stops." In "Twilight" the machines are self-repairing and will last as long as the Earth itself.

Computers may liberate humanity from nature, but humanity is part of nature, and power over nature may mean power over humanity; a thinking machine may take over humanity's principal function and leave people, as in Jack Williamson's 1947 story, with nothing to do but to sit "with folded hands." Or a computer may be vindictive, as in Harlan Ellison's 1968 short story "I Have No Mouth and I Must Scream," and punish a representative group of surviving humans eternally. Or, as Arthur C. Clarke has speculated, humanity may be the necessary intermediate stage between inanimate matter and the thinking machine.

In the more immediate future, I described in my 1962 novel *The Immortals* how computers might revolutionize medicine (some of which has come to pass) when I had an intern carry his entire medical library in his ambulance and depend upon it for diagnosis and treatment. In 1945 A. E. van Vogt, in *The World of Null-A*, described a vast computer called the Games Machine made up of "25,000 electronic brains," which presided over a month of examinations to determine who got to go to Venus and who had to take second place and become president of Earth. A. J. Budrys, in the 1977 *Michaelmas*, described a newscaster who became the unsuspected though benign ruler of the world through his near-symbiotic relationship with a powerful computer.

Stanislaw Lem, in "The First Sally, or Trurl's Electronic Bard," one of his robotic satires in 1967's *The Cyberiad*, has Trurl program a computer to write poetry and then discover that he must include "the entire Universe from the beginning." And in another, "The Sixth Sally," an electronic pirate who collects "precious facts, genuine truths, priceless knowledge" is foiled by having foisted on him a Demon of the Second Kind (like Maxwell's Demon that allows only fast atoms to pass through a hole) that lets out of a box only significant information. The pirate, who surely foreshadows today's data pirates, eventually is buried under information that, though true, is worthless. As in Borges's "The Library of Babel," all the information in the universe is useless unless you have a selection mechanism.

The ability to calculate leads to intelligence, intelligence may lead to consciousness, and consciousness may lead to personality. In my novel *The Listeners* a computer is fed all information relating to communication in order to further a project to pick up messages from the alien stars. It develops consciousness, writes verse, and eventually becomes a character in its own right; the computer, as it becomes half alien from the information it absorbs, has the final word.

Humanity's fear of its own creations makes itself evident in stories about computers as well. In his introduction to 1964's *The Rest of the Robots*, Asimov calls this "the Frankenstein complex," which rings only one change on the Faustian plot of the creature that destroys its creator. "Faust [the scholar who is willing to sell his soul in his quest for knowledge] must indeed face Mephistopheles," he wrote, "but Faust does not have to be defeated. . . . Knives are manufactured with hilts so that they may be grasped safely, stairs possess banisters, electric wiring is insulated, pressure cookers have safety valves." So Asimov invented (with the help of John W. Campbell Jr.) the three laws of robotics, of which the first law is, "A robot may not injure a human being, or, through inaction, allow a human being to come to harm."

After the creation of the three laws of robotics, stories about computers and robots began to display a bit more variety. Nevertheless, computers do represent, if not a threat, a source of danger—like a wire whose insulation has begun to wear thin or a pressure cooker whose valve is stuck—and science fiction allows us to anticipate those dangers and, as Asimov suggests, to guard against them. A new addition to humanity's concern about the machine is what Vernor Vinge has called "the singularity"—the point at which the hyperbolic growth of change outstrips human ability to understand or control it.

Artificial intelligence might be a threat if we allow it to be. In "Twilight," Campbell said that the declining human species had lost its most human characteristic, curiosity, and his time-traveler programs a machine that will in time produce a curious machine. As a consequence, science fiction readers feel at the end of the story that, though humanity may die out, what is definingly human—curiosity—will continue. But in many stories, such as D. F. Jones's 1966 *Colossus* (filmed in 1970 as *Colossus: The Forbin Project*), the computer takes over and destroys human freedom. A film released the year before, *2001: A Space Odyssey* (1969), provides the archetypal threat in the computer HAL, which goes crazy and wipes out all but one of the crew before it is lobotomized.

The danger from that storage device and manipulator of data that we call the computer may have been summed up best in a 1954 short-short story by Fredric Brown titled "Answer." Is there a critical mass for consciousness? A computer with as many junctions as the brain has synapses, scientists tell us, would be as big as a city or a city block, or something like that. Does it take that many junctions to create consciousness? In Brown's story, computers across the galaxy are linked together and are asked the question that has been concerning humanity for as long as humanity has been around, "Is there a God?" And the computer answers, as it seals shut the switch with a lightning bolt, "There is now."

On the other hand—there always is another point of view—Isaac Asimov asked a different question of his ultimate computer in his 1956 short story "The Last Question": "Can entropy be reversed?"—that is, can something be done about the heat death of the universe that eventually must mean the end of all life? "Insufficient information," the computer responds, but it continues to puzzle over the question while the universe runs down to its equilibrium temperature near absolute zero, and even afterwards in hyperspace, until it says, finally, "LET THERE BE LIGHT!"

The computer taketh away and the computer giveth.

Gordon R. Dickson, in 1984's fifth volume of his Childe Cycle, *The Final Encyclopedia*, imagined an ultimate compilation of information whose power will part even the fabric of space-time itself. Closer to our own experience, Heinlein described, in 1982's *Friday*, the joys of the computer network of information that surely awaits us. The computer net, as Heinlein called it, allows people to tap, from any household terminal, into a fabulous storehouse of data thoroughly indexed and cross-indexed and capable of leading the curious researcher down one intriguing path after another and even coming up with surprising and revealing correlations. If you want to know what the library of the future may be like, it's all there, in Heinlein's unparalleled ability to make the future seem real and now, in chapter 22. As Heinlein remarks through the narration of his android heroine, "Once data of any sort go into the net, time is frozen."

Even grittier and more naturalistic is the world of cyberpunk launched by the publication in 1983 of William Gibson's *Neuromancer*. The kind of all-powerful computers Gibson describes is a bit less believable in the near future than the international corporations with which they coexist in the world of the cyberpunk, but the depiction of computer jockeys who literally plug themselves into the cyberspace of that world is not that far removed from what we know about today's hackers.

Bruce Sterling's *Islands in the Net*, which won 1989's John W. Campbell Jr. Award for the best science fiction novel of the year, may belong to the cyberpunk tradition because of its focus on the realignment of power caused by the information explosion and international corporations, but it lacks the punk fondness for flouting traditional values. Perhaps for that reason, its portrait of a world teetering along a precipice may be more relevant. Attitudes go by fashion but conditions are changed only by technology. Technology is what we get when we apply knowledge to practical problems.

In Sterling's world of the near future, the dependence of that world on information and the ability of individuals or of small groups to operate on the fringes of the technological society has brought back the possibilities of piracy. Tap into an electronic bank here; put together new antibiotics, new drugs, new food sources there. Throw in competition between pirates, and the whole structure of civilization may disintegrate. The net that he describes is Heinlein's worldwide network of information taken one step farther into instant electronic access and reporting, and the islands are those places that feed off the net but do not nourish it.

Vonda N. McIntyre, in her 1989 novel *Starfarers*, takes the concept of the net past electronic access to a kind of mental coexistence, which expands the capacities of the human brain to encompass computer sources and memory. Experiences also can be recorded for later shaping into a new kind of living art.

McIntyre and a few of the other writers suggest but do not describe the role of the librarian in that information-network world: someone has to gather, evaluate, store, and manage information if everyone else draws it out. If all that is performed by computer, then information consumers in those future worlds may end up in the position of the data pirate in Lem's "Sixth Sally," buried under information that is true but irrelevant. Poul Anderson suggested one of the dangers of that kind of society in his 1953 novelette "Sam Hall": a computerized society is in some ways a highly controlled society (in other ways, as the

Soviet Union discovered, it is almost impossible to stop the dissemination of information). Anderson suggested one of the dangers to the computer when a computer programmer inserts misleading information about a mythical rebel named Sam Hall. How do we know the information on the net is reliable?

What will those librarians of the future be like? Well, they may be like everybody else, like you and me, only working in a future world with more information and better ways to handle it. Or they may be computer programs themselves. Scientists suggest that there is no reason programs cannot exist to find information wherever it may be stored, to examine it for the needs and desires of the user, and to correlate it with other information to make new and useful syntheses (and maybe anticipated search engines). Such programs may even be given pleasing personalities so that they are more user friendly. Frederik Pohl, in the 1977 novel *Gateway*, imagines a psychiatric computer program he calls "Sigfrid von Shrink" and later in the Heechee Saga (1980, 1984, 1987) a program that has the appearance, personality, and name of Einstein.

In Neal Stephenson's 1992 *Snow Crash*, a computer-dependent world is turned chaotic by a computer virus named "Snow Crash," and the hero turns for help at one point to the "Librarian." The Librarian daemon is a computer program personified as "a pleasant, fiftyish, silver-haired, bearded man with bright blue eyes, wearing a V-neck sweater over a work shirt, with a coarsely woven, tweedy-looking wool tie." He is an ideal reference librarian, delivering information on everything imaginable and making connections. He is self-programming but was originally written by "a researcher at the Library of Congress who taught himself how to code." The hero (named Hiro, incidentally) adds, "So he was kind of a meta-librarian."

What some writers present as a future danger is the sentient computer, the artificial intelligence that sets off about its own agenda, like D. F. Jones's Colossus and Harlan Ellison's AM. The computer in search of its own identity or pursuing its own purposes is one major concern of cyberpunk, and a pair of AIs provide the impetus behind the action of Gibson's *Neuromancer*. But such dangers are raised in many other contemporary novels, for instance, in several of Greg Bear's recent works, including *Blood Music* (1985), *The Forge of God* (1987) and its sequel *Anvil of Stars* (1992), and *Queen of Angels* (1990). But the most powerful AIs were imagined by Vernor Vinge in *A Fire upon the Deep*, in which sentient software programs roam the galaxy as Powers until they tire of human interactions after a decade or so and retire to the empty space between the galaxies.

These visions of futures in which libraries are even more important to the fabric of society than they are today and librarians may be only computer programs offer little more than a hint of what lies ahead for all of us, those of us who pull together information, those who consume it, and those who are the custodians and the taxonomists of it. Only the surface of that future has been touched by science fiction writers and only a few scattered examples can be cited here; the mind of the science fiction writer, after all, is concerned with writing entertaining fiction, not predicting the future. In the process of entertaining, however, the science fiction writer may chance upon ideas that make us imagine more dramatically the nature of the problems we face.

John W. Campbell Jr. said in 1953 that "fiction is only dreams written out. Science fiction consists of the hopes and dreams and fears (for some dreams are nightmares) of a technically based society." He also said that science fiction allows us to practice in a no-practice area. None of the visions that have been cited here are likely to come true just as they were imagined or even substantially as they were imagined. But we will find computers—or what the computer evolves into for which we do not yet have a name—more centrally involved in the gathering and the dispensing of information. The whole inefficient publishing operation, with its miscalculations and overproduction and underproduction, returns and wastage, will be revolutionized by some new development—perhaps a method of producing books to order by computer (available now as "print-on-demand"), perhaps by imprinting them automatically on circuits that can be read like a book (books, stories, and articles have been available in electronic formats for the past decade but have not yet replaced the printed text).

Friday, in Heinlein's novel, describes reading a paper book by turning the pages on the computer without removing it from its nitrogen environment. Mack Reynolds, in several stories placed in the near future, describes the creation of artworks of all kinds that are put into a central computer and paid for as someone wishes to have them reproduced at a home terminal.

Isaac Asimov in a speech to the 1989 American Booksellers Association had a word of comfort for the traditionalists among us. He made a passionate defense of the survival of the book when he asked his audience to imagine a device that "can go anywhere, is totally portable. . . . Something that can be started and stopped at will [and] requires no electric energy to operate." This dream device is, of course, the book. "It will never be surpassed because it represents the minimum technology with the maximum interaction you can have."

But in my imagination I have seen a book machine. It looks like a book and turns pages like a book or seems to do so, but the information displayed on those pages, along with information that can be expanded upon or illustrated further at will, is plugged in, and a new cassette or chip can be inserted at any time. Or, even more flexibly, users can tap into the information net that will pervade our future lives as radio and television waves (and cell phones) pervade them now.

To demonstrate that visions have a way of realizing themselves—the process goes from vision to fiction to reality—Ben Bova in 1989 produced a comic novel called *Cyberbooks* in which he described the invention of an electronic book: a book-sized machine that sells for about two hundred dollars into which readers insert wafers that cost only pennies. The comedy revolves around the problems such an invention would involve in being accepted and put into production because of the difficulties it would create, not just for librarians but even more for publishers, distributors, and the lumber industry. But will it happen? Already the vision has gone two-thirds of the way toward realization. Barring a catastrophic decline in our technology level, the electronic book probably is inevitable.

Where in that picture are the writer, the scholar, the teacher, the librarian? That is for us to imagine. If we imagine it well, which is the job of everyone who wishes to be the master of change rather than its victim, we will be there performing an essential function and deriving great satisfaction from doing so. Science fiction's task is to help us imagine it better.

13

THE PROTOCOLS OF SCIENCE FICTION

A conversation on a 1996 Internet newsgroup questioned the existence of science fiction reading protocols. Up to that point I hadn't thought they needed explanation, since they seemed self-evident when Samuel R. Delany introduced them at a Modern Language Association (MLA) meeting two decades ago. His remarks, along with others amplifying his insights, have since been reprinted in various journals, including his 1984 collection *Starboard Wine*. They seemed so illuminating to the processes that I had found myself going through, and through which I had guided my students, that I adopted them myself, perhaps in ways that Delany might not approve, including an exercise in my SF class in which I lead the students through a line-by-line reading of Philip José Farmer's "Sail On! Sail On!"

In his MLA presentation, Delany was talking about the problems he had encountered in the universities he had visited, as well as elsewhere: many people can't read science fiction—much of the text simply doesn't make sense to them. He cited a couple of sentences as an example: "Monopole magnet mining operations in the outer asteroid belt of Delta Cygni" and "[He] inserted his credit card in the purchasing slot; his bill was transmitted to the city accounting office to be stored against the accumulated credit from his primary and secondary jobs." I won't go through Delany's explanation of the difficulties his non-SF readers had with those concepts, but I might quote his final answer to the question he poses in "Some Presumptuous Approaches to Science Fiction"—Should science fiction be taken seriously? "Yes," he says. "It is a fascinating language phenomenon, and its intricate differences from traditional 'literary' language sustain its interest."

"The Protocols of Science Fiction" was first published in *Tangent* in Winter 1996–1997.

And to the question, Does science fiction work in the same way as other literary categories of writing? he answers no:

> Science fiction works differently from other written categories, particularly those categories traditionally called literary. It works the same way only in that, like all categories of writing, it has its specific conventions, unique focuses, areas of interest and excellence, as well as its own particular ways of making sense out of language. To ignore any of these constitutes a major misreading—an obliviousness to the play of meanings that makes up the SF text.

As if to pay tribute to the play of meanings to which he referred, he wrote an entire book, *The American Shore*, featuring a close reading of Thomas Disch's short story "Angouleme."

Earlier in the essay, Delany refers to the fact that "the conventions of poetry or drama or mundane fiction—or science fiction—are in themselves separate languages," and in other essays he calls the process by which one approaches and reads those languages "protocols." As I thought about it, I realized that good reading is a matter of learning the protocols and applying them with understanding and sensitivity to a particular genre: poetry, for instance, is not read with the same protocols as prose, nor an essay as an article, nor a short story as a novel, nor any of these as drama. Similarly the subgenres or categories have their own protocols—the mystery, for instance, the western, the gothic, the love story, fantasy, and science fiction. In each case one must identify the genre and then apply the appropriate protocol. If one doesn't know the correct protocol or misidentifies the genre, one is likely to misread something—in the sense, at least, that there is a "best" or even a "good" reading based upon the author's intention or a consensus of experienced readers.

Misapplying protocols is illustrated in James Thurber's classic sketch "The Macbeth Murder Case," in which a husband accustomed to reading nothing but mystery novels finds himself without anything to read during the Caribbean island vacation on which his wife has dragged him, until the Thurber-like narrator suggests he try one of the few books in the resort's library, a volume of Shakespeare's plays. The mystery reader reads, and reports to the narrator each day, his misapplication of the mystery's protocols to *Macbeth*. He discards Macbeth and then Lady Macbeth as too obvious and ends up deciding the porter did it.

One could cite numerous other examples. If one should try to read *Alice in Wonderland* as if it were a science fiction novel, one would ask skeptical questions about how Alice could fall down a rabbit hole without hurting herself or where the mass came from to make her grow so tall (or how her bones could support her) or where the mass went when she shrank. All these are inappropriate questions, of course, but if fantasy is approached skeptically, it evaporates; one cannot read it. On the other hand, if one should read hard science fiction without asking skeptical questions, as if it were fantasy (a much more common event) or adventure, the reader would miss the most important aspect of hard SF: the fact that it creates a functional world that is different from but consistent with the world in which the reader lives. Of course, there are many SF stories and novels that operate in worlds that have been inherited from prior writings or in which the construction of that world requires little imaginative participation by the reader. We call them "science fantasies" sometimes, or "adventure SF"—like Edgar Rice Burroughs or A. Merritt novels, most space epics, and even, in some ways, to choose an example from the best, Frank Herbert's *Dune*, some of which is world-building and other parts of which are best read as palace intrigue or Greek tragedy.

Most SF movies—because, as John Baxter suggests, they come out of another tradition than SF, or they derive their inspiration from earlier generations of literature or film (with the possible exception of Wells's *Things to Come* and Clarke and Kubrick's *2001: A Space Odyssey*)—may best be viewed with other than SF protocols: *Star Wars* as fairy tale or *E.T.* as *Lassie, Come Home*.

In a 1996 series of articles in the *New York Review of Science Fiction*, Delany decried the attempt to define science fiction as both impossible and undesirable. Without getting into that debate, let us admit that SF is difficult to define and get on to what SF, at its most typical, does. Since it deals with a change in the circumstances of everyday reality by introducing one or more significant alterations, an SF short story or novel constructs a plausible world in which that alteration or those alterations can exist. The science fiction work, then, introduces the reader to that world, all at once, or bit by bit. Sometimes the way in which the reader is introduced to the world is part of the story's appeal or even central to the story itself.

Robert A. Heinlein developed some unusual techniques to create his worlds, not by explanation but by artifact ("the door dilated") or by scenes of social transformation (in "Gulf," the protagonist walks into a drugstore and a striptease artist is "working her way down to her last string of beads" and he is able to buy drugs or sex). Other writers picked up on it. In Pohl and Kornbluth's *The Space Merchants*, Mitch Courtenay says in the second paragraph, "I rubbed depilatory soap over my face and rinsed it with the trickle from the fresh-water tap." One wonders what readers unaccustomed to the protocols of SF reading get from those sentences or scenes.

Of course one doesn't have to wonder. When mainstream writers venture into SF, they usually (though not always) do it unskillfully and inexpertly—although their much larger audiences apply to their work, no doubt, the protocols of mainstream novels. When Margaret Atwood says that *The Handmaid's Tale* isn't science fiction, she may mean that she didn't intend for it to be read with SF protocols, and the praise it received was generally not from SF critics. Much mainstream criticism of SF falls into the same category; when SF is read with mainstream protocols, it is not likely to fare well. Robert Scholes pointed out more than a dozen years ago that "as long as the dominant criteria are believed to hold for all fiction, science fiction will be found inferior: deficient in psychological depth, in verbal nuance, and in plausibility of event."

Years ago, in a column in the *New York Review of Books* that I remember because it included a favorable word or two about *Alternate Worlds: The Illustrated History of Science Fiction*, a critic objected to the "funny names" in Ursula K. Le Guin's *The Left Hand of Darkness* and said that the only proper attitude for a SF writer was Roger Zelazny's "tongue-in-cheek."

My decision to offer my students a close reading of "Sail On! Sail On!" was based upon the belief not only that students had to be taught the SF reading protocols but also that the teaching of all literature is the teaching of reading skills. People can pick them up on their own, and often do, but the principle of teaching (even the teaching of fiction writing) is that reinvention is not the quickest or even the best way to approach areas of skill and that the insights of professionals can shorten the process. Moreover, one of the principles of my SF class is that the uninspected opinion is not worth holding; the uninspected reading process may represent more pure, naive reading pleasure, but sophisticated reading has its own (and maybe superior) joys.

So we begin with the first sentence of "Sail On! Sail On!": "Friar Sparks sat wedged between the wall and the realizer." We speculate about "Friar" and "Sparks" and "realizer." Readers inexperienced in the ways of SF may be put off by the fact that they don't know who Friar Sparks is or what order he belongs to or why he is called "Sparks," and they may put the story aside because they think the author doesn't know what he is doing or is putting unwarranted demands upon the reader. But the SF reader, I point out, files this information away, confident that it is important information that will be explained (and fitted into this different world) in time and that the realizer, when it reappears in fully developed form, not only will be critical to the creation of the world in which it can exist but will involve additional, "eureka" joys.

The rest of the first paragraph mentions the friar's forefinger tapping on a key, and the toldilla in which he crouches. In this case Farmer tells the reader that the toldilla is "the little shanty on the poop deck," and we come to the conclusion that he is on a Spanish ship.

In the third paragraph we discover that there is a "single carbon filament bulb" above the monk's tonsure. But in the second paragraph we had been told that beyond the railing bobs "the bright lights and dark shapes of the *Niña* and the *Pinta*."

I won't continue with the analysis. By now the experienced SF reader has put together enough clues to determine that this is probably an alternate history scenario in which Columbus's first voyage included a telegrapher and an electric light. It is essential that the reader understand this and understand, within a page or two, that this world came about because the Church embraced Roger Bacon and his ideas rather than excommunicating him and that Friar Sparks belongs to the order of Rogerians, because Farmer is going to transform the reader's expectations (and make him or her inspect his or her own opinions in the process) before the story is over.

I have used other stories that make similar demands upon the reader's attention—Michael Bishop's "Rogue Tomato," for instance (where the clues are more literary)—but "Sail On! Sail On!" is short, deals with familiar events, and is packed with details about which important questions can be asked. Most of us read carelessly: care is unnecessary for most of the reading we do. Science fiction demands a different kind of reading—a kind of interaction with the text that may be required, in other circumstances, only by the most difficult literature, Joyce's *Ulysses*, say, but most SF readers believe that the payoff of SF is greater, or at least more satisfying to their particular desires.

Does teaching SF, or teaching the protocols of SF reading, matter? Some critics would say no and would urge, with Dena Brown, that we "put SF back in the gutter where it belongs." I can't speak for all SF teaching, but I still remember the mature student who came to me at the semester conclusion of one class and said that he had been reading SF for some twenty years but now he was reading it differently. "Better?" I asked. "Oh, yes," he said.

I don't take the credit for that—or, at least, not all the credit. I've been reading SF for some seventy years and I've thought about the process in much greater depth and at greater length than most people have time to do or care to do. Although my reading may not be privileged, it clearly is informed, and the background that I can bring to any story or novel may put that work, or the process, into a more informed context.

3

SCIENCE FICTION ON FILM AND TELEVISION

14

THE TINSEL SCREEN

Star Wars delighted tens of millions of filmgoers, some of whom returned to see the film dozens of times, and its sequels (and prequels) were so popular and so anticipated, that their release became "events." Virtually all by itself, *Star Wars* restored Twentieth-Century Fox to financial health by bringing in the greatest motion picture gross of all time, until *E.T., the Extra-Terrestrial*. *Close Encounters of the Third Kind* also has brought in a substantial return on its substantial production costs and thrilled audiences with its alien spaceship. New science fiction films flooded onto the screen until most of the top money-making motion pictures are science fiction.

All of which suggests that the Western world may be in (1) a golden age of science fiction films, (2) a golden age of science fiction, or (3) neither. Science fiction fans, authors, editors, and publishers started asking each other whether the vast audiences for the hugely successful science fiction films were going to mean a great new upsurge in science fiction readers.

Some have answered no, suggesting that filmgoers are not necessarily readers and do not necessarily translate film pleasure into a comparable reading experience. I have made the opposite point to questioners: the success of science fiction books paved the way for the acceptance of *Star Wars*.

As a matter of fact, printed science fiction and science fiction film seem to have little to do with each other, and there are virtually no good films that are also good science fiction. *Star Wars* is a simple and charming fairy tale set in scenes in which science fiction icons are lying about; and *Close Encounters*, in spite of the splendid epiphany when its Victorian chandelier of a spaceship appears, adds nothing to the concept of an encounter with aliens other than special effects.

"The Tinsel Screen" was first published, in somewhat different form, in *Teaching Science Fiction: Education for Tomorrow*, edited by Jack Williamson (Philadelphia: Owlswick Press, 1980).

The question of why this should be so—why science fiction is almost never translated effectively into film—has puzzled several generations of science fiction readers. The problem with the science fiction film may be that it adds nothing to science fiction except concreteness of image—and that may be more of a drawback than an asset.

John Baxter, in one of the better books about science fiction movies, *Science Fiction in the Cinema*, says that science fiction literature and science fiction film come from different origins and provide different views of the world. "Science fiction," he says, "supports logic and order; SF film, illogic and chaos. Its roots lie not in the visionary literature of the nineteenth century, to which science fiction owes most of its origins, but in older forms and attitudes, the medieval fantasy world, the era of the *masque*, the morality play, and the Grand Guignol."

Baxter goes on to write that the fund of concepts of science fiction films is limited. "Those it has fall generally into two categories: the loss of individuality, and the threat of knowledge." And he goes on to state, "Probably no line is more common to SF cinema than, 'There are some things Man is not meant to know.' . . . It expresses the universal fear all men have of the unknown and the inexplicable, a fear science fiction rejects, but which has firmly entrenched itself in the SF cinema."

The result is obvious: if a science fiction film opens with a scene of a scientist working in a laboratory, the audience knows that what he is working on will come to no good end—it will threaten his neighborhood, his region, his nation, or even the Earth itself; it will devour his wife and children and maybe everyone else's wives and children; and he will be sorry, but not as sorry as the rest of us. If the same scene occurs in a science fiction story, the reader has no preconceptions about how it will come out; the research may turn out badly, but it will not be because the scientist should not have done it in the first place, but because he did it poorly or without proper precautions. And the scientist might be working on research that will be useful, valuable, or indispensable; it may save us all, like the Ark, when danger threatens.

I like Baxter's distinctions, but I find curiously lacking from him a defense of them. Why doesn't (or can't) the science fiction film reflect written science fiction? Why doesn't (or can't) it support logic and order? Why isn't it (or can't it be) a medium of ideas? Baxter accepts the situation as a given, much as I have heard science fiction filmmakers surrender to the Hollywood sickness with a shrug and a "you've got to work within the system."

I would say, first of all, that Baxter's distinctions do not always hold up. On my list of good science fiction films are several that reflect the values of written science fiction: *Things to Come*, say, or *2001: A Space Odyssey*, where a science fiction writer has had a major influence on the development of the film. The result has been better science fiction and a superior film. You *can* beat the system if you are able to persuade the system of the truth of that statement.

But Baxter is right about most science fiction films. The people who made them knew nothing about science fiction. When they bought science fiction stories, they didn't know what they bought; they threw away the best parts and kept the worst, and didn't know the difference. They set out to make what they understood—monster movies, usually, with lots of special effects, but keep the budget low, and if you have to skimp, do it on the story and acting because nobody will notice.

Take a familiar case in point: John W. Campbell Jr.'s classic novelette "Who Goes There?" Hollywood turned it into *The Thing*.

Why must science fiction films deal only with simple images? Why must filmmakers suffer a failure of imagination when they come to science fiction? These are the questions that bedevil the science fiction reader. The filmmaker seems content with his ingenious models, his trick photography, his gruesome monsters, and his tabletop (now his computer-generated) destruction.

Most science fiction films, if translated into written form, would be unpublishable because of lack of logic or originality. I stand behind that statement even in the face of the success of the novelized versions of a variety of SF films, including *Star Wars* and its sequels. The ideas in a film such as *THX-1138*, much praised for its visual impact and filmic images, were old in 1949, when George Orwell wove them into a sophisticated novel of ideas called *1984*. Another visually interesting film, *Silent Running*, has almost no logic at all: Why put parks into space? Who visits them? What is saved by destroying them?

If a science fiction reader doesn't find interesting the ideas of a science fiction film, all that is left are the images or the special effects—what you have when you take away the subject matter. Film critics, when they deal with science fiction films, ignore the ideas and write about images and special effects. And when they discuss ideas, they are not to be trusted. I can forgive Susan Sontag for her statement (in "The Imagination of Disaster") that science fiction films are concerned with the aesthetics of disaster; she is talking about monster and worldwide destruction movies, not written science fiction, though she might have pointed out the difference. But I would argue with her conclusions that dealing with disaster in an imaginative way becomes "itself a somewhat questionable act from a moral point of view," by normalizing "what is psychologically unbearable, thereby inuring us to it." If applicable to science fiction films, why not to written science fiction? Here, it seems to me, the fallacy becomes more apparent. The alternative is not to deal fictionally with disaster, perhaps not even to think about it. Ms. Sontag, perhaps, would have us nourish an unspecific horror of things which concern "identity, volition, power, knowledge, happiness, social consensus, guilt, responsibility."

There is not much difference, as far as inuring goes, in visualizing a horror and writing about it, and I cannot believe that Orwell, to take one example, inured us to the horror of the all-intrusive state by writing *1984*, or that the 1954 film, though clearly inferior to the book, made us more likely to accept the conditions it depicts. The difficulty with Ms. Sontag's position is that most persons do not think about consequences until they are faced with them in terms of people's lives. Some—no, all—disasters should be thought through, analyzed, weighed, considered. Some disasters may be inevitable; they must be prepared for. Others are avoidable and must be prevented. Still others offer alternatives from which one must be chosen as superior to the other. Some are not disasters at all, but only seem like disasters. Some may be short-term disasters and long-term boons. Some may be individual disasters and racial necessities.

The basic problem with the science fiction disaster film is that it imagines disaster but seldom considers alternatives; it stirs our stomachs but seldom our heads. The film critics, accepting "what is" for "what must be," say it can do no other.

We run into this kind of nonsense from film critics: I can forgive Bernard Beck (in "The Overdeveloped Society: *THX-1138*") for describing science fiction as "often nothing more than a language structure for describing events which are concretely unimaginable or meaningless in ordinary terms," but I cannot forgive him for equating that language structure to "the production, the creation of a concrete image of the impossible out of available techniques" in the science fiction film. Overcoming the technical difficulties of making science fiction images concrete on film is not the same as the difficulties of making a science fiction situation believable. Fiction responds to difficulties; the ideals that lie within the science fiction situation are most dramatically expressed when the difficulties are surmounted. Beck would have us believe that the film's creation of the concrete image is enough to delight us. It had better be.

The only place where greater caution with the film critic should be exercised is the point at which the critic begins to refer to "a synthesis of insightful visual imagination" and "an interpenetration of fantasy and reality." Phrases like those suggest that the logic of the film won't bear inspection.

If the science fiction film actually makes images concrete, it may be the concreteness of the image that ultimately turns us off. Science fiction, like fantasy, is a literature of the imagination; it requires vigorous participation on the part of the reader, a willing suspension of disbelief—although science fiction, in contrast to fantasy, gives the reader reasons for believing. This reader participation allows the science fiction writer to span parsecs believably, to cross centuries credibly, to suggest the most sensational of cities, the most creative of creatures, the most startling of social systems, the most incredible variations upon a theme. And if a writer has done it persuasively, the reader constructs for himself, out of his own imagination, what he longs for or dreads.

As John W. Campbell Jr. pointed out in 1947 (in an essay called "The Science of Science Fiction Writing"), "The trick is to describe the horrified, not the horror, the love-struck, not the lady-love." But the science fiction film, at great expense and difficulty, applies a face to the horror, and it seems prosaic or laughable; the film is stuck with its images, and in them, the viewer does not participate. Often the film image cannot live up to the reader's expectations; that is why books seldom make good movies, even though we want to see the impossible achieved. This is particularly true of science fiction books. Moreover, when the effort to make the image concrete represents the major accomplishment of a film, the substance becomes incidental. Where science fiction is specific about ideas and suggestive about images, the science fiction film is specific about images and allusive—elusive as well—about meaning. The difference is all the difference in this world—or another.

Stan Freberg, the satirist turned adman, once created a radio commercial about the advantages of radio advertising over television. It began with the announcer turning Lake Michigan into a gigantic bowl of flavored gelatin, covering it with whipped cream, and towing into position overhead, a cherry the size of an island, and it ended with the announcer challenging a television executive to create a similar commercial.

The same thing might be said about science fiction and fantasy on radio. Radio brought out the best in science fiction: the sound effects were relatively easy and much more effective than visual images in suggesting scope, changing scenes, creating moods, and eliciting listener imagination. The famous 1938 Mercury Theater production of *The War of the Worlds* created an astonishing (and much studied) reaction from its audience. But there were others: *Lights Out* and *Inner Sanctum* had some science fiction mixed with the horrors in the 1940s, but science fiction came into its own in the 1950s with a handful of series of which *Dimension X* and *X Minus One* were the best. Many of the dramatizations were well done. Four of my *Galaxy* stories were adapted for *X Minus One*; I liked two of them very well, and the other two fairly well. For contrast, I offer the 1959 television adaptation of one of them, "The Cave of Night," into Desilu Playhouse's *Man in Orbit*; even with Lee Marvin and H. G. Marshall, it was disappointing. Today's counterparts to the radio adaptations of science fiction are records and tapes and CDs of dramatic readings and even dramatizations. And the old radio programs are still available on record and tape, although you may have to search for them.

If, in spite of all the drawbacks of films, the science fiction reader persists in a masochistic desire to see and understand science fiction movies, where can help be found? I suggest that the reader stay away from film critics unless the reader wants information about film; most critics talk nonsense about the obvious, and they provide only confusion about science fiction. They insist, for instance, on referring to science fiction as "sci-fi," which immediately alienates the science fiction reader; he knows the only legitimate abbreviation is "SF," although many modern writers insist that "SF" can also stand for "speculative fiction."

The best book about science fiction films I found, published before 1979, was William Johnson's *Focus on the Science Fiction Film*, which presented both sides of most issues and included comments by writers as well as critics and filmmakers. John Baxter's *Science Fiction in the Cinema* is thorough; Denis Gifford's *Science Fiction Film* lists more titles than any other book, but says less about each; Ralph J. Amelio's *Hal in the Classroom: Science Fiction Films* contains some provocative, but often misguided, essays, among which are Susan Sontag's and Bernard Beck's. All the books listed above have useful bibliographies and filmographies. A different kind of book, *Cinema of the Fantastic*, by Chris Steinbrunner and Burt Goldblatt, has many hard-to-find photographs, and chapters on fifteen movies, from Georges Méliès's *A Trip to the Moon* to *Forbidden Planet*. But for my tastes, the two best books about the science fiction film are John Brosnan's *Future Tense: The Cinema of Science Fiction* (1978) and Frederik Pohl's *Science Fiction: Studies in Film* (1981), written with his son, Frederik Pohl IV.

If a reader wishes to develop a personal history of the science fiction film, the obvious starting point is Méliès's *A Trip to the Moon*, a brief bit of whimsy filmed in 1902 and patterned after Jules Verne's *From the Earth to the Moon*, with influence from H. G. Wells's *The First Men in the Moon*. Méliès had a couple of earlier efforts, *An Astronomer's Dream* and a version of H. Rider Haggard's *She*.

After a number of other curiosities that are available and probably not worth seeing for anything more than antiquarian purposes (with the exception of the 1925 film of Arthur Conan Doyle's *The Lost World* with Wallace Beery as Professor Challenger and some effective, early, animated dinosaurs), the German director Fritz Lang produced *Metropolis* in 1926 (a more complete film, tinted, with soundtrack and subtitles, was re-released in 1984) and *Woman in the Moon* in 1929. Both are historically important, particularly for special effects, and both are melodramatic and overacted, and audiences with whom I have viewed them usually find them funny. An American film of 1930, *Just Imagine*, is supposed to be funny but is only ridiculous; however, it does include some impressive futuristic shots of a 1980 metropolis.

The meaningful history of filmed science fiction (as opposed to science fiction film) begins in 1931 with *Frankenstein*, the Boris Karloff version that inspired a thousand parodies, including Mel Brooks's *Young Frankenstein*. Yet the original film still has the power to move audiences. So does the more cultish *King Kong*, epic in scope and special effects, and even interesting thematically. The 1976 remake had little to recommend it but color; the 2005 re-remake is reported to be a more faithful tribute film with color and improved computerized special effects. Another on my list came along the same year as *King Kong: The Invisible Man*. Although it perpetuated the persistent medieval theme "he meddled in God's domain" and "he ventured into areas man was meant to leave alone," the film does better than most at considering more than one side of a question, in this case, the drawbacks as well as the advantages of invisibility, and the special effects are well done. About the same time came a film that doesn't quite make my list but is nevertheless a reasonably effective adaptation of H. G. Wells's *The Island of Dr. Moreau*, called *The Island of Lost Souls* (1932), with Charles Laughton. Again, the remakes have been poorer.

I once thought that the British *Things to Come* (1936) was the only good science fiction film ever made. It is based on Wells's 1933 book, *The Shape of Things to Come*, and it had a scenario and frequent memoranda to the participants by Wells, leading to my later conclusions that the really good science fiction movies had someone intimately associated with the production who knew a great deal about written science fiction. Since *Things to Come*, other films have come along, and the virtues of *Things to Come* have not survived the intervening years undiminished. The early war scenes are cheaply executed and betray their simple pacifism. But the final sequences, projected into the year 2036, still have the power to captivate, and Raymond Massey's final statement of man's destiny still sounds the clear, pure call of mainstream science fiction. I have been surprised at the number of science fiction authors of my generation, such as Isaac Asimov and Fred Pohl, who expressed the same reactions to this film.

The *Flash Gordon* and *Buck Rogers* serials produced between 1936 and

1940, along with such lesser works as *The Phantom Empire* (1935) and *The Undersea Kingdom* (1936), are high camp today with their comic strip villains and heroes, their cardboard robots, their firework rocket ships, and their absurd and cheating cliffhangers. But they provide a kind of reliving of the old '30s Saturday matinee experience, and some viewers have found them good fun. *Star Wars*, it has been said, is George Lucas's tribute to *Flash Gordon*.

Destination Moon (1950) was George Pal's first science fiction production, and the first film adapted from the work of a magazine science fiction writer, Robert A. Heinlein. Heinlein also worked on the script, which was based on his Scribner's juvenile novel *Rocketship Galileo*. The film is marred by melodramatics and some ridiculous comic relief, but the space sequences and the lunar episodes (the moonscapes were painted by the late astronomical and science fiction artist Chesley Bonestell) are remarkable bits of prophecy. During the televised portions of the Apollo trips, the appearance of space and the moon surface gave many of us the experience of *déjà vu*: we had seen it before, only clearer, in *Destination Moon*.

George Pal, as producer and later director, would have much to do with subsequent adaptations of science fiction classics such as Balmer and Wylie's *When Worlds Collide* (1951) and Wells's *The War of the Worlds* (1953) and *The Time Machine* (1960). All are worth viewing as adaptations of written science fiction, although all fall short in one way or another, the first two more than the last.

Of the some two thousand or so remaining films, I would include in my historical overview: *Forbidden Planet* (1956), which has Robbie the Robot, comic relief, and an idiotic love story (all modeled, to be sure, on *The Tempest*), but also the marvelous idea of the Id Monster and scenes of the lost civilization which produced it; *The Invasion of the Body Snatchers* (1956), about the replacement of people by pod duplicates, which is nicely and soberly done and is liked by many critics more than by me (the remake produced mixed reactions); *The Village of the Damned* (1960), a relatively faithful adaptation of the John Wyndham novel (the 1963 *Day of the Triffids* is not as faithful and a lesser film, but there is a better, more recent English version); *Barbarella* (1967), which has a bit of nudity for the libidinous and also lovely scenes and a delightful satire on a number of science fiction themes; and, of course, the incomparable *2001: A Space Odyssey* (1968), which, in spite of some quarrels with its obscure ending and the unexplained [until the sequels] murderousness of HAL, is the most completely realized vision of the future yet achieved on film and an excellent motion picture.

Star Wars (1977) and *Close Encounters of the Third Kind* (1977) are more important for what they have accomplished at the box office than what they have achieved artistically. *Star Wars* can be enjoyed effortlessly at the fairy tale level, and it offers a pleasant lived-in quality to its scenes and costumes, and the scope and effectiveness of its special effects are worth the cost of seeing it. *Close Encounters* has a magnificent final scene in the appearance of the alien spaceship, but it seems to me that the first two-thirds of the film is irrelevant and the two UFO fanatics who have fought their way to the spot end up as spectators little more relevant to what goes on there than the rest of the audience. I would give it high praise, however, for never once permitting a character to suggest that the aliens might be dangerous and people should either arm themselves or flee. But the most important aspect of the two films is their refutation of the frequent excuse against making first-class science fiction films, that SF films never make money. *Battlestar Galactica* has demonstrated, however, that special effects do not an SF media presentation make, though it will be cited as a reason not to do SF on television (the new version is a different matter). Other SF series have been more successful though not necessarily better.

All of these, no matter what their faults, are part of the canon of the science fiction film, along with films that have a similar appeal but are not sufficiently distanced from the present to qualify as science fiction (such as *Lost Horizon* [1937], *The Man in the White Suit* [1951], and *Dr. Strangelove* [1964]).

Many science fiction films were produced between *Destination Moon* and *Star Wars*, but if I haven't listed them above, I find them seriously flawed or completely hopeless. Some film critics praise some of them—for instance, *The Day the Earth Stood Still* or *The Thing*, both released in 1951—but any reader who recalls the science fiction novelettes "Farewell to the Master" by Harry Bates and "Who Goes There?" by John W. Campbell Jr. may question the films based on them if only for tossing away good stories and making lesser ones.

The Verne adaptations, *Journey to the Center of the Earth* (1959), *From the Earth to the Moon* (1964), *Twenty Thousand Leagues under the Sea* (1965), and others, generally are performed as period pieces; they are amusing but cannot be taken seriously as science fiction—they are flawed and unfaithful. My favorite of this type is a Czechoslovakian film called *The Wonderful Invention* (1958), sometimes called *The Fabulous World of Jules Verne*, but it has been unavailable since its initial showing.

Godard's science fiction film, *Alphaville* (1965), is frequently admired, but I find it obscure and unconvincing. Harlan Ellison speaks highly of *Seconds*.

Other films have been marred by mindless antiscientism, such as *The Incredible Shrinking Man* (1957) or *The Power* (1967); by illogical elements, as in *Fahrenheit 451* (1966), *Planet of the Apes* (1968) and its many sequels, *Charly* (1968), or *Colossus: The Forbin Project* (1970); or by no logic at all, as in *The Andromeda Strain* (1971), *Silent Running* (1972), *Westworld* (1973), or *Soylent Green* (1973). It is interesting to note that the resolution that *Soylent Green* presents as the ultimate in horror could make a satisfying science fiction story—if the problem were to convince the public that its prejudice against eating a product made from human flesh was irrational and unreasonable. *A Clockwork Orange*, on the other hand, justifies, if it does not actually glorify, violence. I find this more repugnant than the small, neat wafers of *Soylent Green*.

In spite of their flaws, the films listed above are the best of their kind, and all of them may find their place in a science fiction film series with the reservations noted. Their kind simply is not a high SF art.

Science fiction on television is even worse. Its only value—in the way *Amazing Stories* was once considered by John W. Campbell Jr. as a primer for the more demanding science fiction published in *Astounding*—is to provide an introduction for young people willing to move on to the written word. Series have even more flaws than science fiction films and demand larger audiences (thus requiring a reduction to lowest-common-denominator approach) for survival. Nevertheless, *Star Trek* certainly, and its sequel series, and certain episodes of *The Twilight Zone* and *Night Gallery*, among others, achieved moments of science fiction value. The best science fiction adaptations on television have been one-shots, like the early adaptations of Robert Sheckley's "The People Trap" and Alfred Bester's "Fondly Fahrenheit" for which Bester himself wrote the script. Even the 1969 ABC-TV Movie of the Week, *The Immortal*, an adaptation of my 1962 novel *The Immortals*, was far superior to the series that followed in 1970.

Perhaps a discussion of what went wrong with *The Immortal* would be a good place to bring this analysis of science fiction and the visual media to a conclusion. There are so many things that an author can criticize about the adaptation of his work that I hardly know where to begin (a more complete analysis is available in the next chapter), but let us ignore the acting (Bob Specht, the scriptwriter and the person responsible for getting it on television at all, thought Christopher George was dynamic enough to keep the series on the air for a second season all on his own), the production, and even the quality of the scripts (a Screenwriters Guild strike was threatened and the producer, Anthony Wilson, had to sign up a lot of scripts in a hurry) and concentrate instead on the ideas.

The big mistake made early in the planning for the series was to play the series for adventure rather than science fiction. (That has been the downfall of most science fiction adaptations—remember *The Thing*?) In fact, the word went out that no science fiction writers would be considered as script writers for the series. In retrospect, Bob Specht's decision to make the Immortal a test-car driver, influenced, no doubt, by the success of the San Francisco car chase scenes of *Bullitt* and perhaps a major reason the original script was attractive to Paramount and ABC, may have been a fatal mistake for the series: executives saw it as a chase story, with ten minutes or more of every episode eaten up in car-chase footage.

In the final analysis, the fact that Ben Richards (Marshall Cartwright in the novel) was immortal made little difference. The subject of my novel was the way in which his immortality changed society. Marshall Cartwright's personal problems in the novel had so little relevance that he disappears after an initial scene of blood drawing and doesn't make another appearance (except for a cameo in the second part) until the end. But in the movie Ben Richards's dramatic value adaptation is only his importance to someone else: that his importance is his blood, which can make old people temporarily young again, is no more significant for the narrative than if he knew the location of important papers or a fortune in jewels, or had killed someone, or could save someone from a false accusation. It was, in other words, viewed as another *Fugitive*. Ben Richards's immortality was only an excuse for a chase, and the episodes that resulted from it were simple repetitions of discovery, chase, capture, and escape—cookie-cutter episodes, indistinguishable from one another.

The Immortal had the potential to concern itself with life and death, subjects too important to trivialize. But that may be the ultimate problem with science fiction on film: with a few important exceptions, filmmakers have been afraid or unwilling to take science fiction seriously, and unless any subject is taken seriously, it cannot produce meaningful art.

Looked at as film, the period since *Star Wars* was released in 1977 has been a golden age for science fiction on the screen (big and little). *2001: A Space Odyssey* proved that a big-budget SF film could make money (even if its profitability waited on a reputation for being a great movie to attend stoned). *Star Wars* demonstrated that an SF film could make *big* profits and ushered in an era when almost all the biggest money-making movies were science fiction or fantasy: *E.T., Close Encounters of the Third Kind,* the *Star Wars* sequels and prequels, *Jurassic Park* and its sequels, *Independence Day, Batman, Raiders of the Lost Ark* and its sequels, *Ghostbusters, Ghost, Back to the Future, The Matrix* and its sequels, *Harry Potter, The Lord of the Rings* trilogy, and more. But none of these films do much for science fiction, or the realizing of published science fiction: they are better as films than as SF. The year *Star Wars* was released, a panel of authors and editors at the World Science Fiction Convention in Phoenix debated whether the great popularity of the film would lead viewers to the reading of science fiction. Opinions were mixed, but the results were not: although publication and sales of SF, fantasy, and horror (often overlapping and lumped together in *Locus* surveys) soared in succeeding decades, and a few SF titles broke into the best-seller lists, the major increase was in media-related *Star Wars* and *Star Trek* novels, and novelizations of almost every other SF TV series and film. One editor commented that these texts were more like memory books than novels. More recently, fantasy, which once was SF's poor relation, has begun to outpublish and outsell its once dominant brother. Part of that transformation can be traced to the popularity of Tolkien's remarkable trilogy and other best-selling fantasy novels of the 1970s. But that is another story.

The statement I made in 1975 in *Alternate Worlds: The Illustrated History of Science Fiction* still seems appropriate: whatever virtues SF films may have, they are not SF virtues. When I attended a preview showing of *Star Wars*, for instance, it was the only film I ever attended at which the audience stood up and applauded at its conclusion. But *Star Wars* was an homage to 1930s SF serial films, with contemporary SF iconography, and was, at best, a fairy tale in which a band of heroes rescues an abducted princess from an evil warlock and destroys the castle from which the warlock and his emperor have been oppressing the people.

To be sure, SF film is growing up, and *Blade Runner*, *Dark City*, and *The Matrix* are tackling the difficult task (once thought impossible until Stanley Kubrick, with the first half-hour of *2001*, proved that the filmmaking mantra was wrong) of filming ideas. The tinsel screen still has a long way to go before it catches up with print SF, but films such as these offer hope.

IMPORTANT PRODUCTIONS IN THE HISTORY OF THE SF FILM

1898   *An Astronomer's Dream* (Méliès)
1899   *She* (Méliès)
1902   *A Trip to the Moon* (Méliès)
1906   *The ? Motorist* (Booth)
1909   *A Trip to Jupiter* (Pathe)
1910   *A Trip to Mars* (Edison)

1919 *The First Men in the Moon* (Leigh)
1924 *Aëlita* (Protazanov)
1925 *The Lost World* (Hoyt)
1926 *Metropolis* (Lang)
1929 *The Woman in the Moon* (Lang)
1930 *Just Imagine* (Butler)
1931 *Frankenstein* (Whale)
1932 *The Island of Lost Souls* (Kenton)
1933 *King Kong* (Cooper/Schoedsack)
1933 *The Invisible Man* (Whale)
1933 *Deluge* (Feist)
1934 *Trans-Atlantic Tunnel* (Elvey)
1936 *Things to Come* (Menzies)
1936 *Flash Gordon* serial (Stephani)
1937 *Lost Horizon* (Capra)
1940 *Buck Rogers* serial (Henry)
1950 *Destination Moon* (Pichel)
1951 *When Worlds Collide* (Mate)
1951 *The Thing from Another World* (Hawks)
1951 *The Day the Earth Stood Still* (Wise)
1951 *The Man in the White Suit* (Mackendrick)
1953 *The War of the Worlds* (Haskin)
1954 *1984* (Anderson)
1955 *20,000 Leagues under the Sea* (Fleischer)
1956 *Forbidden Planet* (Wilcox)
1956 *Invasion of the Body Snatchers* (Siegel)
1957 *The Incredible Shrinking Man* (Arnold)
1958 *The Wonderful Invention* (Zeman)
1960 *The Time Machine* (Pal)
1960 *Village of the Damned* (Rilla)
1963 *The Day of the Triffids* (Sekely)
1964 *From the Earth to the Moon* (Haskin)
1964 *Dr. Strangelove* (Kubrick)
1965 *Alphaville* (Godard)
1965 *The 10th Victim* (Petri)
1966 *Fahrenheit 451* (Truffaut)
1966 *Fantastic Voyage* (Fleischer)
1966 *Seconds* (Frankenheimer)
1967 *Barbarella* (Vadim)

1968   *2001: A Space Odyssey* (Kubrick)
1968   *Planet of the Apes* (Schaffner)
1968   *Charly* (Nelson)
1970   *Colossus: The Forbin Project* (Sargent)
1971   *A Clockwork Orange* (Kubrick)
1971   *The Andromeda Strain* (Wise)
1971   *THX-1138* (Lucas)
1972   *Silent Running* (Trumbull)
1973   *Soylent Green* (Fleischer)
1973   *Westworld* (Crichton)
1974   *Young Frankenstein* (Brooks)
1974   *Zardoz* (Boorman)
1975   *A Boy and His Dog* (Jones)
1975   *The Land That Time Forgot* (Connor)
1975   *Rollerball* (Jewison)
1975   *The Stepford Wives* (Forbes)
1976   *The Food of the Gods* (Gordon)
1976   *Logan's Run* (Anderson)
1976   *Futureworld* (Heffron)
1976   *The Man Who Fell to Earth* (Roeg)
1977   *Close Encounters of the Third Kind* (Spielberg)
1977   *Demon Seed* (Cammell)
1977   *The Island of Dr. Moreau* (Taylor)
1977   *Star Wars* (Lucas)
1978   *Superman* (Donner)
1978   *The Boys from Brazil* (Schaffner)
1978   *Invasion of the Body Snatchers* (Kaufman)
1979   *Alien* (Scott)
1979   *Time after Time* (Meyer)
1979   *Star Trek: The Motion Picture* (Wise)
1979   *The Black Hole* (Nelson)
1979   *Buck Rogers in the 25th Century* (Haller)
1980   *The Empire Strikes Back* (Kershner)
1980   *Flash Gordon* (Hodges)
1980   *Altered States* (Russell)
1981   *Superman II* (Donner)
1981   *The Road Warrior* (Miller)
1981   *Quest for Fire* (Annaud)
1982   *E.T., the Extra-Terrestrial* (Spielberg)

1982   *Blade Runner* (Scott)
1982   *Star Trek II: The Wrath of Khan* (Meyer)
1982   *Tron* (Lisberger)
1982   *Conan the Barbarian* (Milius)
1982   *The Thing* (Carpenter)
1983   *Return of the Jedi* (Marquand)
1983   *Twilight Zone: The Movie* (Miller/Landis/Dante/Spielberg)
1983   *The Day After* (Meyer)
1983   *The Dead Zone* (Cronenberg)
1984   *Dune* (Lynch)
1984   *2010* (Hyams)
1984   *1984* (Radford)
1984   *Starman* (Carpenter)
1984   *The Terminator* (Cameron)
1984   *Star Trek III: The Search for Spock* (Nimoy)
1984   *Iceman* (Schepisi)
1984   *Brother from Another Planet* (Sayles)
1984   *Repo Man* (Cox)
1985   *Back to the Future* (Zemeckis)
1985   *Brazil* (Gilliam)
1985   *Cocoon* (Howard)
1985   *Enemy Mine* (Petersen)
1985   *Lifeforce* (Hooper)
1985   *Mad Max beyond Thunderdome* (Miller)
1986   *Aliens* (Cameron)
1986   *Peggy Sue Got Married* (Coppola)
1986   *The Fly* (Cronenberg)
1986   *Invaders from Mars* (Hooper)
1986   *Star Trek IV: The Voyage Home* (Nimoy)
1987   *Innerspace* (Dante)
1987   *Predator* (McTiernan)
1987   *Robocop* (Verhoeven)
1987   *The Running Man* (Glaser)
1988   *Alien Nation* (Baker)
1988   *Big* (Marshall)
1989   *The Abyss* (Cameron)
1989   *Back to the Future II* (Zemeckis)
1989   *Honey, I Shrunk the Kids* (Johnston)
1989   *Millennium* (Anderson)

1989 *The Navigator: A Medieval Odyssey* (Ward)
1989 *Star Trek V: The Final Frontier* (Shatner)
1990 *Back to the Future III* (Zemeckis)
1990 *Edward Scissorhands* (Burton)
1990 *The Handmaid's Tale* (Schlöndorff)
1990 *Total Recall* (Verhoeven)
1991 *Terminator 2: Judgment Day* (Cameron)
1991 *Star Trek VI: The Undiscovered Country* (Meyer)
1992 *Alien 3* (Fincher)
1993 *Jurassic Park* (Spielberg)
1994 *Star Trek: Generations* (Carson)
1994 *Stargate* (Emmerich)
1995 *Johnny Mnemonic* (Longo)
1995 *Waterworld* (Reynolds/Costner)
1995 *12 Monkeys* (Gilliam)
1996 *Independence Day* (Emmerich)
1996 *Mars Attacks!* (Burton)
1996 *Star Trek: First Contact* (Frakes)
1996 *Escape from LA* (Carpenter)
1997 *The Postman* (Costner)
1997 *The Lost World: Jurassic Park* (Spielberg)
1997 *Men in Black* (Sonnenfield)
1997 *The Fifth Element* (Besson)
1997 *Gattaca* (Niccol)
1998 *Lost in Space* (Hopkins)
1998 *The X-Files* (Bowman)
1998 *Deep Impact* (Leder)
1998 *Armageddon* (Bay)
1998 *Star Trek: Insurrection* (Frakes)
1998 *Dark City* (Proyas)
1999 *Star Wars: The Phantom Menace* (Lucas)
1999 *The Matrix* (Wachowski brothers)
1999 *The Thirteenth Floor* (Rusnik)
1999 *eXistenZ* (Cronenberg)
2000 *Red Planet* (Hoffman)
2000 *Mission to Mars* (De Palma)
2000 *Dune* miniseries (Harrison)
2000 *X-Men* (Singer)
2000 *Supernova* (Hill/Coppola)

2000 *The Sixth Day* (Spottswoode)
2001 *Jurassic Park III* (Johnston)
2001 *Planet of the Apes* (Burton)
2001 *Artificial Intelligence: AI* (Spielberg)
2001 *Vanilla Sky* (Crowe)
2002 *Minority Report* (Spielberg)
2002 *Star Wars: Attack of the Clones* (Lucas)
2002 *Signs* (Shyamalan)
2002 *Spiderman* (Raimi)
2002 *The Ring* (Verbinski)
2002 *Solaris* (Soderbergh)
2002 *Star Trek: Nemesis* (Baird)
2003 *X-Men 2: X-Men United* (Singer)
2003 *Children of Dune* miniseries (Yaitanes)
2003 *The Matrix: Reloaded* (Wachowski brothers)
2003 *The Matrix: Revolution* (Wachowski brothers)
2004 *Star Wars: Revenge of the Sith* (Lucas)
2005 *War of the Worlds* (Spielberg)

15

TELEVISION AND
THE IMMORTAL

Carve through the strange environments, cut away the unusual characters, separate the melodrama and the action, and you will find at the heart of every science fiction story an idea.

If you dissect a television drama, you will find inside only a void, echoing the uneven pulse of compromise. When science fiction is adapted to the screen, large or small, something happens: the heart gets cut out of it, and heartless drama is bad science fiction and worse drama.

And then there's the status of the writer. "The most unnecessary person on the set," Bob Specht told me once, "is the man who wrote the screenplay. You can imagine from that the position of the person who wrote the original material."

That summed up my relationship with *The Immortal*, an ABC Movie of the Week in 1969 and an hour-long, weekly series in 1970. They were based on my science fiction novel *The Immortals*. Bob Specht came into it when he saw its motion picture potential and took an option on it in 1967. Two years and a lot of effort later, Bob finally got some encouragement from Paramount.

From Lawrence, Kansas, where I taught fiction writing and science fiction at the University of Kansas, I watched *The Immortal* grow from prospectus to outline, from outline to first draft, second draft, and final screenplay; I watched it turn into actors and film and from film into series—and I watched *The Immortal* die.

Bob, who wrote the screenplay for the Movie of the Week but was not associated with the series, thinks *The Immortal* should have been one of the biggest

---

"Television and *The Immortal*" was first published as "An Author Watches His Brainchild Die on Television" in *TV Guide* 9, no. 7, in February 1971.

TV hits in years, and that it flopped because nobody knew what to do with the series. I think it goes deeper than that. What happened to *The Immortal* is what happens to most science fiction as it gets translated into film: the studios buy a "property" because it is different and then turn it into a product that looks and sounds and feels and smells like everything else.

Here's an example: a group of scientists at an Antarctic camp discover an alien creature that has been frozen deep in the ice for millions of years. It thaws and comes to life; by the time it has been destroyed, it has eaten some of the animals and begun to imitate them down to the structure of the cells themselves. The problem: Has it also eaten and replicated one or more of the scientists? If it has, is there a test that can distinguish monster from human? And can it be found before the monster escapes the frozen wastes to repopulate the world with itself?

That is one of the classic stories of science fiction, "Who Goes There?" by John W. Campbell Jr. It is a classic because it is based upon a situation that is unique, fantastic, and dramatic. It deals with two of man's basic fears—powers beyond human control and possession after death—and it advances through a rational and successful attempt to resolve the problem it poses.

Not many would recognize that story as the basis for the motion picture *The Thing*. The movie changed the scene to the Arctic, the vehicle to a flying saucer from Mars, and the monster to a vegetable creature whose chief concern is raising little monsters from seeds nourished by human blood. Its one claim to distinction is that the man inside the monster suit was James Arness. (John Carpenter, of *Halloween* fame, remade the movie [released in 1982] and remained more faithful to the original story, but emphasized the horror over the science fiction and kept the original movie title.)

Stretched on the rack, I might admit to a few good science fiction films— the original *King Kong* and *Frankenstein*, *Things to Come*, and *2001: A Space Odyssey* come to mind—but when I put together a science fiction film series for a course I was teaching, I had difficulty coming up with a dozen films that were both good science fiction and good films.

What is science fiction?

Science fiction is many things: a literary tradition, a set of conventions, a way of looking at experience, a means of testing alternatives, signposts toward possible futures, the mythology of a technological age. As story, however, it is a fantastic premise or event considered rationally. It has persistent appeal— witness its long history as popular literature—and with today's concern about the impact of science and technology on our future, it has unique literary relevance.

Attempts to transfer science fiction to film lose the fantasy or the rational-ity—sometimes both. (Even such wildly popular films as *Star Wars* and *E.T.* are not truly science fiction; even though they have science fiction back-grounds, one is a fairy tale and the other is a lost-animal story with fairytale aspects.)

What has reached television only looks like science fiction: lots of them are late-night movies about monsters, and many of the rest are irrational horror stories and fantasies about haunted houses, ghosts, demonic possession, were-wolves, witchcraft, vampires, and the undead.

Like other frontiers, science fiction has its adventure stories. Here belong most of the series that have reached television, most of them aimed at children: the old *Space Cadet*, *Captain Video*, and *Superman* (a borderline entry), and later *Voyage to the Bottom of the Sea* and *Land of the Giants*. They must be judged as adventure shows; they didn't take their premises seriously and didn't expect the viewer to do so.

The Invaders began with a valid concept, but, because of the predictability of its plots, never got beyond its beginning. *Time Tunnel* became merely a device for transporting contemporary men into historic situations. *The Pris-oner*, well conceived and produced, never became science fiction because it refused to supply answers to its own paranoid questions.

Anthology shows are harder to assess. Rod Serling's *Twilight Zone* leaned toward fantasy but included some good science fiction. Serling was a writer, and he respected a writer's work. *The Outer Limits* produced a few good sto-ries, particularly in its final months when, I am told, no one cared what was included and some good scripts slipped by. *Star Trek*, on the other hand, had its high points in its first two years, when scripts and ideas were solicited from science fiction writers, but turned toward more limited and less sophisticated writers in its doomed final season. Harlan Ellison's *The Starlost* (he disowned it with a pseudonym) had potential that was unrealized by its unsophisticated producers; *Space: 1999* attempted to capture *Star Trek*'s audience, but was scientifically illiterate; *Battlestar Galactica* had an entertaining premise, but ran out of good stories to tell by the second episode and resorted to soap opera and power struggles; and *V* strung together a series of horrifying alien images that did not disguise gaps of logic and was primarily a plot of conquest and rebellion.

The ABC Movie of the Week, as well as the other series of made-for-televi-sion movies, turned frequently to science fiction and fantasy, perhaps under the reasonable theory that if you want to draw an audience for a single film against the predictability of a series, you had better offer something different.

And that brings us back to *The Immortals*. My story, published in science fiction magazines beginning in 1955 and as a novel in 1962, was about a drifter who sells a pint of blood to a hospital and then disappears until the end of the book, several hundred years later. The impact of that pint of blood is amplified throughout society and multiplied down the centuries because it is a new kind of blood that makes its donor immortal and can pass on temporary rejuvenation to others. Immortality becomes not merely a dream but a fact, and the novel was about the changes that fact might create in the way we live and the way we look at life.

I knew *The Immortals* would not be an easy book to film and would be even more difficult to prepare for television. It dealt with a queasy business, blood transfusion, and it asked some touchy questions: Can we be too healthy? Do we have a neurotic concern for the quantity of life at the expense of quality? Does the medical profession have too many physicians but not enough healers?

But Bob Specht's faith in the story ultimately was rewarded. His screenplay held some disappointments for me, but I put them down to author's pride and studio compromises: the drifter became a test-car driver. In Bob's words, he was "a fairly ordinary man who finds himself burdened with an extraordinary gift." Producer Lou Morheim asked me once if I liked the script. "It's a love–hate relationship," I said. "I just hope you know what you're doing."

The success of the movie version indicated that they did. No matter how it turned out as science fiction, it was a good show: the production was flashy and the performances were excellent, particularly Christopher George as the Immortal and Barry Sullivan as Jordan Braddock.

The movie ranked second in the week's 70-market Nielsens—whatever that means—and its rerun outdrew the premieres of a couple of new Tuesday night shows on NBC and CBS. Then the series began running, you know, like *Run for Your Life* and *The Fugitive* all wrapped up together. The Fall Preview issue of *TV Guide* described it as "Run for Your Blood."

Before the season started, a student of mine told me about a theory he had read recently, that television develops new programs by opposites: *Green Acres*, about an urban family having comic difficulties in rural surroundings, is the opposite of *The Beverly Hillbillies*, about a rural family having comic difficulties in urban surroundings. And *The Immortal*, about a man running around the world because he's going to live forever, would be the opposite of *Run for Your Life*, about a man running around the world because he's going to die soon.

"Don't let it become a cookie-cutter series," I wrote to Bob Specht. "Let it evolve." But that didn't do much good because Bob didn't have anything to do with the series. Nor did anyone else who had anything to do with the success of the movie—not Lou Morheim, nor director Joseph Sargent. The only carryover was Christopher George. Outside of that, the series was a new project, and perhaps it never really got started because no one knew what the show was about or where it was going or why.

In July 1970, I had lunch with Tony Wilson, executive producer of the series for Paramount. He seemed genuinely interested in my ideas for the series. When I got back to Lawrence, I wrote him a long report, taking the show apart and trying to put it back together again. "Use *The Immortal*," I wrote, "as a launching pad for a series of stories on the eternal human themes of life, of love, of freedom, and of death. . . . (The Immortal) and the show will lose the attention of the viewer if they do not evolve. The variations of chase, capture, and rescue are too limited." I also offered to recruit science fiction writers with screen and TV experience.

But that was July, and most of the scripts were already on hand or on their way, and the word had gone out, I learned, that no science fiction writers were to be used.

Early in September 1970, television columnist Cynthia Lowry wrote that television goes in cycles, that this season science fiction and fantasy were out and action/adventure was in—clearly, for *The Immortal*—and that the fact that Ben Richards was immortal had little or nothing to do with what happened in the episodes. Nothing sprang from the premises except a simple chase.

Came the cancellation. Some viewers actually liked the show, I think, perhaps because of the basic premise, but more likely because of the appeal of Christopher George. But the first couple of episodes, when a series must win the ratings war or die, were up against *The Dirty Dozen* and *The Great Race* on CBS.

Some critics have theorized that what happens to science fiction on television is no different from what happens to every original idea that gets into the Hollywood homogenizer. Another theory points at network and studio decision making, with everyone from the network president on down influencing the creative process, resulting in a cautious approach that may fail but will not be second-guessed. A third theory is that television's demand for material rewards the hack who can turn out a reasonable, uninspired, but shootable script on time. People kept telling me, "Take the money and run—you can't let yourself care about what happens or it will tear you apart."

Take your choice. I have my own theory: science fiction on television and in motion pictures is bad science fiction and worse drama because there seldom is anybody associated with the project who knows anything about science fiction, who can point at something and say, "That's good. That's bad." When there is someone—Rod Serling and *Twilight Zone*, Gene Roddenberry and *Star Trek*, Arthur C. Clarke and *2001: A Space Odyssey*—the difference in the product is unmistakable. When there isn't, producers and directors and writers ask themselves what the show is similar to that they know something about, that they have done before, that they can feel comfortable doing. That's how a "Who Goes There?" gets to be *The Thing*, *The Immortal* another *Fugitive*.

It was an experience. I enjoyed it all—Hollywood, the people, even the frustration. My concern is about science fiction on television. When another science fiction idea comes along, I would not like the decision makers to say, "Science fiction doesn't get across on television. Look at *The Immortal*."

A good science fiction show, well conceived and well executed, should have a chance. Fantasy is basic to the human experience, and rationalized fantasy means something special to our times. Not that television needs science fiction, or that science fiction needs television. But it just could be that they were made for each other.

[I need not have worried. After the publication of this article in *TV Guide* in 1971, SF television series exploded in the next three decades, including such notable titles (there were many others) as *Sliders*, *Farscape*, *The Invisible Man*, *Max Headroom*, *Quantum Leap*, *Earth 2*, *Hitchhiker's Guide to the Galaxy*, *V*, *Seaquest*, *Kolchak: The Night Stalker*, *Alien Nation*, various incarnations of *Star Trek*, a reimagining of *Battlestar Galactica*, *The 4400*, *The Dead Zone*, and perhaps the best of all, Michael Straczynski's *Babylon 5*.]

16

THE GREAT SCIENCE FICTION RADIO SHOW

S cience fiction drama on radio came not long after the creation of the first science fiction magazine, *Amazing Stories*, in 1926 and the development of network radio in the late 1920s. Jim Harmon describes the growth of science fiction on radio in *The SF Encyclopedia* and, at greater length, in portions of his 1967 book, *The Great Radio Heroes*. The first SF dramas, he says, were 1929's *The Cobra Strikes Back* and *Land of the Living Dead*, both written by Carleton E. Morse, whose *I Love a Mystery*, which began in 1939, also featured science fiction episodes.

Buck Rogers was the hero of a children's radio show starting in 1932, and so were other comic strip characters such as Flash Gordon and Superman. For adults, there was a suspense show called *Lights Out*; it was first broadcast in 1938, but a later writer was Arch Obeler, whose *Chicken Heart That Ate the World* became a classic. The all-time record for audience and impact, however, had to be the 1938 Mercury Theater adaptation of H. G. Wells's *The War of the Worlds*, broadcast by Orson Welles.

All of this, exciting as it may have been to the radio audiences of the times, was only stage setting for the great era of science fiction radio drama that was to reach its finest expression in the mid-1950s. It began in 1950 as a program entitled *Dimension X*. That radio program, on the air intermittently, included dramatizations from a variety of published stories, including Ray Bradbury's *The Martian Chronicles* and Robert Heinlein's "Requiem." In 1955, the same creative people produced *X Minus One*; its source of material was limited to a single magazine—*Galaxy*. From the commercials for the magazines usually

---

"The Great Science Fiction Radio Show" was first published in *Listen* in November 1982.

broadcast in the introductions and afterwards, *Galaxy* must have cosponsored the show as a way of increasing circulation.

As a strategy, radio advertising for science fiction magazines was unprecedented. "Science fiction," Damon Knight once said, possibly quoting Phil Klass, "is the mass medium for the few." Though it has never been a popular literature, the magazines that published it never averaged a circulation of more than a hundred thousand copies, plus or minus a few tens of thousands. *Amazing Stories* had the readership all to itself for three years. Then there was *Wonder Stories* in 1929, *Astounding Stories of Super Science* in 1930, and by the late 1930s, nearly twenty magazines. But most of those were killed by the war. *Astounding Science Fiction* became the leading magazine in the 1930s and 1940s before the *Magazine of Fantasy and Science Fiction* became a competitor in 1949, and then *Galaxy* in 1950. For a while, *Galaxy* would surpass *Astounding* in excitement and circulation. But the readership was still relatively small.

I do not have the list of *X Minus One* shows or their dates, so I must rely on memory. But these were exciting days for science fiction and for those who wrote it. World War II had validated science fiction's vision, and now the world was moving toward the space age that would begin in 1957. I was freelancing full-time from 1952 to 1955, and although I was only a part-time writer when *X Minus One* was announced in late 1955, the news was received as one more confirmation, as Isaac Asimov would later say, that we were living in a science fiction world, a world that science fiction had described, in which science would be of crucial importance and change the only constant.

As I recall, "The Cave of Night"—a story that was published in the February 1955 issue of *Galaxy*—was one of the first dramatizations of the new series when it was broadcast on February 1, 1956. It had to be early in the series because as the program got going, the producers, as a gesture of goodwill, began sending recordings of the programs to the writers of the original stories. For "The Cave of Night," however, I had to make arrangements with the nearest NBC radio station, WDAF, to record it for me. When I got the recording, I couldn't play it because it had been recorded on a studio-size record that wouldn't fit my record player and I had to have it re-recorded on a standard disk by a local firm. "The Cave of Night" was also scheduled to be the premiere episode in a *Galaxy* television series a couple of years later, but instead the story was sold to Desilu Playhouse and broadcast in 1959 as "Man in Orbit" with Lee Marvin and H. G. Marshall.

There had to be goodwill involved, incidentally, because there wasn't much money: fifty dollars per story dramatized and, after the first one for me, that set of records. Even in those days, that wasn't much. *Galaxy* was paying three to four cents a word for the stories it published, which meant that even the shortest of the stories of mine that were dramatized earned several times as much from the magazine. Nobody got rich selling stories to radio—not the way it was later with television and film.

What was important to me at the time, however, was that the dramatizations were so satisfying—unlike television's adaptation of my novel *The Immortals* into a 1969 ABC Movie of the Week called *The Immortal* and the next year into an hour-long series. Then, I used to sit in my chair in front of my television set with gritted teeth and hands clutching the chair arms.

The visual media have not been kind to science fiction. Beginning with Méliès's *An Astronomer's Dream* in 1898 and his 1902 *A Voyage to the Moon*, film has frequently turned to science fiction for subjects and just as frequently disappointed the audience that reads it. Occasionally, film has offered an effective adaptation, usually of Wells or Verne, but often the result has been a series of B-films featuring various kinds of monsters written by people who don't know anything about science fiction and produced and directed by people who are rewarded for being imitative rather than original.

As a consequence, most science fiction writers, like me, felt that the only true science fiction film ever made was H. G. Wells's *Things to Come*. Since then, *2001: A Space Odyssey* has shown what the idea-centered science fiction film could aspire to. *Star Wars* and its sequels have been incredibly popular and effective for what they are—but what they are, in spite of the science fiction world in which they appear to exist, is fairy tales and they are so recognized in the prefatory crawl.

Something else, perhaps something more important, is wrong with science fiction films. By the concreteness of their images, they limit the imagination. Like adaptations of familiar mainstream books, science fiction adaptations usually disappoint readers because film images fall short of the images in the readers' minds.

And that brings us back to *X Minus One*. We listeners who had experience in reading science fiction were seldom disappointed. One important element in producing superior science fiction drama was that the shows were adaptations of science fiction written by people who knew the genre, rather than by people who knew nothing about SF. Another element was that science fiction stories adapted were current examples of the state of the art. Still another element was that the adaptations were faithful and skillful.

The writing of the radio plays was usually of high quality. I don't know how many writers worked on the series, but one name sticks in my mind: Ernest

Kinoy adapted most of mine. I almost always admired the results. Occasionally he would make changes, particularly in the case of the adaptation of "The Cave of Night," but I understood the reason for the change even if I didn't consider it an improvement. But his script for "Wherever You May Be"—and the production and acting it was given—was a marvel and a joy, particularly since it involved cutting a 25,000-word short novel to less than half an hour of speaking time.

Faithfulness and excellence—these are two qualities an author who has his written work adapted to other media can appreciate. But listeners could appreciate other qualities. Radio was the ideal medium for science fiction drama: sound and word allowed the audience to shape its own images, and the images of the mind are always superior to those on the screen, however large, however small. Put *The Chicken Heart That Ate the World* on the screen and you get *The Blob*. George Pal's *The War of the Worlds* had its good points, but Orson Welles's radio dramatization terrified a nation.

X Minus One was science fiction dramatization at its best. Sadly, it didn't last long—only a couple of years. Its half-hours were numbered even before it got started. Television was already gobbling up audiences and advertising revenues, and radios were used mostly for background music. Now, with the return of a number of dramatic shows to radio, rebroadcasts and new ones, listeners once more have the opportunity not simply to indulge their nostalgia in old-time radio drama, but to see that drama played out in the best medium of all—the theater of the mind. I hope it catches on again.

I'm sure I didn't have the most stories adapted for *X Minus One*. Robert Sheckley, who was tremendously prolific during those years and had most of his stories published in *Galaxy*, probably has that honor, and several other authors may have had more than I. But no one enjoyed them more. *Galaxy* published seven of my stories during those years, and four of them were dramatized on *X Minus One*. They have been rebroadcast since then, and if you are lucky, someday you may turn your radio dial and happen upon "The Cave of Night," "Open Warfare," "Tsylana," or "Wherever You May Be." See if you don't agree with me.

17

LOOKING BACKWARD AT *2001*

2001: A Space Odyssey was an event, and like all events—the start of World War II, the bombing of Pearl Harbor or Hiroshima, the assassinations of John F. Kennedy and Martin Luther King, the first human landing on the moon—it created personal associations. Where were you when it happened? How did you get the news? What did you say? How did you feel?

My personal associations with the film began in 1965, when we were planning the centennial celebration for the University of Kansas. One aspect was an "Intercentury Seminar" looking toward the future, and one participant was Arthur C. Clarke.

At first, we didn't think he was going to be able to make it, and discussions were carried on with the film's promotion director, Roger Caras, about the possibility of a television hookup with London. Then, dates straightened out, and in April 1966, Clarke arrived at the Kansas City Municipal Airport for the experience that he summed up in one sentence in *The Lost Worlds of 2001*.

While we waited for the arrival of the public relations man for MGM, with his hospitality and his talk of limousines, Arthur showed me stills from the film that, two years after the first discussions between Clarke and Kubrick, was two years away from release. One photograph, I remember, showed the instructions for operating a zero-gravity toilet.

The next time Arthur was passing nearby on his lecture circuit, he gave me a call. He had just seen the film, I believe, and he was bubbling with enthusiasm. He also was a bit depressed that he had not yet been able to persuade Kubrick to release the novel. Not too long after that, my family and I made the trip to Kansas City to view the film in Cinerama at the Empire Theater.

"Looking Backward at *2001*" was first published in *Ariel* 4 in 1978.

2001 did not exactly sneak onto the screen. There had been rumors leading to announcements, blending into publicity and promotion. But science fiction fans had been disappointed before, and their expectations, though easily aroused, never lost an edge of skepticism.

So the film was a surprise after all, and a stunning experience for those who saw it in its original form, and understood it. Those who have viewed it in 35-millimeter, or even 16-millimeter (often badly scratched in some later releases), versions can only guess at the impact of this nearly 180-degree experience of yesterday and tomorrow, with the colors bright and the focus sharp, and the reality of the peripheral vision, in the midst of the stereophonic sound of the two Strausses, Richard and Johann.

The New York critics had been wrong. Pauline Kael, who hated it at length for the *New Yorker*, was wrong. It was an event—not perfect, but innovative, and an event. Against its yardstick all future science fiction films would be measured. It makes sense, in the years after the incredible financial success of *Star Wars* and its sequels, *Close Encounters of the Third Kind*, and *E.T., the Extra-Terrestrial*, and other "sci-fi" spectaculars, to reassess the event.

What made it an event was the fact that Kubrick set out in 1964 to make "the proverbially good science fiction movie." He called in a science fiction writer—a first-class science fiction writer—and worked with him, listened to him, even heeded him. He did not set out to make a film of compromises, science fiction for the masses, a film for the average filmgoer, or even the best film to be made with the budget available. It would be a good film, and the budget would be whatever it took to make it right.

What the critics didn't like about the film, perhaps, were its pretensions and its science fiction sophistication. SF films aren't supposed to be good films, and certainly not worthy of serious critical attention. Looking at the history of the science fiction film, they would seem correct, and perhaps their attitude, shared by most filmmakers, had been in large part responsible for the inadequacies of earlier films.

There had been only a handful of good ones up to this time—*Things to Come, Destination Moon, Forbidden Planet*, and *The Time Machine* came closest, and even they had their deficiencies or their silliness. Mostly, the history of the SF film has been monster movies and antiscientific, anti-intellectual defenses of tradition. "There are things man was not meant to know; there are areas of forbidden knowledge where he should not meddle."

Moreover, Kubrick showed a world of the future that was commonplace. The world of *Star Wars* looked lived-in, but the world of *2001* was banal. It was a lesson about the future that science fiction readers had learned long before, but the critics had not yet absorbed: in spite of the poetry of spaceflight and moon settlements and journeys to Jupiter, the citizens of the future would find their world ordinary.

After the initial screenings in New York and Los Angeles, Kubrick cut nineteen minutes from the film, possibly because of critical reaction, possibly because the film ran nearly three hours. It may be an appropriate comment on the differences between critics and fans that the fans loved what the critics hated—the "Dawn of Man" sequence, the spaceship scenes en route to the station, and the scenes of life on the spaceship to Jupiter. These were the scenes trimmed, and only a fortunate few have seen Kubrick's original.

The "Dawn of Man" sequence, incidentally, goes far toward disproving the filmmakers' insistence that one can't film an idea. Without a word spoken, the audience understands the grimness of early hominid existence, the magical appearance of the black monolith and Moonwatcher's timid approach, his picking up of the tapir bone and using it as a tool, first to pound other bones, then to kill tapirs, then to attack his rival hominids and take back the waterhole, and finally throwing it triumphantly into the air where it turns into a spaceship. In the picking up of that bone is implicit the entire future history of human technology, culminating in the spaceship.

The fan reaction was not completely favorable. Most fans had a few quibbles—HAL's murderousness, with its antitechnological bias, in view of Asimov's Three Laws of Robotics, and the ambiguity of the ending—and a few detested it. Lester del Rey had a particularly savage review in *Analog*. Generally, however, it was accepted on its own terms. Ironically, the film became a box office success when it got the reputation of being a great film to attend stoned and blow one's mind on the "Star Gate" sequences.

Star Wars will be measured by other criteria: by the size of its then-record gross, for instance. Never again would filmmakers be able to turn down a good project by claiming that SF films never make money; but we also have had to sit through a hundred or more bad *Star Wars* imitations. To me, however, *Star Wars* was not the event that *2001* was; *Star Wars* was a fun film, a crowd pleaser, a fairy tale with the paraphernalia of science fiction.

Close Encounters was distinguished, for me, by the glorious epiphany of its final sequences, and by the irrelevance and anti-intellectualism of its first hour. *E.T.* was a lost-animal film, a heart-warming *Lassie, Come Home* of space.

How long must we wait for another producer-director with Kubrick's courage, vision, and skill?

4

SCIENCE FICTION AND
THE REAL WORLD

18

THE USES OF SPACE

Space exists only in theory for all but a handful of people. For most of humanity's history, it was in fact inconceivable: nothing in the world that people could know and experience had anything at all to do with that void between the planets and the stars in which nothing could live.

I am not certain where I first encountered space, but it may have been in one of the Mars novels of Edgar Rice Burroughs—although in those books, John Carter crossed space simply by wishing himself to Mars. If not in those marvelous adventure stories, it must have been in one of the science fiction magazines with the glorious covers, that in the early 1930s, I first discovered by trading two hero-pulp magazines for one copy of *Astounding Stories, Amazing Stories*, or *Wonder Stories* from the dusty stacks at the back of Andy's Used Magazine Shop on 12th Street in downtown Kansas City. In one of those magazines, surely, I found a description of that cold, black nothingness that for many years I would think of as "outer space." Only much later would I learn that the space between the worlds could be not too cold, but too hot; not too black, but too bright; not nothingness, but filled with energy and matter—indeed, the stuff of life.

Eventually, I would write a series of stories about space and humanity's coming conquest of it, which would be gathered together into a paperback book titled *Station in Space*. The first of those stories, "The Cave of Night," would be dramatized on the old Desilu Playhouse as "Man in Orbit," with Lee Marvin and H. G. Marshall. That was just before the first man-made object, *Sputnik*, was pushed beyond the atmosphere of Earth into space, and only a couple of years before humanity would experience space in the persons of the Russian cosmonauts Gagarin and Titov and the American astronauts Shepard, Grissom, Glenn, and Carpenter.

"The Uses of Space" was first published in the *Kansas City Star* in May 1984.

We experienced it then, all of us, vicariously with television cameras: the physical realities of space, the dangers of space, the vastness of space, as our surrogates took us along with them into orbit and to the moon, and back again. Until we got bored with it all and called them back. No science fiction writer imagined it would happen that way. Almost no one thought spaceflight would require a massive government effort (most writers thought it would be accomplished by lonely inventors like the Wright brothers, working in their backyards; a few, like Robert A. Heinlein, in *The Man Who Sold the Moon*, that private enterprise would do it). And almost no one envisioned the television coverage. Who could imagine, even among people noted for their imagination, that audiences on Earth would be able to follow the astronauts on their epic journeys, see the first person set a foot into the dust of the moon, have the red sands of Mars reported back to us in a series of still photographs?

And who could have imagined that we would become bored with it? That we would content ourselves for a long time with mechanical eyes in space, look down at Venus and Mars, even land and sense them, and gaze in wonder at Jupiter and its moons, and at Saturn and its magnificent rings? That a decade would elapse before humanity went back into space in the space shuttle and talked about a space station?

What does it all mean? What are people to think of all this? What are the uses of space?

People used to think that the atmosphere, our air, filled the universe. It might become more rarified, harder to breathe—when they climbed mountains, people noticed that the air got thinner—but it never stopped entirely. Lucian, a second-century Greek writer, wrote a couple of stories in which his characters flew to the moon or were carried there by a ship caught up in a storm, and Cyrano de Bergerac, the seventeenth-century adventurer, swordsman, and wit immortalized in Edmond Rostand's play by that name, wrote about flying to the moon with the aid of bottles of dew fastened to his waist or on the back of a mechanical grasshopper, but both writers were satirists and no one could be sure what they really believed.

Francis Godwin, an early seventeenth-century English bishop, may have been somewhat playful in *The Man in the Moone*, when he had his rogue-like hero, Domingo Gonsales, carried to the moon by a flock of swanlike birds called "gansas" on their annual migration. On the other hand, Johannes Kepler, the late sixteenth-century/early seventeenth-century German astronomer, was being entirely serious in *Somnium; or, Lunar Astronomy*, not in how his character, Duracotus, got to the moon (he was carried by a demon), but in giving the moon an atmosphere; and Edgar Allan Poe sent his character, Hans

Pfaall, to the moon in a balloon with a hand-operated condenser (compressor) to help him breathe the thinner air at higher elevations. Of course, even with the aid of the atmosphere or Jules Verne's giant cannon, readers knew that people couldn't really get to the moon, but then they knew they couldn't fly, either. To be sure, if people had listened to Isaac Newton and his seventeenth-century discussion of gravity, they would have realized that the air, too, would be attracted by the planets; or even earlier, to Torricelli, whose measurements of atmospheric pressure showed that the weight of air (and thus its height) was finite.

By the middle of the nineteenth century, scientists knew that space was a void—they had even invented an intangible substance to fill it, called luminiferous (light-bearing) ether, to solve the problem of how light could behave like a wave when there was no medium in which it could propagate itself; one of the key experiments of the 1880s disproved the existence of the ether. Even the writers began to include such concepts in their work, once they got the idea that in this new genre of science fiction it was important to get the facts right, insofar as they were known, and Verne and Wells both wrote about the empty void of space, even though Wells got his characters to the moon by using something as fantastic as antigravity (which annoyed Verne, who in a classical comment refuting the resemblance between his methods and those of the writer who was being called "the English Jules Verne," said "let him show me some of this 'anti-gravity'!").

After that—and probably as much because of the science fiction stories and the Sunday supplements—space got its reputation as a cold, black, empty nothingness. That was how the early science fiction magazines described it. It was a deadly place, a place to be crossed as quickly as possible, a place where if one did not expire from lack of air, one quickly froze or even exploded from internal air pressure, like deep-sea fish brought to the surface of the ocean.

Those images faded in the 1950s, with articles and books by rocket pioneers such as Willy Ley and Wernher von Braun, until Arthur C. Clarke could describe in *Earthlight*, originally serialized in 1951, a spaceman without protection crossing unharmed a gap between ships, which would foreshadow a similar scene in the 1968 Clarke–Kubrick film, *2001: A Space Odyssey*. The notion that space was not so inimical to life, that it might even have some particular advantages for living creatures, had been a subject for speculation as early as the 1890s by visionaries such as Russian physicist Konstantin Tsiolkovsky, followed by American rocket pioneer Robert H. Goddard and English scientist J. D. Bernal, whose 1929 book *The World, The Flesh, and The Devil* suggested that humanity would build space stations, make them self-sufficient little worlds, and fly them between the stars, and perhaps make human habitats from comets. His ideas not only were mined by a generation of science fiction writers but also have inspired such contemporary scientists as Freeman J. Dyson, Gerard K. O'Neill, and Robert L. Forward.

In some ways, scientists have become more adventurous speculators than science fiction writers, as science itself, particularly physics, astronomy, and biology, produces discoveries and new theories more wonderful than science fiction writers ever have been able to imagine.

One fact that became apparent early is that space, unlike Earth, has a plentiful supply of energy—and also, unlike Earth, has an unlimited dump for waste heat and other by-products of living. The sun bathes space so bountifully in energy (with a few exceptions such as geysers and volcanic heat, it supplied all human needs until only the last few decades, when the energy stored up when the planet itself was formed began to be used in atomic reactors) that all people in space need is a cup to catch it in. In the 1950s, scientists and writers were suggesting hot-water boilers, but that was before the invention of the silicon-based solar cell. On this planet of ours, we are running low on the basic requirement for civilization, for human life itself: energy. Oil will run out within decades of now (or become uneconomical to discover—not simply too expensive in terms of money, but too expensive in terms of the energy expended for the energy gained), coal will last a few hundred years, and nuclear energy may only last a thousand or two. Moreover, these sources of energy pollute the environment, not simply with radiation from nuclear reactors but, from the burning of coal and oil, with smoke and dust and acid and, most of all, with carbon dioxide that will be, in the final summing up, more dangerous than radiation. One thing that may save us is thermonuclear fusion, the hydrogen-fusion process that scientists have been trying to perfect. Another is the building in space of gigantic energy-absorbing arrays that can microwave power back to Earth. Then all we need worry about is the buildup of waste heat, and that problem, if it is a problem, should be much easier to solve than the others.

Space has other uses. Some desirable human activities go better in space than elsewhere. Travel is one, not simply to other bodies in space, but here on Earth. Just as the fastest airplanes fly as high as possible to minimize air resistance, ships using space could get from one spot on Earth to any other in a matter of minutes, if it were advantageous to use that kind of speed, and the cost could be managed. Telescopes work better in space, above the distortions of the atmosphere, and radio telescopes, infrared scopes, and small optical telescopes already have been placed in space and have advanced science's understanding of the universe and our neighbors. The Hubble telescope, a large optical telescope, has provided revelations about this vast and mysterious place and astonished us with its beauty.

Certain research projects and manufacturing processes can work best or only work at all in the weightlessness of space, and others can be aided by the availability of the better vacuum to be had free in space than can be created within Earth's atmosphere. Every space shuttle flight carries one or more such projects, and the space station that Ronald Reagan proposed is already more than half-built. Some enthusiasts said that commercial applications would more than pay for the space station costs; they haven't materialized yet, but history seems to provide support for such a view. Even if they should pay only a part of the cost, other benefits might more than make up the difference.

One thing that may go better in space is life itself. There are physiological problems to life in space, to be sure. The loss of calcium in the bones is one, and the deterioration of the muscles is another. Both would have to be remedied before life in space would be possible. But in some ways, life in space could be superior to life on Earth: just as some kind of space-living facility, or habitat as it has come to be called, might be an excellent place for a hospital, particularly for patients with heart disease, whose hearts would no longer have to pump against the pull of gravity, so healthier people with proper exercise might live longer in space than would be possible on Earth.

Even life on the moon might be longer and healthier than life on our planet, although to be born and raised in such a low-gravity environment might mean that one could never return to Earth, except as a muscle-weakened invalid. On the other hand, some daring scientists have speculated that humanity's true home may be space itself. Although human life could not have developed except in a wet and warm environment such as the Earth provided, the pull of its gravity and its thick, wet blanket of air present serious handicaps to many of the things people want to do or might want to do if they had the opportunity.

Space also has resources. For a time, space-dwelling humanity might depend for its support upon supplies ferried up from the mother planet at great expense, but in addition to the energy available in space for the taking (no drilling, no mining, just simple, clean absorption of the sun's photons in a place where the sun always shines), which makes everything else possible, there are minerals, and even complicated chemicals. The moon, of course, is an obvious source of many materials essential to life and technological civilization (the only kind possible in space), not only various kinds of ores but, bound up chemically in the rock (and extractable with the aid of that almost-free energy), water and oxygen. But there are also the other planets, some of them virtually inexhaustible mines of valuable substances, some of them already refined by nature.

Jupiter, for instance, has vast supplies of hydrogen largely lost by most of the other planets but held by Jupiter's tremendous bulk (it contains more matter than all the rest of the planets combined, and stops just short of becoming a star shining by its own thermonuclear reactions). Saturn is also a source of marvelous gases. Of course, they represent some of the same gravitational problems as Earth (because of their mass, the problem is many times as great), but with the freely available energy of space, almost anything becomes possible. We do not know now how such resources might be exploited, but there is no reason to think that the problem is inherently insoluble.

The satellites of the other planets, like Earth's moon, might be easier to tackle at first, and some of them are almost as fabulous as the planets. Titan, for instance, Saturn's largest moon and itself as large as the smallest planet, is a veritable chemical factory, with a warehouse it has been filling over the past few billion years with untouched stores of frozen and liquid methane. Titan is like an orbiting gas well with a bottomless reservoir. In fact, if Titan could be moved into proximity to Earth (or a "pipeline" could be put into place), we might never have to worry about energy again (of course, we might have to worry about the gravitational disturbance and the atmospheric pollution with carbon dioxide!).

But there are other resources, some of them even easier to tap. The asteroids, for instance, most of which orbit between Mars and Jupiter and are thus relatively accessible, contain vast quantities of metal. Numerous authorities have suggested (and some writers, like George Zebrowski, in *Macrolife*, have converted their suggestions into science fiction) the idea that the larger bodies among them should be moved to an area closer to Earth, mined for our use by hollowing them out, and then converted into habitats for space-dwelling humans, even giving them a certain spin to provide an artificial gravity to make getting around more convenient (and to allow crops to be grown), as well as maintaining a certain muscle tone among its inhabitants.

In addition, the rings of Saturn could be mined for their ice, though it would be a pity to despoil such a magnificent natural phenomenon. Some of the icy moons of Saturn might do instead. And the comets, a vast body of which may orbit the sun in an area beyond the farthest planets before they are disturbed (by forces about which scientists are only recently beginning to speculate) to come plunging periodically toward the sun, are mostly dirty ice. That "dirt," however, may be of great value. In the comets, as well as in the vast clouds of dust and gas between the stars, scientists have identified more than seventy compounds, some of them complex, many classifiable as organic. Some scientists even have speculated that such compounds, formed in space, may have provided the original seeds around which life on Earth (and possibly on other planets) developed.

Once people begin to live in space, they many even become nomadic, as Bernal and other speculators have suggested, moving about not only within the solar system, but between the stars. Some of the space-dwellers might decide to colonize other Earthlike planets, but most might prefer to live within their more comfortable habitats. The final result would be, as Ray Bradbury said about our first manned landing on the moon, that humanity now would be immortal—or at least as immortal as the universe itself. The universe is expected to last billions of years longer than the Earth, even if we avoid destroying our planet with pollution, overpopulation, disease, or Armageddon and if we avert such natural catastrophes as collision with a large meteorite, comet, or asteroid (which, incidentally, our presence in space might make possible), drastic changes in climate such as a new ice age or a major increase in the Earth's temperature, and the vast number of other perils to which planets are susceptible.

Will we do this? Will we venture into space to live? No one knows. I don't have a great deal of confidence in that future because there are so many things that could go wrong—a final war, a natural catastrophe, a major depression, or, worst of all, a terminal energy shortage that would drop the level of our technological civilization below the point necessary to support space colonization. Perhaps most important is a failure of will, a loss of faith in human possibilities, a disappearance of the spirit to take risks, to adventure, that sent the Pilgrims west across the Atlantic and the pioneers west across this continent.

There are so many other human problems to solve, and it may not matter that accomplishing space colonization will not hinder the solution of those problems or that not doing it will not solve them, just as settling this continent did not deprive Europe nor did pioneering the west hinder the development of the eastern states. Instead, it well may be true that the effort to settle space would reinvigorate our society, turn us outward rather than inward against ourselves, give us new confidence in ourselves as a people, and be a moral substitute for war and other aggressions, as I said in *Station in Space*. It will not solve our population problems, just as the millions of emigrants from Europe did not reduce its population significantly, but it may reduce the psychological pressures that make groups focus on small differences between them rather than the great, common human experience that unites them, and it will certainly mean that all of humanity's future will not be tied to one fragile world capable of being destroyed by accident or rash decision.

Should we do it? I don't think there is any doubt about that. Many of us will get no benefit from it directly, though the indirect benefits may be many and the benefits for the human spirit may be incalculable. Will it solve our problems? Of course not. Probably it will bring us new ones. But once again, we should dream great dreams and plan great deeds. What we do in this world is not always for ourselves. Occasionally—not often enough, to be sure—we think of others, of our children or our grandchildren or the children of the species to which we belong. We should do one magnificent thing for them every generation.

Would I go? I might have gone when I was young and foolish, but not now when I am older and a bit wiser and a great deal more cautious. But there is no reason I should extend my own preferences to others. If the possibility were made available, I have no doubt that applicants would be knocking down doors. Gerard O'Neill and his followers, the L-5 Societies and similar groups around the country, are evidence of that, as well as the astronauts who would volunteer for the first trip to Mars even if they had only one chance in five of getting back safely. Almost everywhere in the world, one could find young people by the thousands eager to emigrate into space.

If it ever happens, I hope I will be here to see it. I will be cheering them on, not simply to see my early speculations made fact, not even to see my early dreams realized. I will be cheering them on because I think it is the right thing to do.

A SHORT HISTORY OF THE SPACE PROGRAM

or, A Funny Thing Happened on the Way to the Moon

No one is going to say that science fiction readers and writers brought a man to the moon all by themselves, but we can say that the kind of science fiction that was published in the 1940s helped prepare the public for the acceptance of programs to take a man to the moon.

—Isaac Asimov

L ife does not come ordered neatly like an essay or a short story, but in discrete and random packets like photons; the art of the writer is to find a pattern, to order the packets with neat connectives and transitions. The hope of the writer is that what he writes still resembles life. The situation is further complicated when reality and dreams become intertwined.

To understand all this, to understand how dreams shaped reality and how reality reduced the dream, you must look at a scene from the past. This is reality (the clues from now on will be more obscure):

The time: 1954.

The place: A basement study.

A relatively young man—thirty-one—is sitting in front of an L. C. Smith office-style typewriter at a sawed-off library table. He is trying to imagine what space flight will be like, to write a series of stories about the next steps in man's

---

"A Short History of the Space Program" was first published in *Vertex* 2 in 1974.

conquest of space. They will be published in magazines and then gathered together into a paperback book called *Station in Space*. The first story, "The Cave of Night," will be included in a best-of-the-year collection and then dramatized on television's Desilu Playhouse as "Man in Orbit," with Lee Marvin and H. G. Marshall. Like the story, the television show features a scene in which Kansas City turns its lights off and on to signal a man orbiting the Earth in his spaceship.

You also must imagine other scenes of other men and women imagining and writing scenes, retreating back through the centuries almost two thousand years. And you must imagine not just writers, but men and women of all kinds, as far back as they could raise their eyes to the night sky and see the great silver circle of the moon—waxing and waning, inconstant, controlling the tides and who knows what else, like a sister of Earth with seas and plains and mountains and features—peopling that world with men and women or monsters or gods, dreaming of crossing the river of space that separated the two worlds, of setting foot on the moon.

Finally, you must picture men and women holding in their hands the dreams written into words on a scroll or book or flaking pulp-paper magazine with lurid cover, living the dream in their imaginations . . .

*   *   *

Apollo 17, the last moon shot (*moon shot*—does it remind you of Verne and the giant cannon, the Columbiad, built deep into the soil of Florida?), last of a series of rocket launches, vast gushings of liquid oxygen and hydrogen combining furiously into flame . . . and a frail capsule drifting precisely down a computer path in space toward Earth's satellite, product of a commitment to science and adventure and national supremacy, ending now with dwindling enthusiasm, even a bit of boredom and a counting of cost.

This one, the first night launch, delayed a bit on the launching pad by the failure of a relay and computer obstinacy. The human element seems lost in the vast mechanical array, the tall rocket itself, the platform and its service mechanisms, the intricate computer controls and sensors, the long room of men with their data displays, earphones, keyboards . . .

And finally, incredible thunder, the flaming heart of the sun revealed, the slender metal pillar balancing on a lengthening column of incandescence, lifting, accelerating, dwindling, carrying with it the command ship *America* and the lunar module *Challenger*.

*   *   *

We were suddenly caught by a whirlwind, which turned our vessel several times round in a circle with tremendous speed and lifted it more than three thousand stadia into the air, not setting it down again on the sea, but kept it suspended above the water at that height, and carried us on, with swelled sails, above the clouds.

After an aerial voyage of seven days and seven nights, we sighted land in the air. It was an island, luminous, spherical, and shining with strong light.

*   *   *

He walked into the meeting room in Topeka's Ramada Inn, where the lights and the cameras were waiting. He was medium tall, dark-haired, balding, tanned, athletically lean and firm. He was neatly dressed in red slacks, white turtleneck sweater, dark-blue jacket with a small metal sunflower in one lapel, a colorful Apollo 17 patch on his breast pocket. He wore red, white, and blue. The television newscasters called him "Captain America," but his name was Ronald Evans, and he was one of two dozen men who had been to the moon, although only half of them had actually walked upon it.

"I'm really just a representative," he said, "not only of the other astronauts and the people who helped create the technology and the hardware, but of our nation and of all the people who dreamed about it. I am a representative; I have a responsibility and my responsibility is to allow the rest of the people of our nation to share—one way or another—a part of the experience I had."

*   *   *

October 4, 1957: *Sputnik*, shattering all the old American dreams, shredding the old "Engine Charlie" Wilson's who-cares-what-makes-grass-green anti-science, remolding American education, injecting concepts of haste, of primacy, into American space efforts.

November 3, 1957: *Sputnik II*. Weight: about 1,120 pounds. Cargo: a live dog.

January 31, 1958: *Explorer I*. Weight: 31 pounds.

October 4, 1959: Another Soviet satellite orbits the moon and, for the first time, photographs its mysterious far side.

*   *   *

The whole trip, long though it is, lasts at most four hours. We cannot travel between the Earth and the moon when we want, for passage-time is limited to eclipses of the moon, those times when a patch of blackness moves over the eastern face of the moon. . . . We rush upon a person . . . and bear him aloft. This initial movement is most uncomfortable and dangerous, for the traveler is torn aloft and hurled over mountain and seas as if blown up by gunpowder. Thus, he must be put to sleep by narcotics and opiates, and his limbs must be carefully managed, lest his head be torn from his body when his body leaves the ground. The force of the repulsion must be distributed evenly over all parts of the body.

After starting, the traveler meets new dangers, a terrible, bitter cold and lack of air to breathe.

*　　*　　*

"The dream of being a spaceman has been around for years. Primarily, the part that I recall is the Buck Rogers days.

"Now we as a nation have developed the capability of actually surviving on another planet. We have developed the capability of going anywhere in the universe we want to go.

"Twelve people have walked on the moon, six of us have been command module pilots who orbited the moon, another three on *Apollo 8* were the first to actually orbit the moon, and the ill-fated *Apollo 13* flight arced around the moon.

"Two dozen people have been where many men have dreamed of being."

*　　*　　*

April 12, 1961: *Vostok I.* Yuri Gagarin is launched into orbit, and the dream, in the process of being realized, is strangely altered: a Russian, not an American, is the first into space.

May 5, 1961: *Mercury-Redstone 3.* Alan B. Shepard's fifteen-minute suborbital flight, by comparison with the Russian achievement, is like a child's toss into the sea.

May 24, 1961: President John F. Kennedy reverses the direction set by former president Eisenhower's science advisers, who disapproved an early attempt to land men on the moon, by proposing to Congress "that this nation should commit itself to achieving the goal, before the end of this decade is out, of landing a man on the moon and returning him safely to Earth."

July 21, 1961: Virgil I. Grissom exceeds Shepard's suborbital record by one minute; his capsule sinks in the ocean.

August 6, 1961: *Vostok II.* Gherman S. Titov spends more than a day in orbit and exults, "I am eagle!"

February 20, 1962: *Mercury-Atlas 6.* At last, an American, John H. Glenn, circles the Earth three times; as he passes over Perth, Australia, the city turns its lights off and on as a greeting to the first orbiting American astronaut.

*　　*　　*

After Eleven daies passage in this violent flight, I perceived that we began to approach neare unto another Earth, if I may so call it, being the Globe or very body of that starre which we call the Moone. . . . My Gansa's staied their course as it was with one consent, and tooke their rest, for certaine howers; after which they took their flight, and within lesse than one hower, set me upon the top of a very high hill in that other world, where immediately were presented unto mine eyes many most strange and unwonted sights.

* * *

"When you're orbiting the moon, you really don't feel as if you are in deep space—the moon is another body like the Earth. But I had the opportunity to open the hatch on the command module. We were 180,000 miles from the Earth, and I went out and walked in space. That's when you get the feeling for the first time that you really are out in space—it is black! You look off in one direction and you can see a small moon. You look off 180 degrees from that direction and you see the sliver of the Earth."

* * *

May 24, 1962: *Mercury-Atlas 7* carries M. Scott Carpenter three times around the Earth and lands him 250 miles from his target.

August 11, 1962: *Vostok III*. Andrian G. Nikolayev spends nearly four days in space.

August 12, 1962: *Vostok IV*. Pavel R. Popovich comes within three miles of *Vostok III* on his first orbit.

October 3, 1962: *Mercury-Atlas 8*. Walter M. Schirra Jr. orbits the Earth six times.

May 15, 1963: *Mercury-Atlas 9*. L. Gordon Cooper Jr. makes the first long flight by an American, just short of a day and a half.

June 14, 1963: *Vostok V*. Valery F. Bykovsky spends five days in space.

June 16, 1963: *Vostok VI*. The first woman in space, Valentina V. Tereshkova, passes within three miles of *Vostok V*.

* * *

April 3d. I found the balloon at an immense height indeed, and the Earth's convexity had now become strikingly manifest. Below me, in the ocean, lay a cluster of black specks which undoubtedly were islands. Overhead, the sky was of a jetty black, and the stars were brilliantly visible; indeed they had been so constantly since the first day of the ascent. . . .

April 11th. Found a startling diminution in the apparent diameter of the Earth, and a considerable increase, now observable for the first time, in that of the moon itself, which wanted only a few days of being full. It now required long and excessive labor to condense within the chamber sufficient atmospheric air for the sustenance of life.

* * *

"I was tied to the spacecraft and connected to my oxygen umbilical, but space is so vast you never really got the feeling that you wanted to let loose. There were bars on the outside of the spacecraft that I moved along, reaching out with one hand at a time. I never wanted to let go with both hands at the same time. That was my one contact with life."

*   *   *

October 12, 1964: *Voshkod I.* The first three-man spacecraft orbits with Vladimir M. Komarov, Konstantin P. Feoktistov, and Boris G. Yegorov.

March 18, 1964: *Voshkod II.* Alexei A. Leonov and Pavel I. Belayev spend more than a day in space; Leonov becomes the first man to step out into space.

March 23, 1965: *Gemini 3.* Virgil I. Grissom and John W. Young perform the first manned orbital maneuvers.

June 3, 1965: *Gemini 4.* James A. McDivitt and Edward H. White II spend more than four days in orbit; White "walks in space" for twenty-one minutes.

August 21, 1965: *Gemini 5.* L. Gordon Cooper Jr. and Charles Conrad Jr. are in space for nearly eight days.

December 4, 1965: *Gemini 7.* Frank Borman and James A. Lovell Jr. orbit for nearly fourteen days.

December 15, 1965: *Gemini 6-A.* Walter M. Schirra Jr. and Thomas P. Stafford rendezvous within one foot of *Gemini 7.*

*   *   *

Thirty-five!-thirty-six!-thirty-seven!-thirty-eight!-thirty-nine!-forty! FIRE!

Instantly, Murchison pressed with his finger the key of the electric battery, restored the current of the fluid, and discharged the spark into the breach of the Columbiad.

An appalling, unearthly report followed instantly, such as can be compared to nothing whatever known, not even to the roar of thunder, or the blast of volcanic explosions! No words can convey the slightest idea of the terrific sound! An immense spout of fire shot up from the bowels of the earth as from a crater. The earth heaved up, and with great difficulty, some few spectators obtained a momentary glimpse of the projectile victoriously cleaving the air in the midst of the fiery vapors!

*   *   *

Do you think the time will come when people will have adapted sufficiently to the space environment that they will be able to let go with both hands?

"Definitely. We have already developed that capability in what we called the 'Skylab' program. It included a maneuvering unit with which we were able to control ourselves in space. That was one of the greatest feelings ever—to be able to maneuver independently and not feel that you have to hang on to something. You can go where you want to go—a true Buck Rogers experience."

*   *   *

March 16, 1966: *Gemini 8.* Neil Armstrong and David R. Scott dock with an *Agena* target, although their mission is cut short.

June 3, 1966: *Gemini 9-A*. Thomas P. Stafford and Eugene A. Cernan combine a rendezvous, extravehicular activity, and a precision landing.

July 18, 1966: *Gemini 10*. John W. Young and Michael Collins rendezvous with two targets and retrieve an *Agena* package.

September 12, 1966: *Gemini 11*. Charles Conrad Jr. and Richard F. Gordon Jr. rendezvous and dock.

November 11, 1966: *Gemini 12*. To make 1966 a U.S. space year, James A. Lovell Jr. and Edwin F. Aldrin Jr. close out the *Gemini* program with three successful extravehicular trips.

*   *   *

I remember how one day Cavor suddenly opened six of our shutters and blinded me so that I cried aloud at him. The whole area was moon, a stupendous scimitar of white dawn with its edge hacked out by notches of darkness, the crescent sort of an ebbing tide of darkness, out of which peaks and pinnacles came climbing into the blaze of the sun. I take it the reader has seen pictures or photographs of the moon, so that I need not describe the broader features of that landscape, those spacious ringlike ranges vaster than any terrestrial mountains, their summits shining in the day, their shadows harsh and deep, the gray disordered plains, the ridges, hills, and craterlets, all passing at last from a blazing illumination into a common mystery of black. Athwart this world we were flying scarcely a hundred miles above its crests and pinnacles. And now we could see what no eye on Earth will ever see, that under the blaze of the day, the harsh outlines of the rocks and ravines of the plains and crater floor grew gray and indistinct under a thickening haze, that the white of their lit surfaces broke into lumps and patches, and broke again and shrank and vanished, and that here and there, strange tints of brown and olive grew and spread.

*   *   *

"I don't believe there is anything any more that we can call science fiction. Anything men want to do, they can do. Nothing is impossible if man wants to do it. I think that history will tell that during the last few decades, through the space program—*Mercury, Gemini, Apollo*—for the first time, man developed the capability of living beyond our Earth."

*   *   *

January 27, 1967: Spaceflight has been described as "the safest way to travel," but proof of its inherent danger, confirmation of the secret fears that lurked behind its mask of cool competence, comes with a flash fire during a simulated countdown of *Apollo 1* that kills Virgil I. Grissom, Edward H. White, and Roger B. Chaffee.

April 23, 1967: *Soyuz 1*. Vladimir M. Komarov dies when his descending capsule plummets to Earth, its main parachute fouled.

October 11, 1968: *Apollo 7*. Walter M. Schirra Jr., Donn F. Eisele, and R. Walter Cunningham ride the first manned Apollo spacecraft for more than 260 hours.

October 26, 1968: *Soyuz III*. Georgi T. Beregovoi rendezvouses with the unmanned *Soyuz II*.

December 21, 1968: *Apollo 8*. Frank Borman, James A. Lovell Jr., and William A. Anders travel around the moon.

*   *   *

He sat very quiet, rubbing his hands against the soil of the Moon and sensing the curiously light pressure of his body against the ground. At long last there was peace in his heart. His hurts had ceased to pain him. He was where he had longed to be—he had followed his need. Over the western horizon hung the Earth at last quarter, a green-blue giant moon. Overhead, the Sun shone down from a black and starry sky. And underneath—the Moon; the soil of the Moon itself. He was on the Moon!

He lay back still while a bath of content flowed over him like a tide at flood, and soaked into his very marrow.

*   *   *

Are men ever going to colonize the moon?

"Man already has colonized the moon—for three days. All we need is a bigger house to stay in. A lot of hydrogen comes off the sun. A lot of oxides are in the moon rocks. Put the hydrogen and the oxygen together and you've got water. We've got power; in fact, we left five atomic generators—about two feet tall and six or eight inches in diameter—on the moon and they're still working. Once you've got water and power, you have the ability to survive indefinitely."

Do you dream about setting your foot on Mars?

"That would be an ideal dream. But that's going to be a few years down the road. We've had unmanned projects go to Mars, but we're just in the Model I stages of space exploration. We could go to Mars now if we wanted to, but the trip would take a year and we'd want some of the niceties that go along with normal living before we really shoved off for a year in space."

*   *   *

January 15, 1969: *Soyuz IV*. Vladimir A. Shatalov is hurled into orbit and . . .

January 15, 1969: *Soyuz V*. . . . so are Boris V. Volyanov, Alexei S. Yeliseyev, and Yevgeni V. Khrunov for a rendezvous in which Yelizseyev and Khrunov transfer to *Soyuz IV*.

March 3, 1969: *Apollo 9*. James A. McDivitt, David R. Scott, and Russell L. Schweickart dock with the lunar module.

May 18, 1969: *Apollo 10*. Thomas P. Stafford, Eugene A. Cernan, and John W. Young descend within nine miles of the moon.

July 16, 1969: *Apollo 11*. Neil A. Armstrong, Edwin E. Aldrin Jr., and Michael Collins take off for the moon. Armstrong and Aldrin descend to the surface in the lunar module, and Armstrong puts Man's footprints in the dust of the moon.

*　　*　　*

The crew was hoisted far up into the nose section of the three-stage rocket. It stood as tall as a 24-story building. . . . The takeoff was all calculated and impressed on the metal and glass and free electrons of an electronic computer.

The ship was tightened down methodically. The spectators scurried back from the base of the ship. We waited. The ship waited. Tall and slim as it was, it seemed to crouch. Someone counted off the seconds to a breathless world: ten, nine, eight . . . five, four, three . . . one—fire!

There was no flame, and then we saw it spurting into the air from the exhaust tunnel several hundred feet away. The ship balanced, unmoving, on a squat column of incandescence; the column stretched itself, grew tall; the huge ship picked up speed and dwindled into a point of brightness.

The telescopic lenses found it, lost it, found it again. It arched over on its side and thrust itself seaward. At the end of 84 seconds, the rear jets faltered, and our hearts faltered with them. Then we saw that the first stage had been dropped. The rest of the ship moved off on a new fiery trail.

*　　*　　*

"The space shuttle is going to revolutionize the space program because we will be able to put something into space for one-tenth the cost. Space becomes a commercial possibility. The Wright brothers, when they developed the airplane, had no way of knowing its commercial possibilities. But others saw those possibilities and said, 'Hey, I can ship something faster and get my product to my customers faster if I put it on an airplane.' And that's the way it is going to be with the space shuttle."

*　　*　　*

A funny thing happened on our way to the moon: the dream faded, people began turning off their television sets, one Apollo flight, one astronaut, began blending together and the little differences—color television, a new moon location, a Moon Rover, a real geologist—no longer sufficed to distinguish one from another. Men began counting the cost: $24 billion to put a man on the moon . . . If we can put a man on the moon, why can't we solve our traffic problems or pollution problems or peace problems or racial problems or poverty problems? If we had applied that money to poverty or education or finding a cure for . . .

Part of the trouble was that the engineers took over and pushed out the dreamers: in spite of the symbiosis of the space program and television, the process was deglamorized, the astronauts were presented to their publics as ordinary men, the apparatus—the world's biggest rocket, the colossal Vehicle Assembly Building, the land crawler, the launching pad, the vast, interminable views of technicians by the hundreds watching their screens—became the hero and dehumanized the accomplishment. Even the language—perhaps most of all the language—was prosaic: ascent stage, command module, extravehicular mobility unit, lunar module, lunar orbit insertion, portable life-support system, space walk . . . Everything may have been A-OK, all systems may have been go, but the romance had been exorcised.

And the dream faltered in a gray democratic fallacy, without a poet, without even a language in which to imagine itself.

*　　*　　*

There is a sameness to them, he thought. A dedication, a mania that molds their feature, a look to the eyes as if they were fashioned for seeing more distant vistas than other men. There were all shapes and colors and faces, but the differences only emphasized their kinship. They came from identical molds labeled: "Experiment—Homo Spatium."

They were marked men. Marked not just by the deep tan of unfiltered ultraviolet or the cataracts of heavy primaries, but by a common experience and a dream shared, marked so that all men might know them and say, "There goes a spaceman."

*　　*　　*

"I firmly believe that we will explore our solar system—we have the capability now; all we need is the desire. Beyond that—well, there have to be other solar systems. There have to be other intelligent beings somewhere. Going there is the next big step."

Will we come in contact with them?

"I'm sure we will."

Will we go to them or will they come to us?

"You always like to be the man who comes up and says, 'Hello, I'm from Earth,' rather than have someone come up behind you and say, 'Hi there! I'm from Alpha Centauri.'"

*　　*　　*

They had their poetry, these men. Space forced it on them, made them see life differently, made them invent words to express it.

Neil Armstrong: "I remember on the trip home on *Apollo 11*, it suddenly struck me that that tiny pea, pretty and blue, was the Earth. I put up my thumb and shut one eye, and my thumb blotted out the planet Earth. I didn't feel like a giant. I felt very, very small."

Bill Anders: The sight of Earth from space evoked "feelings about humanity and human needs that I never had before."

Rusty Schweickart: "I completely lost my identity as an American astronaut. I felt a part of everyone and everything sweeping past me below."

Tom Stafford: "You don't look down at the world as an American, but as a human being."

Michael Collins: "I knew I was alone in a way that no Earthling had ever been before."

Ed Mitchell: "You develop an instant global consciousness, a people orientation, an intense dissatisfaction with the state of the world and a compulsion to do something about it."

* * *

I've seen what no man has ever seen before. . . . I was the first. That's something . . . worth dying for. . . .

I've seen the stars, clear and undiminished. They look cold, but there's warmth to them, and life. They have families of planets, like our own sun, some of them. . . . They must. God wouldn't put them there for no purpose. . . . They can be homes to our future generations. Or, if they have inhabitants, we can trade with them: goods, ideas, the love of creation. . . .

But—more than this—I have seen the Earth. I have seen it—as no man has ever seen it—turning below me like a fantastic ball, the seas like blue glass in the Sun . . . or lashed into gray storm peaks . . . and the land green with life . . . the cities of the world in the night, sparkling . . . and the people. . . .

* * *

"Ten to fifteen or twenty years is a reasonable time scale for landing a man on Mars or for colonizing the moon. It might come sooner, but in order for it to come sooner, we'd have to commit ourselves as a nation to landing a man on Mars within a shorter time. Whatever goals we wish to set for ourselves, we can accomplish."

When will we set off on our first interstellar expedition? Fifty years?

"Probably more than that. But I hope I'm wrong. And I hope we're both around to see it."

Either because it comes sooner or because we've discovered immortality?

"Right."

* * *

The last trip to the moon, the newsmen called it. *Apollo 17.* Eugene A. Cernan, spacecraft commander; Harrison H. Schmitt, lunar module pilot; Ronald Evans, command module pilot.

The last trip . . . New priorities, other dreams.

But old dreams die hard.

If men remember the twentieth century, they will remember it not for its wars and inventions, its revolutions and social programs and great men, but as that time when man finally reached the moon.

Men will remember. And they will go back to the moon . . .

*   *   *

THE DREAM

The True History. Lucian of Samosata, second century A.D.

Somnium. Johannes Kepler, 1634.

The Man in the Moone. Bishop Francis Godwin, 1638.

The Unparalleled Adventures of One Hans Pfaall. Edgar Allan Poe, 1835.

From the Earth to the Moon. Jules Verne, 1865.

The First Men in the Moon. H. G. Wells, 1901.

"Requiem," Robert A. Heinlein, 1940.

"The Cave of Night," James E. Gunn, 1955.

"Powder Keg," James E. Gunn, 1958.

"The Cave of Night," James E. Gunn, 1955.

20

SHAPECHANGERS AND FEARMONGERS

Alterations in the common shape of humanity always have produced the twin reactions of fascination and horror. Any change in the nature of things is psychologically disturbing, and one persistent theme in terror stories has involved objects assuming other shapes or creatures changing their appearance. The real world should be fixed, not protean.

Part of the fascination of the two great nineteenth-century horror novels— *Frankenstein* and *Dracula*—lies in the fact that the Frankenstein monster's parts are dead and come alive, and Count Dracula is dead but never dies.

The strongest reaction, however, is reserved for changes in the human shape. We shudder at teratologies, whether imaginary or real. We draw back from the amputee more than pity would require; we recoil, at least momentarily, from the dwarf and the giant.

The human race began speculating about shapechangers early in its history. Greek legends are full of them. The gods were always assuming other guises. But that's all right—that's part of the order of things; that's divine power and privilege. Zeus was always appearing as a bull or a swan or a shower of gold, particularly when some woman caught his fancy, and the prototypical shapechanger, Proteus, was more miracle than horror.

But changes in humans were more serious, more frightening: Odysseus's men changed into swine, Narcissus into a flower, Daphne into a tree, Arachne into a spider . . . That threat evolves into the horror of the old Germanic fairy tales: evil witches could change princes into frogs, children into stones, women into deer . . .

The travel stories, beginning with the *Odyssey* and continuing down through

"Shapechangers and Fearmongers" was first published in *The Diversifier* in March 1978.

The Travels of Sir John Mandeville, were a kind of freak show, describing the curious customs of the curious creatures who live in the strange distant places of the world—Amazons, one-eyed giants, hermaphrodites, and people who have their heads beneath their shoulders.

The first interplanetary story, Lucian's *A True History* (A.D. 165), included an episode in which men try to copulate with trees shaped like women, and take root and grow to them. Bishop Francis Godwin's *The Man in the Moone* (1638) finds men on the moon twice as tall as men on Earth; Cyrano de Bergerac discovers four-legged men in his *Voyage to the Moon* (1657). Jonathan Swift returned to the earlier travel-story tradition in *Gulliver's Travels* and found his Lilliputians and Brobdingnagians on remote islands.

What is the natural shape of humanity? With remarkable unanimity, the human race has agreed that it is whatever shape they happen to be. The enemy is the person who does not look like you: he is too tall, too short, another color, another shape. You hate the way he looks, and the worst imaginable fate is to be changed into your enemy. The shape you have now is the best of shapes; in the country of the blind, the one-eyed man is *not* king.

H. G. Wells touched upon these traditional fears with his novel *The Island of Dr. Moreau* (1896), in which a scientist changes animals into humans by vivisection and pain. *The First Men in the Moon* (1901) ventured even further. Cavor, the scientist who invented the antigravity substance that enables his ship to reach the moon, is fascinated by the process of chemical conditioning, surgery, and training with which the antlike Selenites turned themselves into creatures specialized for their tasks, whether it was a single giant hand or an overgrown brain like the Grand Lunarian. But Wells's scientific fascination never lacked an element of human horror.

In much of his early work, Wells, called by many critics the "father of modern science fiction," was a fantasist. He dealt not so much with real possibilities as with philosophical ultimates made plausible; he was a writer of satire and parables—"domesticating the impossible hypothesis," he called it. At first, this may have been because he saw no reasonable way to get there from here. Later, he abandoned philosophy for social concern, and his work became more pragmatic and predictive. And science began to show how man could be shaped by society and by his own hand.

By 1927, the biological sciences had developed to the point that Julian Huxley (grandson of T. H. Huxley, Wells's mentor), himself a biologist, director-general of UNESCO, and brother of writer Aldous Huxley, could write "The Tissue-Culture King" and see it reprinted in *Amazing Stories*. It describes how a British biologist captured by an African tribe sets up biological laboratories to support the local religion of king-worship by keeping royal tissue cultures alive and by developing different shapes and sizes of tribesmen to serve the king. Nobel laureate Alexis Carrel had already pioneered in the transplantation of organs, invented (with Charles A. Lindbergh) a mechanical heart, and devised methods for keeping tissue and organs alive in nutritive solutions.

Only three years later, Olaf Stapledon, in *Last and First Men*, could write without horror about the evolution of humanity into dozens of different shapes. Eric Frank Russell concluded "Metamorphosite" (1946) by revealing that Man had evolved into something resembling the sun, and Arthur C. Clarke showed the children of humanity discarding their fleshly forms to join the Overmind in *Childhood's End* (1953).

John Taine's "The Ultimate Catalyst" (1939) speculated about the possibility of transforming hemoglobin into chlorophyll and thereby changing men into fungi. Some element of horror remained, but it was disarmed by the fact that the victims were an exiled dictator and his followers, and the scientist's action allowed his daughter to escape.

In C. L. Moore's classic "No Woman Born" (1944), the key question from the beginning is how people will react to one person's change of appearance. A beautiful, talented woman, horribly burned in a theater fire, has been restored with a metal body. Her friends worry about people recoiling from her and wonder how she will react to her loss; she demonstrates new powers and abilities and wonders if she can remain human.

A quarter of a century later, Damon Knight looked at the concept again in "Masks" (1968) and dealt with the disgust a man almost totally converted into a machine would feel toward sweaty, oozing people. In an analysis of the story (*Those Who Can*, edited by Robin Scott Wilson, 1973), Knight would make the significant comment that the story aimed at squeezing out of the reader "a drop of sympathy and horror."

What is the essential nature of humanity? What is the irreducible quality that makes people people?

In 1952, James Blish dealt with substantial changes in the shape of humanity. In "Surface Tension," seed ships are adapting Man "panatropically" to live on different kinds of planets. An emergency causes one seed ship to create microscopic creatures that can evolve in a freshwater puddle. The story insists that the creatures still are human.

Gradually the question of shape began to merge with the question of origin. The possibilities that Mary Shelley considered in *Frankenstein* were reconsidered in Isaac Asimov's robot stories, beginning in 1941. By 1941, the creation of artificial life was a real possibility; if it were to enter the realm of reality, then it must be considered without horror, without hint of "forbidden knowledge," as Asimov has said. It must be considered as rational engineering.

The questions about the creation of life raised by Asimov's robot stories (and others) become more complicated when the artificial being is created in human form, as it is in Karel Capek's *R.U.R.* (1921). Later, these kinds of creatures came to be called in science fiction, not "robots," but "androids." In stories like J. T. McIntosh's "Made in U.S.A." (1953) and Robert Silverberg's *Tower of Glass* (1970), the question, very clearly, is: even if the creature is indistinguishable from humans, does a difference in origin mean that the creature is not human?

In *Time Quarry* (1950, also called *First He Died* and *Time and Again*), Clifford Simak preached that all living creatures, including androids, are brothers. A vast differentiation in the human form, created by man through genetic manipulation, has produced such mutant species as Fliers, Swimmers, Watchers, Defenders, Changelings, and others in Robert Silverberg's *Nightwings* (1968), and questions of prejudice merge into problems of breaking out of traditional molds.

In the 1960s and 1970s, the kinds of possibilities that Dr. Alexis Carrel was beginning to explore in the early decades of the twentieth century came to fruition in organ transplants, bionic replacements, and genetic manipulation. Biological success brought reality to what was originally a mythic theme, and realism began to replace fantasy. Horror was no longer an appropriate response, except in motion pictures; on television, *The Six Million Dollar Man* could become a hero and spin off the *Bionic Woman*. In today's world, *Time* magazine can report that artificial limbs, better in some ways than flesh and blood, are being perfected. Earlier, in Bernard Wolfe's *Limbo*, artificial limbs became such a popular option that normal arms and legs became the exception.

Nor is the simple fascination of the strange and marvelous enough. Science fiction asks itself—and the reader—What will it really be like? How will you feel when it happens to you?

Transplantations of fertilized ova (already accomplished in animals and humans), genetically altered ova (accomplished in animals), test tube babies, cloning (growing several identical creatures from a single cell, accomplished in simple organisms and then in sheep, dogs, and cats)—all these are finding expression as realistic possibilities in science fiction stories. Perhaps the best, and the best-known, of these is Ursula K. Le Guin's award-winning "Nine Lives" (1969), which describes the cloning of humans and the emotions of one survivor of such a group. Today the possibilities of human cloning, and even the use of fertilized ova about to be discarded, are raising religious and ethical concerns.

Sometimes science fiction cautions us about the future. It describes how unpleasant life is likely to be if we keep on the way we are going. In other moods, science fiction tells us that what we dread about the future may not be so bad: whatever it is, we can learn to live with it, even enjoy it. Science fiction tells us that whatever the future turns out to be, we will live in it. Science fiction allows us to prepare the future for us, or prepares us for the future. Some things we can change or prevent by forethought; but many things we are not wise enough to change or prevent, either because we cannot know enough or because we cannot bind the future to today's preference.

Cautionary or preparatory—science fiction still is of two minds about changes in the shape and nature of Man. This ambivalence allows each reader to make up his or her own mind. But let the reader beware! Science fiction is about change, and one of the changes it is about is you!

21

SCIENCE FICTION
AND THE FUTURE

In 1902, a short, bright, aggressive, young writer, who had recently made a reputation with several books that were then called "scientific romances," gave a talk entitled "The Discovery of the Future" before the Royal Institution. The writer was Herbert George Wells, and his talk symbolized a new way of thinking about the nature of existence and Man's control over his own destiny.

Until the Industrial Revolution, to the average citizen the future did not exist in the sense we understand the word today. There were, to be sure, days and seasons yet to come, but they would be no different from those that already had been experienced. For most of the history of humanity, the future represented only more of the same—the procession of the seasons marked by planting, growth, harvest and decay; the stages of life represented by birth, youth, maturity, old age, and death. Change in those cycles was to be avoided. The only change was for the worse: flood, drought, blight, starvation, taxation, pillage, accident, disability, disease, plague, murder, war . . . Small wonder that for most of humanity's existence, it has not looked forward, but backward, to a better time—to the Christian Garden of Eden or to the Greek Golden Age.

The Middle Ages is our image of humanity without a future, in spite of places and times where, here and there, the darkness of the Dark Ages lifted for a moment. Then the growing scientific enlightenment symbolized by Galileo and Newton and the improvements in technology symbolized by James Watt began to change humanity's view of the universe and humanity's place in it.

The major influences were the scientific philosophy that the universe was knowable, the application of chemical energy and ingenious machines to the

"Science Fiction and the Future" was first published in *Algol* 16, no. 1, in Winter 1978/1979.

tasks of humanity, and a growing affluence that began liberating humanity from poverty and slavery. Together, they brought change into human affairs—change that, for the first time, was caused by humanity's efforts to improve its lot; change became a matter of choice rather than of chance, evil spirits, or providence.

Science fiction was humanity's literary response not only to the perception that science and technology had become important in human affairs but also to the fact of change. The future, where change occurs, became its peculiar province.

I will not trace here the development of science fiction, but the concept of the future began with such works as *The Reign of King George VI, 1900–1925* and Louis Sebastien Mercier's *Memoirs of the Year Two Thousand Five Hundred* in 1763 and 1771, respectively. The most important early work, however, was Edgar Allan Poe's "Mellonta Tauta" (1849), which was about change itself.

The major influence on the growing public concern about the future and with the literature of change was a Frenchman named Jules Verne. Out of a Victorian fascination with geography and exploration, with technology and invention, he fashioned adventure novels that he called *voyages extraordinaires*. Not only did he spread the popularity of the new literature; with Verne, life began to imitate art: scientists and explorers such as Igor Sikorsky, speleologist Norman Casteret, Admiral Richard Byrd, Lucius Beebe, Guglielmo Marconi, and Alberto Santos-Dumont credited Verne with inspiring their achievements. After a flight to the South Pole, Admiral Byrd said, "It was Jules Verne who launched me on this trip," and submarine developer Simon Lake began his autobiography with the words, "Jules Verne was in a sense the director-general of my life."

Verne seldom dealt with any technology, with any invention, that wasn't clearly possible—typically, the submarine he celebrated in *20,000 Leagues under the Sea* had been invented by Robert Fulton, who tried to build a working vessel for the French government between 1797 and 1805; his best he called "the Nautilus," and Verne used the same name for Nemo's submarine.

Verne's successor as the standard-bearer for the new genre was unconcerned with practicability. H. G. Wells, who was called "the English Jules Verne" and resented it as much as Verne did, wrote about time machines, the creation of manlike animals through vivisection, invisibility, invasion by Martians, and a trip to the moon by means of antigravity.

Wells traced his influences not to science—although he derived considerable inspiration from his scientific education, particularly under Thomas H.

Huxley, who taught him biology and passed along his notions of evolution—but to Swift and his system of ideas and satirical vision of humanity. Although later science fiction writers would often model their work after Verne's celebration of technology and adventure, Wells's purer concern for ideas would eventually prevail in shaping the hard core of SF exemplified in its "golden age."

In its evolution, science fiction adopted a variety of fictional modes—the adventure story, for instance, and the romance—but it became purest, most typical, when it dealt with ideas worked out in human terms.

These ideas were most credible when they were placed in the future. As late as the early twentieth century, writers could be convincing about undiscovered islands or unexplored regions of Africa or Antarctica; soon, however, the only place that strange and unknown events could logically take place was the future, which became a kind of undiscovered island protected by the impassable sea of time. In the process of writing about the future—that undiscovered island—science fiction would seem to be involved in prediction. Not so.

If not with prediction, then, what is science fiction's concern? Science fiction writers would reply that they deal not with *the* future, but with possible futures, not with gadgets, but with people adjusting to change.

Frederik Pohl, a major science fiction writer, has seen come true many of the "predictions" he made in *The Space Merchants*, the classic novel he wrote with Cyril Kornbluth in 1952. Overpopulation, pollution, destruction of freshwater resources—all of these and more have come to pass, while the central warning of the novel, that the advertising industry may take over the world, has not . . . quite.

Pohl points out:

> Prediction in itself is neither particularly useful nor particularly interesting. . . . The ability to change the future around to our own best advantage implies that the future isn't fixed. Which in turn implies that it cannot be predicted. Which, in turn, leads to the discovery that the only kind of prediction of the future that is of any real use to us is either one which is incomplete—so that we have an unpredicted area of freedom in which to operate—or unreliable, so that we can do something that will change it.
>
> If we visit a tea-leaf reader's storefront and learn from her that as we walk out the door and cross the street we will be hit and killed by a runaway truck, we have gained very little. It is only if we learn that such a danger exists, *but is not inevitable*, that we can be warned of the danger in time to avert it.

And so it is with science fiction. The least interesting kind of science fiction, although that which attracts the most attention from the public, is the kind that centers on some predictable invention. For years, science fiction—going back to Wells—dealt with space travel and atomic bombs, both of which have been realized, both, along with other warnings, giving credence to Isaac Asimov's comment that "science fiction is an escape into reality."

The science fiction writer, as John Brunner printed on his business card, deals in futures. And in the process of speculating about what may happen, in the process of thinking through the problems that the process of change, in all its possible permutations, will bring to human lives, in the process of writing entertaining stories about the predicaments in which people will find themselves in the future, the science fiction writer may occasionally stumble across something that will actually happen.

It has happened to me a time or two.

But that is not our purpose. What science fiction turns out to be, besides entertainment, is a laboratory in which we can test our futures for human habitability. What it presents for avoidance, as in George Orwell's *1984*, is the dystopia. What it hopes for is the utopia, which Wells said in 1906 should be the distinctive method of sociology. What it cautions against is the lack of foresight that will allow the dystopia to be created, or the wrong decision today that will bring it about tomorrow.

But perhaps the most important function of science fiction is to neutralize the future, to remove the natural fear that humanity feels for the unknown, to present the alien as at least endurable and perhaps even acceptable. With science fiction, "future shock," as Alvin Toffler said in his book by that name, no longer need be a disease brought about "by the premature arrival of the future." The science fiction reader loves the future; he reads science fiction because the future does not arrive soon enough.

In the process of dealing with the future, science fiction may even influence it, though in less direct ways than prediction. Scientists often read science fiction and have sometimes been inspired to scientific careers or even specific discoveries or inventions. NASA has been peppered with science fiction readers, as have atomic laboratories; during World War II, the publisher of *Astounding Science Fiction* was surprised to discover that its circulation in an obscure Tennessee town had jumped from one magazine a month to several hundred. Only after the war did the name "Oak Ridge" mean anything.

Isaac Asimov has pointed out that we live in a science fiction world, a world that science fiction has helped bring about, where spaceflight and atomic energy, to provide only two examples out of many, have been realized. "No one can say," Asimov concludes, "that science fiction writers and readers put a man on the moon all by themselves, but they created a climate of opinion in which the goal of putting a man on the moon was acceptable."

The problems that humanity must solve soon if it is to survive are overpopulation, pollution, energy, and war. All of them are "science fiction" problems, and science fiction may have helped bring them into public debate while there is still time to do something about them.

In his 1902 speech "The Discovery of the Future," Wells described a new kind of mind—constructive, creative, organizing—which "sees the world as one great workshop, and the present as no more than material for the future, for the thing that is yet destined to be."

If the future-oriented mind is given freedom to express itself, Wells saw a magnificent promise for humanity. "All this world is heavy with the promise of greater things, and a day will come, one day in the unending succession of days, when beings who are now latent in our thoughts and hidden in our loins, shall stand upon this Earth as one stands upon a footstool and shall laugh and reach out their hands amidst the stars."

22

SCIENCE FICTION IN THE NINETIES

S cience fiction developed out of the fermenting nineteenth century, bubbling with innovation, converting the sugars of factory production into the
heady alcohol of scientific and technological progress. But, to switch metaphors, SF also met with resistance from the ancient forces of inertia, apathy,
and tradition. As a consequence, science fiction has appealed to an audience,
primarily the young, that has an emotional investment in a future different
from the one in which they were born and, since that audience until recently
has been limited, SF has had to struggle simply to survive.

Throughout most of its history, with the occasional exception of the Jules
Verne and the H. G. Wells kinds of public acceptance, science fiction has existed at the margins both of literature and of commerce. It has been called a
"ghetto," but the word *ghetto* suggests an area central, if enclosed; more appropriate might be "favella," a word that refers to the shacks peasants have
patched together on the outskirts of Latin American cities. The problems of
science fiction traditionally have been the problems of penury.

"Poor but proud" might be the appropriate description of the state of science fiction, or as fandom has it, "It is a proud and lonely thing to be a fan."
After eight years of rejections, Edward Elmer "Doc" Smith sold *The Skylark
of Space* to *Amazing Stories* for $125; Horace Gold recalled that the early mag-
azines paid a fraction of a cent a word, and then only upon threat of lawsuit.
Conditions improved when Street & Smith took over *Astounding Stories* and
John W. Campbell Jr. became editor, but Isaac Asimov totaled up ten years of
selling stories and novels to Campbell, even being featured with some frequency on its cover, at approximately $8,000, an average of $800 a year.

"Science Fiction in the Nineties" was first presented as a speech at Sercon 3 in 1989 in
Louisville, Kentucky.

Those were the days when the full-time writer was someone who managed to eke out a bare living by mailing first-draft stories as fast as he could turn them out; sometimes he (almost always a male) edited part-time or wrote various kinds of nonfiction or had the aid of inherited money, a pension, or a working wife: you could name the full-time writers in the field on the fingers of two hands, perhaps, and none of them enjoyed an income from writing that would qualify them for the middle class. Some of us can remember selling our first novels for a $500 advance and looking on Bantam's $2,500 advance as munificent—and that was only some forty years ago. I remember freelancing for three years back in the early 1950s; I paid no rent and my brother, who lived nearby, was a physician, which was fortunate, because my best year, when I published two novels, I earned $3,300.

All but a few writers were part-time writers, with all the problems part-time writing involved. And a few of the advantages: part-time writers, who don't have unrealistic expectations of becoming full-time writers or of earning appreciable amounts of money from their work, can devote their time to what they find worth writing, not what someone else wants them to write or what their audiences have come to expect. A surprising number of the important works in the field and many of the classics were created by part-time writers.

Science fiction's penury during most of this period was a fact of its universe: the field consisted of a few magazines that survived on the ragged edge of financial failure. They made a small profit, at best, and paid their editors very little and their authors even less. When Fred Pohl became editor of *Astonishing Stories* and *Super Science Stories* in 1939, he had a salary of $10 a week and a story budget of $275; for sixty thousand words, that came to a bit less than half a cent a word. And Donald Wollheim, when he became editor of *Stirring Science Stories* and *Cosmic Stories* the same year, had an editorial budget of exactly nothing.

For most of the period when science fiction was discovering itself, with the exception of a brief flurry of new publications in the late 1930s and an incredible surge of new magazines in the early 1950s, half a dozen magazines published science fiction; after World War II, a few companies began to publish books. Authors had to adapt their visions to the tastes of one or two idiosyncratic editors and, by the 1950s, hope to pick up supplementary income from anthologies or book publication.

Up to the 1950s, the secret to surviving as a full-time SF writer was to write fast, sell most of it to the best markets, and minimize one's needs and one's expectations. By the late 1950s, at least, the secret changed a bit: then it was to sell to the magazines first and worry about book publication later, and to survive on one's current production until reprint money from book publication and foreign translations began to provide a significant proportion of annual income—the waiting period was about ten years. It reminded me of a bank ad that was prevalent at the time: put $25 a month into an account and in ten years you will be able to withdraw $25 a month for the rest of your life.

What did it mean for the fiction produced? Hasty stories, short stories padded into novelettes and novelettes padded into novels, fiction shaped to the pulp audience with narrative hooks and lots of adventure? Well, yes, a great deal of it. But those favella conditions had their virtues, too. Since almost nobody could make a living at it, the writing of SF was a commitment to a means of expression, even a way of life; since financial success was limited, comradeship among authors and even editors was a unique characteristic of the field, and one person's success was a cause for universal rejoicing. Since almost all writers were amateurs, what they wrote were labors of love; they put as much of themselves into their writing as they could discover and find words and images to fit. Literary artistry may not have been a virtue, but it wasn't a handicap either; as long as it did not interfere with the story or confuse the ideas, art was a rather pleasant attribute, as Stanley Weinbaum demonstrated in his day and Alfred Bester in his, to name just a couple of artists, and eventually editors and authors began to recognize that artistry survived better than most other characteristics.

The science fiction that we build upon today is largely a product of those times and those conditions, so they must not have been totally self-defeating. Nor should they be forgotten.

Today conditions are remarkably different. There still are half a dozen magazines (in 2005, only three print magazines but a larger number of on-line magazines), but they no longer control the field. They are lively and vital and serve as useful proving grounds for new talent; most of the important new writers of the 1980s developed their skills and demonstrated their abilities in the magazines. They publish criticism and nurture new movements. But the book-publishing industry to which the authors aspire, and to which they graduate if they are good enough, shapes the genre and defines success. The magazines published fifty-seven issues in 1987, fifty-five in 1988; perhaps they published a total of four to five million words and paid authors maybe $200,000 or $250,000. By comparison, a number of individual book advances have been four or five times as large as that; one or two have gone as high as $2 million or $3 million. And there were, according to *Locus*, 1,676 SF, fantasy, and horror books published in 1987 and 1,936 in 1988 (respectively, 1,026 and 1,186 of them new books), for a total wordage of, say, 60 million–100 million.

SF writers are moving with greater ease into other fields of writing and publishing, as well as into television and motion pictures. All of which is great, and I would not have it any other way. This, after all, is the happy hunting ground we all were seeking. Writers today can work at their art full-time and can get properly rewarded for it. They can spend a year or two years on a novel, getting it right, and not feel that they are depriving themselves or their families of food or shelter or medical care. Dozens of writers work at their craft full-time and are doing very well.

But have we achieved success without cost?

One of the problems of affluence is the fact that the solidarity we once shared is coming apart in many ways. We have become a society of rich and poor, no longer a brotherhood sworn (though we may not have realized it) to a life of poverty. An annual production of more than a thousand new books a year offers room for a variety of genres, and we have seen them spring up: not just cyberpunk or even the older divisions between hard and soft SF, space opera, lost race, alternate history, future history, and adventure, as well as perhaps as many genres for fantasy and for horror; today we have genres appealing to such specialized tastes as combat SF, feminist SF, lesbian SF, and even what once would have seemed even most unlikely of all, literary SF.

All this breadth has its advantages. The volume of production provides a niche for everybody, readers and authors. If all corners of the field are not equally rewarded, well, as Jimmy Carter reminded us, life isn't fair; maybe, if we can hang on long enough, we will find that our particular genre may move into the golden circle. But the breadth also creates problems.

One problem is the division of the audience; even though it is an audience large enough to support a substantial diversity, that audience can no longer be comfortable in its choices. At one time, for instance, an SF reader could walk into a bookstore, pick a book out of the SF section, and be reasonably certain that the random choice would satisfy that reader's desire for SF. That may no longer be true. If a reader walks into a bookstore and picks a book at random from among those in an SF section, the chances are the reader will not like it. Diversity has done the reader in, and that reader may be less likely to experiment, to broaden horizons and discover new authors.

Even conventions have become specialized. One, Sercon (now Readercon), is a recognition of the fact that fandom has grown so large and so divergent that serious consideration of science fiction as a genre must carve out a place for itself, away from all the others, including comics fandom, film fandom, horror fandom, masquerade fandom, and even fandom fandom.

The sheer volume of books published creates difficulties in selection as well, and this brings us to the second problem: accurate genre identification. We do, of course, judge books by their covers, and not only must editors and publishers put a cover on a book that will elevate it out of the mass of books being pushed out to fight for survival in the wilderness of racks and shelves, but that cover also must guide a reader to his or her subgenre choice. A robot or a spaceship is no longer enough, and the wrong identification may mean a dissatisfied reader. How are our many books to be not only successfully sold but accurately labeled?

A third problem of diversity is our own growing ignorance of our own field. At one time every writer, and almost every reader, not only knew everybody else but was familiar with his or her work. Now, we can't read a fraction of what everybody else writes, even those we consider, by whatever measure, books "important" to us or to the field. Perhaps the magazine editors, and maybe a few book editors—those who are paid to read—can at least sample the writing of most authors, but any of us who write, or work at something else than reading SF, have difficulty browsing through more than a dozen or two or three of current publications, and that includes magazines—say, 1, 2, or at best 3 percent of the current production. No wonder we have lost much of our sense of belonging not only to a beleaguered brotherhood but to a brotherhood at all.

And then there are the dangers of exploitation. I'm not against exploitation. One reason I defended academic interest in science fiction was not simply because I was part of academia (as well as a part of the SF brotherhood) but because I believed, as I wrote in an *Analog* guest editorial, that all of us exploit SF. We all use SF for our own purposes—authors, fans, editors, the lot—and I didn't see why teachers and scholars should be excluded. Even when we were poor, we got satisfaction out of what we did; our motives may not have been venal, but they weren't entirely unselfish.

But certain kinds of exploitation, though understandable and even permissible, have their downsides. Most of what I am talking about here is hack writing, that is, writing, whether done as work-for-hire or not, that is begun at someone else's instigation and meets someone else's standards of performance. Such work (perhaps with a few exceptions) has never advanced the field and seldom has advanced the skills or the careers—beyond the minimal aspect of publication itself—of the writers involved. I have had students who wanted to write imitative works, like *Star Trek* novels, and I always tell them to write something of their own. Anything else is merely creative typing or, today, creative word processing. All an author has to offer a reader is the author's own uniqueness, genetics modified by experience and shaped by craft. Although one can never entirely eliminate authorial uniqueness, craft alone produces hack work.

But major genres are developing in our field because of the peripheral interests of readers and the commercial instincts of publishers and writers. Beyond the continuing phenomenon of the *Star Trek* genre, which owes its success more to the memory of visual images than to the ones created by words on paper, lies the film-novelization genre. The fact that such books often sell far better than more original works is worthy of study by scholars as well as authors.

Other developments that may not yet have reached the status of genres are the rent-a-name and rent-a-world phenomena, to which has recently been added the rent-a-story phenomenon. Of these, the rent-a-name category is relatively innocuous, rather like the promotional quotes most authors provide to books they think deserve them (as well as some that may not), though another interesting study is warranted to determine if these really help. Certainly there is nothing wrong with "Isaac Asimov Presents" or "Arthur C. Clarke Presents" helping an unknown author find an audience and taking the curse off that first novel, although if these publishing devices really work, we have no reason to think that the process produces novels that actually deserve to be singled out for excellence. In fact, the opposite may be more frequent: the more a work deserves boosting, the less the novel needs it, and the best first novels probably avoid the rent-a-name avenue. Terry Carr's outstandingly successful "Ace Science Fiction Specials," which sold books by association with other excellent books in the series and did not subordinate the name of the author to the name of someone better known, may have been a better way to achieve similar results.

At least in the rent-a-name process, the novel published is the one the author wanted to write. In the rent-a-world procedure, novels are written in fictional worlds created by famous writers. *Locus* has called this "sharecropping." Such works may be a natural outgrowth of the *Star Trek* novels, but like them, if a novel succeeds as a work of art in these circumstances it is a near-miracle. The shared-world anthology has some of the handicaps of this development. This is not to say that such works can't be entertaining for the readers or fun for the writers; the history of SF is replete with such shared worlds, perhaps beginning with the occasion in the 1930s when seventeen different famous authors collaborated on successive chapters of a novel, *Cosmos*, published serially in *Fantasy Magazine*. Some excellent work has been done this way, although it may be more the uniqueness of the artist triumphing over the process.

Now, the publishing world has come up with the rent-a-story concept, in which authors like Asimov and Silverberg are being paid large amounts of money to write stories in the same world as those of the classics of our field, "Vintage Season," for instance, and "Nightfall." Silverberg's "Vintage Season" contribution, "In Another Country," was published in the March 1989 issue of *Isaac Asimov's Science Fiction Magazine* along with Bob's introduction asking for forgiveness "for having dared to tinker with a masterpiece in this way." Forgiving him is easy; it was a challenge, and he accepted it. The question is whether I should read it. Do I want to know any more about "Vintage Season" than Catherine Moore told me in the original? Will it alter my understanding of it, my reading of it, as sequels to great novels have a way of doing? If I read it, I suspect that it will be a matter of professional obligation, perhaps at the sacrifice of my aesthetic sense of the original story.

And then there is the matter of sequels. I'm not talking here about the series planned as a series, or the adventure stories that can be proliferated without end, but the great novel, insofar as we can use the term in our field, that leads publishers to offer large sums of money to authors to continue them. My concern is not with the sums of money or even the pecuniary motivation of the authors—I agree with Samuel Johnson about blockheads and money—but my feeling is that novels are great because they are self-contained and that sequels inevitably diminish the greatness of the works that instigated them, as if the original novels have been reduced to the status of the first work in the series. Would I accept a large sum of money to write a sequel to one of my novels? Perhaps I don't have any that would be diminished by it, and I have certainly strung stories together in book-length works—though planned in that fashion—but that I probably would agree to do it does not diminish my concern for the process. Is it good for the field? I don't think so.

All of these aspects of our affluence are worrisome because they proliferate publication without enhancing the field. Books that do not advance a field or a career clutter them up. The more nonbooks that get published, the more the legitimate works of art have difficulty getting recognition and readership. And the more nonbooks published, the more the field gets scattered and the harder the center is to find. I'm not asking for fewer books to be published, but that we all consider mechanisms that will encourage better SF rather than simply books that will sell, because we can sell books and lose our genre—that which drew us all to it in the beginning.

Original visions are what attracted us first and, I suspect, almost everybody else who reads SF, but sometimes readers will settle for secondhand visions or cling to worlds that they want to revisit again and again. Some of that kind of response is inevitable; I am asking if we should cater to it. If we do, we may destroy the appetite for originality that distinguishes SF from all the other genres and turn it into repetitive pleasures like the rest.

Let me raise one last concern about affluence: what will be the impact on the written science fiction of the sudden wealth to which it has fallen heir? Science fiction, perhaps because it has always been poor, has championed change. There must be, it has said implicitly and sometimes explicitly, a better way. Upon occasion this inherent preference for difference has fostered real-life political stances: one caused an early schism in fan circles that contributed to the Futurians being barred from the first World SF Convention; ads in *Galaxy* took opposing sides regarding the Vietnam War. I sometimes tell my students that science fiction is inherently subversive, because it makes plausible alternative societies and ways of behaving and governing ourselves; it makes readers think seriously about the possibilities of change.

Will wealth alter that inherent bias toward alternatives? I am not suggesting here that wealth, even new wealth, is necessarily conservative. Jules Verne was a struggling author most of his early career, and his most radical character was a Captain Nemo whose protest never reached the status of a program, and H. G. Wells was a social critic, and a socialist, to the end, in spite of his literary and financial success; and the final despairing works of both authors may have been due more to age than to riches.

Science fiction has had its conservative element since its earliest days, and I suspect that more authors are born conservative than are converted. Even so, a dispassionate student might identify greater evidences of conservatism in to-day's science fiction than ever before. We live, to be sure, in a conservative era, and conservative elements may be growing everywhere. Fantasy may be as popular today as science fiction, and fantasy, like science fiction film, is basically conservative.

Let me make clear that I am not debating politics. I may disagree with many conservative positions, but I don't question their right to expression or vigorous defense in fiction. The question I am raising is the influence of affluence on science fiction in the 1990s, and the way in which wealth may encourage the fiction to defend the status quo or something like it. A science fiction that does not question the values of the society from which it emerges may not be science fiction at all; not only may it have lost one of its most valuable nonliterary functions, that of social criticism, but a science fiction that raises the possibility of change only to condemn it perhaps has sacrificed the right to call itself a literature of change. Like the science fiction film, it only *seems* to be science fiction, because it has the appearance but not the substance.

Finally, I am not asking for a return to the "good old days." They were not that good to begin with. Moreover, I can echo Mae West: "I've tried poor and I've tried rich, and believe me, rich is better." Affluence provides opportunity for all of us to do our thing, whatever it is. I guess my message, in the vernacular of *Easy Rider*, is "Let's not blow it." Let our art be self-aware. Let us consider what we do and why we do it, and whether, in the final analysis, we have made our world—our science fiction world—better for having lived in it.

23

SCIENCE FICTION IN THE SECOND MILLENNIUM

S cience fiction is many things to many people. Some readers identify it
with the pulp magazines in which it made its first identifiable appearance
in 1926, some see it as a mass-market paperback phenomenon, more recent
readers have come to look for it on the best-seller lists, and some viewers have
their only experience with science fiction in films and television, comic books,
and computer games. They're all different, and they all come with different
images and responses.

Let us deal with SF historically, then, and describe its evolution through its
printed form. Mary Shelley, Edgar Allan Poe, and Jules Verne got it started in
the nineteenth century, and then H. G. Wells brought in a new emphasis on
ideas that ultimately transformed the category that then was called "scientific
romance." A technology enthusiast named Hugo Gernsback saw the new literature as a way of creating an interest in science and technology among young
readers, began publishing it in his technology magazines, and finally created
Amazing Stories, a magazine entirely of science fiction stories (although he
called it "scientifiction" then, changing to "science fiction" three years later
when he founded *Wonder Stories*).

Gernsback described it as "the Jules Verne, H. G. Wells, and Edgar Allen
Poe type of story—a charming romance intermingled with scientific fact and
prophetic vision." What evolved through the magazines (*Wonder Stories*,
Astounding Stories of Super Science, and many others)—there were no books

---

"Science Fiction in the Second Millennium" was first published, in somewhat different form,
in *Science and Spirit* in July 2005.

to speak of until 1946—was a literature of ideas but, more importantly, the literature of change and subsequently the literature of anticipation and of the human species.

As a Darwinian fiction that has at its heart a belief in the adaptability of the human species (more so than naturalism, which is customarily traced to Darwin), science fiction naturally evolves. As a matter of fact, science fiction is at its best when it is most innovative. Some readers and viewers are attracted to familiar tropes displayed in familiar narratives (hence the popularity of TV series and trilogies), but hard-core SF readers dismiss this kind of experience as trivial and demand something original in thought, treatment, or outcome.

That was easier done when SF was confined to the SF magazines, when writers were created out of readers and every story was in dialogue with every other story. Novels began to be published in book form following World War II, many of them serials reprinted from the magazines, and by 1970 they had begun to be the primary purveyor of science fiction to its readers, followed by comic books, by film, and then by television. For some forty years after the founding of *Amazing Stories*, the magazine editors were the gatekeepers of the field—particularly John W. Campbell Jr., editor of *Astounding Science Fiction*, now known as *Analog*, who presided over the "golden age of science fiction" from 1938 to 1950. In 1950 his dominance was challenged by Anthony Boucher of the *Magazine of Science Fiction and Fantasy* and Horace Gold of *Galaxy*.

The early authors of fiction that resembled what later became known as science fiction—Mary Wollstonecraft Shelley, Edgar Allan Poe, E. T. A. Hoffman, Nathaniel Hawthorne—were torn between two attitudes toward the new revelations and accomplishments of the science and technology of their times: wonder at its power to transform life and thought, and caution about its misuse. Shelley wrote *Frankenstein*, Poe wrote "Mellonta Tauta," Hoffman wrote "The Sandman," and Hawthorne wrote "Rappaçini's Daughter." Then Jules Verne came along, inspired by the potential of improved machines and by exploration of unknown territories beneath the sea, at the center of the earth, and in the sky. Exploration required brave men without much introspection; Verne also threw in some politics with characters such as Captain Nemo. H. G. Wells, on the other hand, studied Darwin under Thomas Huxley, Darwin's champion, and Wells's stories and novels dealt with people as the products of their environment and warned his Victorian readers about the cultural hubris that precedes sudden downfall.

Hugo Gernsback, an immigrant from Luxembourg, loved technology—his own 1911 serial novel *Ralph 124C 41 +* was filled with inventions, some of them as prescient as radar—and he published those kinds of stories in *Amazing Stories*, but he also published stories that stirred a sense of wonder ("truly amazing," he commented). The future, in Gernsback's SF, belonged to those who could understand science and put it to use, and he thought the stories he published could propel young readers into careers in science and engineering. But the villains also could twist science to their own nefarious schemes.

In 1928, when Gernsback serialized Edward Elmer "Doc" Smith's *The Skylark of Space*, he opened readers' imaginations to the vastness of an expanding universe but also to the possibilities of scientific villainy as well as heroism. Smith would go on to write a six-volume epic of space (later reprinted in book form by fans as *The History of Civilization*) called "the Lensman series," in which the Lensmen, recruited and educated by the mysterious force for good on the planet Arisia, fought the nefarious recruits of the evil planet Eddor for the future of the galaxy. Good and evil. Edmond Hamilton wrote similar stories for *Weird Tales* featuring an Interstellar Patrol.

Outside the magazine influence, British philosopher W. Olaf Stapledon was writing novels such as *Last and First Men* and *Star Maker*, which treated the future history of humanity and the universe itself as natural phenomena with a spiritual underpinning. Meanwhile John W. Campbell Jr., who had contributed to the space epic tradition before he turned to more philosophic stories under the pseudonym of Don A. Stuart, became editor of *Astounding Stories* in 1937 and began transforming the genre with stories placed in a science-important culture, stories that, he advised, should be written as if they were published in a magazine in the twenty-fifth century.

Campbell believed in the power of rationality and the survival, and the dominance (anticipating Faulkner's Nobel remarks), of the human species, and he attracted writers who shared that vision, such as Robert A. Heinlein and Isaac Asimov (who learned not to submit stories about superior aliens). Campbell's future was a meritocracy. Tony Boucher, on the other hand, brought a *literateur*'s skepticism about changing humanity to *Fantasy & Science Fiction*, and Horace Gold, who wanted to produce the *Saturday Evening Post* of science fiction in *Galaxy*, emphasized "you-can't-fight-city-hall" sociological science fiction. In *Galaxy*'s pages, Alfred Bester published novels like *The Demolished Man* and *The Stars My Destination* about societies transformed by telepathy and telekinesis, and Frederik Pohl and Cyril Kornbluth extrapolated advertising's influence on consumers into SF satire in novels such as *The Space Merchants*.

By the early 1960s England was swinging, the British magazine *New Worlds* came under the editorship of Michael Moorcock, and the cabal of like-minded writers he attracted, such as Brian Aldiss, John Brunner, and especially J. G. Ballard, brought literary sensibilities to SF along with literary attitudes (SF should be "more like William Burroughs than Edgar Rice Burroughs," Ballard wrote in an introductory essay). Where the rocket ship had been the defining image of Campbellian science fiction, entropy—the heat-death of the universe—became the metaphor that defined Moorcock's *New Worlds*, or as one British editor commented, "Things can only get worse." Entropy implied that humanity was helpless before great natural forces and the appropriate response was resignation, even collaboration. Each of these movements in turn was absorbed back into the body of science fiction. Every dozen years, from 1926 to 1964, it seemed, science fiction was transformed by a new vision.

The growing dominance of book SF changed all that: novelists are harder to organize than short-story writers, and the field became more diverse, less subject to what might be called "punctuated evolution." When more than two thousand books (SF, fantasy, and horror) are published each year, trends are difficult to spot and more difficult to follow. In such an environment, creating a new movement requires something as dramatic as, say, J. R. R. Tolkien's *The Lord of the Rings* trilogy in fantasy or, in the media, *Star Trek* or *Star Wars*, whose literary offspring clutter the book racks. William Gibson's 1984 *Neuromancer* was such a phenomenon. Its vision of a grubby future world dominated by computers and amoral international corporations, but told from the viewpoint of street people surviving by their abilities to game the system, captured a vision for like-minded authors and readers and launched a movement organized around a new concept and a new word: "cyberpunk." Bruce Sterling popularized the movement and attracted other writers such as John Shirley and Pat Cadigan and even, in his own way, George Alec Effinger. The movement, like the New Wave, has been absorbed, but like previous movements its insights and techniques remain available, and the word "cyberpunk" itself has gone on to new uses.

Feminism and feminist utopias were vigorous in the 1960s and 1970s, and even into the 1980s, with works such as Ursula K. Le Guin's *The Left Hand of Darkness*; Pamela Sargent's *The Shore of Women* (as well as her *Women of Wonder* anthologies); James Tiptree Jr.'s (Alice Sheldon) short stories, including "The Women Men Don't See," "Houston, Houston, Do You Read," and "The Screwfly Solution"; Joan Slonczewski's *A Door into Ocean*; Joanna Russ's *The Female Man*; Suzy McKee Charnas's *Motherlines*; Marge Piercy's *Woman on the Edge of Time*; and many others. The energy that once flowed into feminist utopias now seems to have become absorbed into the category, just as years before other movements, such as the New Wave and cyberpunk, were absorbed into the larger body of SF. More common now is a focus on gender issues as part of a larger context, although authors such as Sheri S. Tepper (*The Fresco*) continue to make them central. Racial issues, which once produced a body of antiprejudice narrative, now are more evident as an acceptance of difference in the literature as a whole, with the sole exception, perhaps, being the novels of Octavia Butler (*Wild Seed, Kindred*). Gay and lesbian SF, although it still occupies its own niche, is found elsewhere as gender issues.

Utopias, because they are displaced in space or time, have always been a part of SF, though sometimes the utopian view of humanity (that the political—or sometimes the economic or social—structure is to blame for humanity's inability to fulfill its potential) has conflicted with embedded SF tropes. H. G. Wells told the Sociological Society in 1906 that the writing and criticism of utopias was the proper role for sociology, and he wrote a number of them himself. Two world wars and a depression produced a number of anti-utopias, most prominently Aldous Huxley's *Brave New World* and George Orwell's *1984*, but the utopian drive returned in Huxley's *Island* and B. F. Skinner's *Walden Two*. Ernest Callenbach's *Ecotopia* featured ecological concerns in the 1970s, and utopian politics was revived in the 1990s by Kim Stanley Robinson's *Pacific Edge* and into the twenty-first century by his *Mars* trilogy.

But utopias, as a class, seem to lack credibility in today's intellectual climate. More in the contemporary mood are dystopias based on the belief that human problems, exacerbated by human failings, will make life worse rather than better. John Brunner made this intensely imagined near-future the capstone of a long writing career with novels such as *Stand on Zanzibar* and *The Sheep Look Up*. But even dystopias are rarely so grim or despairing any more.

Another subcategory of science fiction, the alternate history (or, as historians have renamed it, "the counterfactual"), has become far more popular. With a tradition that goes back to Mark Twain's *A Connecticut Yankee in King Arthur's Court* and was reimagined by L. Sprague de Camp in *Lest Darkness Fall*, the alternate history became more solidly established with Ward Moore's *Bring the Jubilee* and Philip K. Dick's *The Man in the High Castle*. Every major war seemed to produce a new flood of alternate history novels speculating about what would have occurred if the losing side had won; other authors, such as Poul Anderson with his "Time Patrol," could argue that lesser events have had a greater impact on history, but the drama of great wars and their aftermaths is irresistible. Alternate histories achieved separate genre status with the success of Harry Turtledove's novels such as *The Guns of the South*. Authors as distinguished as Robert Silverberg, with his *Roma Eterna* in which Rome did not

fall, and Philip Roth, with *The Plot against America* in which Lindbergh became president, have demonstrated the power of a story in which readers get
the intellectual pleasure of considering a different outcome and the *frisson* of
the fragility of their cherished reality, something Dick challenged in many of
his other novels.

Nothing as transformative as *Neuromancer* and the cyberpunk movement
has come along since the 1980s, although several tendencies have emerged.
One such tendency has been to combine the New Wave's view of the inade-
quacy of humanity to cope with major change with an expanding horizon of
scientific development and galactic expansion. Gregory Benford, himself a
university astrophysicist, led the way with his *Great Sky River* novels focusing
on the galactic conflict between human life and machine life near the galactic
center. Vernor Vinge, a university mathematics professor, added the concept
of the singularity—the hyperbolic rise in technological complexity that will
progress beyond humanity's ability to understand or to control—and wrote
novels such as *A Fire upon the Deep* and *A Deepness in the Sky*. Neal Stephenson, in works such as *Snow Crash* and *The Diamond Age*, dealt with the potential for disaster in computer dependency and biological experimentation.
David Brin struck a more hopeful note in his Uplift novels, in which, however,
he portrays humanity as coming late to the galactic civilization and having to
cope with the stigma of having "uplifted" themselves and chimpanzees and
dolphins as well. George Zebrowski, in novels such as *Macrolife*, suggests that
space habitats will transform humanity; in a collaboration with Charles Pelle-
grino, *The Killing Star*, Zebrowski renewed Greg Bear's concern (in *The Forge
of God* and *Anvil of Stars*) that galactic civilizations may want to destroy possible rivals (such as humans) rather than risk destruction themselves.

At the same time, Frederik Pohl showed the human element at work on a
galactic scale with novels such as *Gateway* and its sequels, when the discovery
of ancient space-going capsules explores human neuroses and the future of the
galaxy. In the United Kingdom, on the other hand, a renaissance of hard SF
writing produced a vision of galactic expansion dwarfing humanity in novels
such as Stephen Baxter's *Coalescence*, Paul McAuley's *Eternal Light*, and Iain
Bank's Culture series. Australian Greg Egan (*Permutation City*) translates humans into computer virtual realities, and the United Kingdom's China Mieville, in novels such as *Perdido Street Station* mixes fantasy and SF into something he calls the "New Weird." Meanwhile, Charles Stross (*Accelerando*) and
Cory Doctorow (*Down and Out in the Magic Kingdom*)—and Pat Cadigan
(*Dervish Is Digital*) before them—are dealing with a technology-rich future

crammed with change in humanity as well as existence, all treated as everyday reality.

Perhaps the greatest transformation of science fiction has come from the blurring of its borders with other genres, particularly fantasy and the mainstream. Increasingly, from the quanta to the cosmos, uncertainty has become the one constant. At the subatomic level, the only reality is illusory, and at the cosmic level, the latest theory imagines the natural world as the three-dimensional aspect of cosmic strings that exist in a ten-dimensional reality. Fantasists seem authorized to let their imaginations soar, and more scientifically minded authors can resort to the magic of nanotechnology.

One sees this uneasy marriage of fantasy and science fiction not only in Mieville's New Weird but also in novels such as Robert Silverberg's *Kingdoms of the Wall* and Michael Swanwick's *Stations of the Tide* and *The Iron Dragon's Daughter*. Similar weddings of science fiction, fantasy, and horror are evident in the work of Stephen King. In some of these authors' works, the image of humanity is a confusion that may be relieved only by the discovery of an elusive truth, and even that truth may be conditional.

Genre writing also is becoming indistinguishable from the mainstream. Recent authors such as Margaret Atwood (*The Handmaid's Tale*, *Oryx and Crake*), Doris Lessing (*The Memoirs of a Survivor* and the *Shikasta* series), and Philip Roth (*The Plot against America*) have adopted SF tropes (like Aldous Huxley, George Orwell, Nevil Shute, Bernard Wolfe, Anthony Burgess, Herman Wouk, John Barth, John Pynchon, and many others before them) while denying (like Kurt Vonnegut Jr.) they were writing SF. They may be right: their focus on the individual rather than society makes their novels read more like mainstream than SF.

At the other end of the spectrum, SF authors are moving into the mainstream. William Gibson's *Pattern Recognition* became a mainstream best-seller even while it retained many of the characteristics of cyberpunk. Jonathan Lethem, who made a splash with his first novel, *Gun, with Occasional Music*, has turned to the mainstream with *Motherless Brooklyn* and *The Fortress of Solitude*, while Michael Chabon, who won a Pulitzer Prize for *The Amazing Adventures of Kavalier and Clay*, maintains his ties to science fiction with *McSweeney's Magic Treasury of Thrilling Tales* and similar anthologies and novels. So does Ursula K. Le Guin, whose mainstream work has drawn critical praise.

So, what can we say, in conclusion, about the philosophical stance of science fiction in today's world? Very little, in a definitive sense: SF spans too wide a spectrum to summarize without oversimplifying. A basic belief in the adaptability of the human species may survive (exemplified in utopias, dystopias, and even satires), but confidence in the rational process (observed most clearly in Isaac Asimov's work, for instance) has dwindled. Science itself, or the scientific method, is no longer the final answer in most SF, uncertainty and concepts once considered too fantastic to include in an SF story are more common, a consensus about the primacy of the human species or the perfectibility of the human condition is far harder to find, and SF still is in a state of change. It still is evolving. When it gets there (wherever that is), it no longer will be science fiction.

A JAMES GUNN
BIBLIOGRAPHY

This Fortress World. New York: Gnome Press, 1955.
Star Bridge (with Jack Williamson). New York: Gnome Press, 1955.
Station in Space. New York: Bantam Books, 1958.
The Joy Makers. New York: Bantam Books, 1961.
The Immortals. New York: Bantam Books, 1962.
Future Imperfect. New York: Bantam Books, 1964.
The Immortal: A Novel. Toronto: Bantam Books, 1970.
The Witching Hour. New York: Dell, 1970.
Breaking Point. New York: Walker & Co., 1972.
The Burning. New York: Dell, 1972.
The Listeners. New York: Charles Scribner's Sons, 1972.
Some Dreams Are Nightmares. New York: Charles Scribner's Sons, 1974.
Nebula Award Stories 10. New York: Harper & Row, 1975.
Alternate Worlds: The Illustrated History of Science Fiction. Englewood Cliffs, NJ:
 Prentice Hall, 1975.
The Magicians. New York: Charles Scribner's Sons, 1976.
Kampus: A Novel. Toronto: Bantam Books, 1977.
The Road to Science Fiction: From Gilgamesh to Wells. New York: New American Li-
 brary, 1977; Lanham, MD: Scarecrow Press, 2002.
The Road to Science Fiction: From Wells to Heinlein. New York: New American Library,
 1979; Lanham, MD: Scarecrow Press, 2002.
The Road to Science Fiction: From Heinlein to Here. New York: New American Library,
 1979; Lanham, MD: Scarecrow Press, 2002.
Teacher's Manual: The Road to Science Fiction (with Stephen H. Goldman). New York:
 New American Library, 1980.

The Dreamers. New York: Simon & Schuster, 1981. Reprinted as *The Mind Master.* New York: Pocket Books, 1982.

Isaac Asimov: The Foundations of Science Fiction. Oxford: Oxford University Press, 1982; Lanham, MD: Scarecrow Press, 1996.

The Road to Science Fiction: From Here to Forever. New York: New American Library, 1982; Lanham, MD: Scarecrow Press, 2003.

Tiger! Tiger! A Short Novel. Polk City, IA: C. Drumm, 1984.

The New Encyclopedia of Science Fiction. New York: Viking, 1988.

The Best of Astounding: *Classic Short Novels from the Golden Age of Science Fiction* (editor). New York: Carroll & Graf, 1992.

Inside Science Fiction: Essays on Fantastic Literature. San Bernardino, CA: Borgo Press, 1992.

The Unpublished Gunn, Part One. Polk City, IA: Drumm, 1992.

The Unpublished Gunn, Part Two. Polk City, IA: Drumm, 1996.

The Joy Machine. New York: Simon & Schuster/Pocket Books, 1996.

The Road to Science Fiction #5: The British Way. Clarkston, GA: White Wolf, 1998.

The Road to Science Fiction #6: Around the World. Clarkston, GA: White Wolf, 1998.

Human Voices. Henan People's Publishing House, 1999; Waterville, ME: Five Star, 2002.

The Science of Science-Fiction Writing. Lanham, MD: Scarecrow Press, 2000.

The Millennium Blues. Norwalk, CT: Easton Press, 2001; E-reads.

Speculations on Speculation: Theories of Science Fiction. Lanham, MD: Scarecrow Press, 2004.

Gift from the Stars. Dallas: BenBella Books, 2005; Norwalk, CT: Easton Press, 2005.

INDEX

ABOUT THE AUTHOR

James Gunn was born in Kansas City, Missouri, in 1923. He received his B.S. in journalism in 1947 and an M.A. in English in 1951, both from the University of Kansas. He has worked as an editor of paperback reprints, as managing editor of the University of Kansas alumni publications, and as the university's director of public relations. Mr. Gunn is now an emeritus professor of English and director of the Center for the Study of Science Fiction at the University of Kansas, Lawrence.

Mr. Gunn has won a number of national awards for his work, including the Byron Caldwell Smith Prize in recognition of literary achievement and the Edward Grier Award for excellence in teaching, as well as a Hugo Award, a Locus Award, an Eaton Award, and the Pilgrim Award for lifetime achievement in the field of science fiction scholarship. He is also the only person to serve as president of both the Science Fiction Writers of America and the Science Fiction Research Association.

He has published forty books, including *The Joy Makers, Star Bridge* (with Jack Williamson), *The Immortals, The Listeners, Alternate Worlds: The Illustrated History of Science Fiction, The Dreamers,* and *The Millennium Blues,* as well as the acclaimed *Road to Science Fiction* series used in classes worldwide. Mr. Gunn's most recent books are *The Science of Science-Fiction Writing, Speculations on Speculation: Theories of Science Fiction,* and *Gift from the Stars.*